Reworlding

Recent Titles in
Contributions to the Study of World Literature

Reworlding

THE LITERATURE OF THE INDIAN DIASPORA

EDITED BY

Emmanuel S. Nelson

Contributions to the Study of
World Literature, Number 42

GREENWOOD PRESS
New York • Westport, Connecticut • London

Library of Congress Cataloging-in-Publication Data

Reworlding : the literature of the Indian diaspora / edited by
    Emmanuel S. Nelson.
        p.   cm. — (Contributions to the study of world literature,
    ISSN 0738–9345 ; 42)
    Includes bibliographical references and index.
    ISBN 0-313-27794-X (alk. paper)
    1. Indic literature (English)—Foreign countries—History and
criticism.   2. East Indians—Foreign countries—Intellectual life.
3. East Indians in literature.   4. India in literature.   I. Nelson,
Emmanuel S. (Emmanuel Sampath).   II. Series.
PR9485.45.N45R48   1992
820.9′891411—dc20   91–40939

British Library Cataloguing in Publication Data is available.

Library of Congress Catalog Card Number: 91–40939
ISBN: 0-313-27794-X
ISSN: 0738-9345

First published in 1992

Greenwood Press, 88 Post Road West, Westport, CT 06881
An imprint of Greenwood Publishing Group, Inc.

Printed in the United States of America

The paper used in this book complies with the
Permanent Paper Standard issued by the National
Information Standards Organization (Z39.48–1984).

10 9 8 7 6 5 4 3 2 1

To my parents, who stayed Home

Contents

Introduction

Emmanuel S. Nelson

Exiles or emigrants or expatriates are haunted by some sense of loss, some urge to reclaim, to look back, even at the risk of being mutated into pillars of salt. But if we do look back, we must also do so in the knowledge—which gives rise to profound uncertainties—that our physical alienation from India almost inevitably means that we will not be capable of reclaiming precisely the thing that was lost; that we will, in short, create fictions, not actual cities or villages, but invisible ones, imaginary homelands, Indias of the mind.

—Salman Rushdie (76)

The chapters that follow critically examine the literature of the Indian diaspora. A term that was first used largely in the context of the Jewish experience outside the Jewish homeland and more recently in the contexts of a variety of transnational ethnic experiences (such as African, Chinese, and Armenian), *diaspora* literally refers to dispersal—the scattering of a people. In all its contexts, however, the concept of diaspora remains problematic, for it raises complex questions about the meanings of a number of related terms, such as nationality, ethnicity, and migrancy. It necessitates, therefore, a broad definition such as the one that William Safran offers. Safran suggests that the "concept of diaspora be applied to expatriate minority communities whose members share several of the following characteristics":

1) they, or their ancestors, have been dispersed from a specific original "center" to two or more "peripheral," or foreign, regions; 2) they retain a collective memory, vision,

or myth about their original homeland—its physical location, history, and achievements; 3) they believe that they are not—and perhaps cannot be—fully accepted by their host society and therefore feel partly alienated and insulated from it; 4) they regard their ancestral homeland as their true, ideal home and as the place to which they or their descendants would (or should) eventually return— when conditions are appropriate; 5) they believe that they should, collectively, be committed to the maintenance or restoration of their homeland and to its safety and prosperity; and 6) they continue to relate, personally or vicariously, to that homeland in one way or another, and their ethnocommunal consciousness and solidarity are importantly defined by the existence of such a relationship. (Safran, 83–84)

In terms of Safran's definition, we may justifiably speak of an Indian diaspora—as one may speak of the Palestinian, or Italian, or Chinese diasporas— yet the problematic nature of such usage still remains. For India, clearly, is not a culturally monolithic entity; it is, on the contrary, a staggering compendium of a multitude of ethnicities, languages, and traditions. To speak of an Indian diaspora, then, is to insist on a claim to an essential psychological and historical unity that undergirds the spectacular Indian mosaic. An equally vexing problem is the concept of "India" itself: the post–1947 India, the political unit, is an artificial colonial construction, carved out of a larger subcontinental collective in order to meet political exigencies. The imposed geographical boundaries, for the most part, are marks of violent dismemberment—scars that testify to the troubled history of the subcontinent. As a diasporic Indian who participates in the discourses of the diaspora, the subcontinental political geography poses for me dilemmas that are academic as well as personal. If I were to limit my definition of the diaspora to people who are linked only to India—the post–1947 political entity—I would be, justifiably, accused of historical inaccuracy and nationalist chauvinism. Yet, if I were to broaden my definition to include all the nation-states of the subcontinent, I suppose I could be viewed with suspicion by some who might consider my inclusiveness a sign of imperialist appropriation and absorption of India's smaller neighbors.

I, therefore, use the term diaspora quite self-consciously, and I use it to refer to the historical and contemporary presence of people of Indian subcontinental origin in other areas of the world. Though I recognize that the subcontinent is not a homogeneous unit, its inhabitants share a common history. And since the major waves of the diasporic movement began during the nineteenth century— and since the diasporic destinations were frequently other parts of the British empire—a forced interaction with colonial hegemony is a fundamental and unifying feature of the diasporic experience. Even the post-independence emigration of highly skilled professionals from the subcontinent to foreign locations is spawned largely by colonial dislocations. In a general sense, therefore, the young subcontinental scientists, professors, surgeons, and architects who now emigrate do have a good deal in common with those Indian indentured workers who braved long voyages on ill-equipped ships to Mauritius, Trinidad, and Fiji during the nineteenth century. And the imaginative literatures that articulate their experiences are indeed comparable.

And I insist on using the term diaspora to refer not only to people who have roots in India—the India created in 1947—but in the other parts of the subcontinent as well. Such inclusiveness is historically valid; it is also an affirmation of our shared subcontinental experience and consciousness.

But this volume sacrifices comprehensiveness for depth. Its chapters cover all *major* areas of the Indian diaspora: the South Pacific, the Caribbean, Singapore, Britain, the United States, Canada, and Africa. It includes discussions of all major writers of the diaspora. And it includes a few writers who have subcontinental, but not specifically Indian, origins, for example, Sara Suleri (Pakistan) and Michael Ondaatje (Sri Lanka).

The application of the concept of diaspora offers a new paradigm to study Indian cultural productions outside the Indian center. Rather than view the works of Indian writers in places such as Fiji, Singapore, and Trinidad merely in national or regional contexts, the diasporic paradigm enables a global approach and initiates a new perspective. Situating the texts in the diasporic context allows us to grasp more fully the unresolved tensions in the diasporic consciousness that shape those texts as well as the ethnohistorical significance of those texts. Furthermore, the diasporic framework creates space for a variety of comparative studies of the different traditions within international Indian writing in English.

This book begins, and appropriately so, with Vijay Mishra's "The Girmit Ideology Revisited: Fiji Indian Literature." Mishra provides an appropriate beginning to the discussion because he became, in 1977, the first prominent scholar in postcolonial studies to theorize the literature of the Indian diaspora. In his present chapter he offers a reassessment of his earlier critical stances and advances a more sophisticated theory of Girmit ideology which, he argues, informs Fiji Indian literature, culture, and consciousness. But beginning this volume with a chapter that focuses on Fiji, I believe, is appropriate on a political level as well.

The history of Indians in Fiji offers on a minor scale an unsettling paradigm of the Indian diasporic experience in general. Indians arrived in Fiji in 1879, first as indentured laborers and then as free immigrants, lured into undertaking a dangerous voyage across the oceans in search of promised but largely elusive prosperity. Their entrepreneurial spirit, however, did ensure their gradual ascendancy in the island's economic and professional life, but their success, coupled with their cultural insularity, led to an uneasy relationship with the indigenous Fijians. Stunned by the 1987 Rambuka coup, which has effectively left them deeply vulnerable, Indo-Fijians now face an uncertain future in a troubled and hostile territory. The experiences of diasporic Indians in other parts of the world are not vastly dissimilar to that of Fiji Indians.

Mishra begins his chapter with an examination of the "Girmit" ideology (Girmit is a vernacular variant of the word "agreement"—the agreement that the Indian indentured workers had with the British authorities who transported them to Fiji), which is at the core of the Fiji Indian diasporic sensibility. It is an ideology, he argues, that has been shaped by thwarted millenarian expectations, by nostalgic links with the cultural traditions of the Indian center, by perceived threats from the indigenous presence, and the political and social apparatuses of control and manipulation installed and implemented by the British colonial administration in Fiji. Mishra points out that it was an ideology doomed to failure from the very beginning; the Rambuka coup, which has paralyzed the Indian community in Fiji, is merely a testament to its failure. He then proceeds to analyze the role of and response to this Girmit consciousness in the works of four major Indo-Fijian writers: Subramani, Raymond Pillai, Satendra Nandan, and Sudesh Mishra.

The betrayals of history, which mark the Indo-Fijian experience, are also the central philosophical concern of V. S. Naipaul, as P. S. Chauhan argues in his pioneering interpretation of Naipaul's vision. A towering figure among contemporary writers, the twice-displaced V. S. Naipaul—a Trinidad-born Hindu Brahmin, now a reluctant resident of England—gives voice to the many ambivalences of the postcolonial diasporic Indian consciousness. His texts are exquisite articulations of his celebrated despair, his obsessive preoccupation with exile, rootlessness, and alienation. But his merciless criticism of newly independent societies and his insistent refusal to engage in "formulaic denunciations of the colonial masters" have, while endearing him to readers of certain political persuasions, elicited angry rebuttals from others. Chauhan cuts through the controversies that surround Naipaul and exposes the ideological fallacies that guide the interpretations of his works by critics from the political left as well as the right. He argues, convincingly, that the vision of history that Naipaul projects in his works not merely condemns postcolonial failures but passes "devastating judgment upon the dreams and the deeds of the colonizer" as well. History mocks at all human endeavor: the seemingly strong, inevitably, grow weak; "what the imperious will to empire proposes, time smoothly disposes—and, not infrequently, in abrupt and violently unsympathetic ways." And Chauhan asserts that such a view of human history is shaped primarily by Naipaul's "Hindu consciousness of the terrible fluidity of things human and nonhuman." Thus, despite Naipaul's ambivalence toward his ancestral homeland, despite even his occasional rejections of it, India, in subtle ways, continues to claim her prodigal diasporic child.

This recognition of the Hindu roots of Naipaul's worldview emerges in Chellappan's chapter as well. In "Voice in Exile: 'Journey' in Raja Rao and V. S. Naipaul," he argues that both Rao's *The Serpent and the Rope* and Naipaul's *A Bend in the River* are quasi-autobiographical testimonies of the authors' own attempts to heal their physical exile from India through oblique spiritual reconnection with that geographical home. India, in Rao's and Naipaul's fiction, and indeed in much of the diasporic fiction, is more than a geographical space: it is a region of the mind. As exiles their characters journey ceaselessly, but all journeys—at least in an emotional sense—lead them back to India.

Craig Tapping, in his "South Asia/North America: New Dwellings and the

Past,'' offers a sophisticated discussion of the works of several significant sub-continental writers in the United States and Canada: Ved Mehta, Sara Suleri, Michael Ondaatji, Bharati Mukherjee, Suniti Namjoshi, and Rohinton Mistry. While Tapping acknowledges that the subcontinental writers in North America are part of the international school of Indian diasporic writing, he locates them more specifically in the context of North American "ethnic" writing. And he argues that an autobiographical impulse, "the desire to name experience and to create identity, to emerge from the dominant language and gaze of 'nonethnic' America,'' is central to Indo-American immigrant literature. Given the autobiographical core of this literature, its most obsessive themes center around issues of identity, sense of displacement, resistance to racism, nostalgia for home, and search for personal and cultural wholeness.

C. L. Chua's chapter also focuses on North America, but he deals specifically with two writers, Bharati Mukherjee and V. S. Naipaul, and comments on the uneasy passage of their protagonists from India to the United States. Especially useful is Chua's detailed discussion of Mukherjee's evolution as an artist—from an insecure young Indian expatriate writer seeking in Naipaul a model for emulation to a confident storyteller who has now enthusiastically redefined herself as an American artist in the immigrant tradition of writers such as Henry Roth, Isaac Bashevis Singer, and Bernard Malamud.

Lawrence Needham's " 'The Sorrows of a Broken Time': Agha Shahid Ali and the Poetry of Loss and Recovery" offers a sensitive commentary on another important Indian diasporic writer in the United States. Needham not only discusses the central themes of Ali's poetry but also, through close readings of individual poems, comments on their technical fluency and explores the impact of diverse poetic traditions—Indian, Persian, British, and American—on Ali's art.

The aesthetics of loss that Needham locates in Agha Shahid Ali's poetry is also at the core of much of the Indian diasporic writing in the Caribbean. Victor Ramraj, in his perceptive commentary titled "Still Arriving: The Assimilationist Indo-Caribbean Experience of Marginality," focuses on the representative texts of several Indo-Caribbean writers: Seepersad Naipaul, V. S. Naipaul, Samuel Selvon, Sonny Ladoo, Neil Bissoondath, and Ismith Khan. In their works he identifies a central tension that defines Indo-Caribbean experience—the tension between the desire for cultural separation and the opposing urge toward creolization, both of which are different psychosocial responses to the same historical event: the loss of India and, consequently, the absence of home. Often unable to negotiate the dilemma, the diasporic Indians in the Caribbean remain perpetual travellers "who find themselves at the harbor contemplating the enigma of their arrival.''

Helen Tiffin, in her "History and Community Involvement in Indo-Fijian and Indo-Trinidadian Writing," provides a useful comparative study of the treatment of and response to history in selected works of Indian writers in the Caribbean and in Fiji. She argues that while history is not "a traditional Indian pursuit or mode,'' the preoccupation of "Indo-Trinidadian and Indo-Fijian imaginative writers with it . . . is at least in part a product of their journey across the black waters, the *kala pani*.'' The identifiable differences in attitudes to history between the two groups, Tiffin posits, reflect their differing reactions to the surrounding non-Indian communities, the relationship of those communities with their own histories and lands, and the presence of different colonial apparatuses in operation in Trinidad and in Fiji. But to both Indo-Trinidadian and Indo-Fijian writers, "adjustment to a new world has seemed to involve an escape from colonial history into the potentialities of a racially hybridized present." In Fiji, however, the 1987 Rambuka coup has disrupted, at least temporarily, any such progress toward hybridization of histories.

Historical tensions also inform Indian writing in Singapore, argues Kirpal Singh in his "Staying Close but Breaking Free: Indian Writers in Singapore." As far back as the fourth century Indians had begun to settle in Singapore and in the adjoining Malayan peninsula, although migration in significant numbers occurred only after the British occupation of these territories in the early nineteenth century. Currently, about 6 percent of Singapore's population of 2.8 million are of subcontinental origin. For the most part they have continued to maintain close cultural links with India, while acknowledging Singapore as their political home. Singh argues that the emotional tension inherent in their conflicting affinities "gives occasion to some intense literary expression." While Singh focuses his discussion on his own work and on that of Chandran Nair, Edwin Thumboo, and Gopal Baratham, he suggests that the desire to reconcile Indian cultural identity with Singaporean national identity is discernible in the works of several young writers as well: Bilahari Kim Hee, Elizabeth Alfred, Qirone Haddock, and Shirley Dhillon, among others.

Harold Barratt's chapter focuses largely on the works of Sam Selvon, who grew up in Trinidad, emigrated to Britain, and now resides in Canada. Barratt's "Sam Selvon's Tiger: In Search of Self-Awareness" traces the initiatory journey of Tiger—Selvon's protagonist in *A Brighter Sun* and *Turn Again Tiger*—his incremental movement out of the insular boundaries of Trinidad's rural Indian community, his gradual creolization, his spiritual reconnection with the land, and his eventual forging of a healing and liberating sense of self. Tiger's ability to achieve a sense of wholeness is, to a considerable extent, a result of his learning to affirm the cultural plurality of his Caribbean environment. Selvon, through Tiger, suggests a model not only for construction of a Trinidadian national identity but also for the formation of an authentic Indian diasporic identity in the Caribbean.

Arlene Elder's detailed chapter, "Indian Writing in East and South Africa: Multiple Approaches to Colonialism and Apartheid," begins with a historical overview of the Indian presence in Africa, surveys the Indian literary representations of individual and collective displacement, and concludes with a thorough analysis of the major themes in the works of three representative writers: Peter Nazareth, Bahadur Tejani, and Ahmed Essop. Elder argues that though "all three writers come from the same continent, and their artistic concerns are similar in that they reflect a colonial or postcolonial world of oppression, their focuses are very different, as are their solutions, styles, and ultimate views about the individual and his/her society.''

The last three chapters in the volume deal with the Indian diasporic experience in Britain. Kamala Markandaya's *Nowhere Man* is the focus of Hena Ahmad's "Kamala Markandaya and the Indian Immigrant Experience in Britain.'' A classic tale of migrant experience and an angry indictment of the pathological racism of the British, *Nowhere Man* offers a particularly bleak vision of the plight of diasporic Indians. The social realism of Markandaya's fiction sharply contrasts with the fabulist-absurdist mode of Salman Rushdie's works, as Vijay Lakshmi points out in her "Rushdie's Fiction: The World Beyond the Looking Glass.'' Rushdie's choice of narrative modes, in itself, reveals a philosophical outlook that has been shaped by the contradictions of his own immigrant experience. Finally, Anuradha Dingwaney provides an engaging discussion of the rhetorical strategies that Rushdie deploys to authorize his voice as he imaginatively reconstructs the history of the subcontinent. She demonstrates that Rushdie employs a complex set of moves that first privileges his migrant sensibility and grants him the authority to speak, but that he also safely deconstructs his authority by "insisting simultaneously on the partiality and fragmentariness of his ultimate fictions.'' Dingwaney's cogent analysis of the rhetorical strategies that Rushdie deploys in constructing his authority has broad relevance to diasporic discourse in general, since the diasporic writers—who are often "unhoused'' more than once—continue to engage in their fictions what they have left behind.

There are, as the chapters in this volume demonstrate, certain common resonances in the literary representations of the Indian diasporic experience in places as varied as Trinidad, Fiji, the United States, Singapore, Uganda, Canada, Britain, and South Africa. A complex system of historical ties, cultural bonds, spiritual affinities, and unifying racial memories generates a shared diasporic sensibility. There are common thematic concerns too: issues of identity, problems of history, confrontations with racism, intergenerational conflicts, difficulties in building new, supportive communities. The responses of individual writers vary widely. There are those who, like V. S. Naipaul, remain incapacitated in their state of homelessness, insisting on an identity that is shaped by exile, loss, and the vast betrayals of history. In contrast, there are artists, such as Bharati Mukherjee and Bahadur Tejani, who call for an end to futile nostalgic engagements with the past and a bold affirmation of the adopted land. Assimilation, they assert, would be the answer to the discontents of the diaspora. (A problematic feature of such a neat solution, however, is the questionable belief that assimilation is feasible.) And then there are writers, such as Salman Rushdie, who exuberantly celebrate the old and the new, India and the diaspora, our myths and our realities, thus imaginatively claiming for us a territory of our own. At the core of all diasporic fictions, nevertheless, is the haunting presence of India—and the anguish of personal loss it represents. It is precisely this shared experience

of absence that engenders an aesthetics of reworlding that informs and unites
the literature of the Indian diaspora.

WORKS CITED

Rushdie, Salman. "The Indian Writer in England." In *The Eye of the Beholder: Indian
    Writing in English*. Ed. Maggie Butcher. London: Commonwealth Institute, 1983:
    75–83.
Safran, William. "Diasporas in Modern Societies: Myths of Homeland and Return."
    Diaspora: A Journal of Transnational Studies 1 (Spring 1991): 83–99.

1

The Girmit Ideology Revisited: Fiji Indian Literature

Vijay Mishra

Any study of the literatures of the Indian diaspora must begin with the original moment of migration and the circumstances that made people leave the lower Gangetic Plains or the "Madras Presidency" in the first instance to help produce the preeminent stimulant, sugar, "an indispensable additive to sauces and pastry, as well as a sweetener for innumerable cups of tea," for the industrializing areas of the Western world (Wolf, 333). What is required is a massive archaeology of the "Girmit" phenomenon—the phenomenon of the experience of displacement summed up by Indian indentured laborers in the vernacularized form of "agreement" (*girmit*)—to be undertaken by historians thoroughly conversant with Indian culture and familiar with the "general project of ethnographic subjectivity and cultural description" (Clifford, 113). Classic studies such as those of Hugh Tinker on general histories and K. L. Gillion on specific histories will have to be supplemented by the histories of younger, "indigenous" scholars such as Brij Lal who have explored the material conditions of migration with a native command of the language. The contribution of literary historians too can no longer exist in a vacuum. They must draw upon the insights of ethnography and literary theory and be willing to engage their object of study with a high level of critical self-reflexivity and "ironic positioning." Though in this chapter I cannot theorize the question of cultural representation in the way in which Said and Clifford have done, it is nevertheless important that we be aware of the need for a kind of cultural polyphony, a plural definition of culture which would qualify our seemingly totalizing critical tendencies with the voice of our informants who are both writers and interpreters. My initial strategy in this chapter is to situate the field or "idea" of Mother India as a controlling mechanism in the lives of the diasporic Indian and examine, furthermore, how cultural linkages between the two were maintained and how in the nostalgic transmission of culture the diaspora itself became a fossilized fragment of the original nation.

A fragment of any nation has the capacity to duplicate in itself the dynamics of the totality of which, at the moment of forced "departure," it was a part. The fragment normally undergoes two stages of change. Its initial stage is marked by a highly imaginative process as it proposes to reconstruct a new world out of the structure of oppositions that made up, in this instance, the Indian center. But the excitement of reconstitution is soon overtaken by a reality principle, marking the second stage. Because the fragment was detached from the center, its inherent principle of dynamic growth, which lay in the contradictions of the center, cannot be reestablished. In jettisoning its Indian part, the fragment simultaneously jettisons its future, and its culture becomes ossified (Hodge and Mishra 1991). In short, a process remarkably akin to the opposing principles of fantasy and reality immediately gets under way. The inherent capacities of a revolutionary fragment, with its potential for change (the end of religious and caste divisions, for instance), are very quickly overtaken by the triumph of the "fossil." At the same time the structural inadequacies of the fragment produce a psychology that leads to the construction of ghostly enemies—the colonial masters, the indigenous race—generating a sense of threat which in turn necessitates the unity of the fragment itself.

The diasporic Indian, however, could not play out this duality upon a *tabula rasa* as the white fragments of Australia, New Zealand, and Canada had done. In these settler colonies, the complex cultural formations of the indigenous races were robbed of their complexities and the races themselves reduced to the status of landless, detribalized, disenfranchised natives. The diasporic Indian had to coexist with highly developed cultures (in Fiji or in Malaya) or other displaced groups (as in the West Indies and Mauritius) whose lives had already been affected by European imperialism.

It is out of the special conjunction of a fragment of India and a Pacific culture of a different social order that a specific Girmit ideology developed. Yet this very Pacific culture was never available to the Indian fragment in an unmediated, natural form. The fact is that the complex culture of the indigenous race in Fiji was given a historical reality and an institutional priority by the processes of imperialism itself. What emerged as a consequence was a Fijian culture that was given expression through an "inauthentic" oligarchic Fijian political structure, which was a construction, in the main, of colonialism as it responded to a perceived counterthreat from the Indian fragment. As a consequence the phantoms constructed by the fossilized fragment were the colonizing power as well as the discursive projections, institutionalized defenses, and mediated reconstructions of a Fijian cultural complex by the same imperialist machinery. In short, the unity of the fragment arose in response to two complex but self-sustaining ideologies. Of course, the fragment mistook these phantoms for reality and engineered a political apparatus based upon the success of nationalist movements elsewhere as a defense mechanism. It was the success of that political apparatus that led to the Fijian rebellion of May 14, 1987 (V. Mishra 1987).

And the incredible success of the rebellion (better known around the world as the "Pacific Coup") left the Girmit ideology bereft of any direction. Unknown to the Indians, the Fijian hegemony, which imperialism had constructed, acted in accordance with a historical predictability that Whitehall clearly understood (since it was its creation) but refused to recognize. The structures that had been put into place—the creation of imaginary constituencies and paramount chiefdoms, the racial homogeneity of the Fiji military forces, and the exclusion of the migrant race from all forms of "Fijian" representations—reacted with a vengeance that shook the Girmit ideology to its very foundation and demonstrated the pathetic inadequacy of that ideology to come to terms with historical realities. An ideology based upon fictions—its own and those of the imperial order— responded by turning inward but found no sustaining oppositions like those of the center it had left behind a century before: the contradictions that lead to dynamic responses in the wake of any threat were no longer there. What the Fijian rebellion of May 14 demonstrated was the degree to which the Indian diaspora, as a fragment, had reconstituted an India that could not interact with the Fijian world, while at the same time this Fijian world, still trapped in an imperialist conception of itself, had not acknowledged the historical reality of the people of the diaspora. The schism that May 14 brought about grew out of a drama authored by colonialism. It was a drama of multiple but false consciousnesses—both Fijian and Indian—trying to find an authentic ground for their existence. The narrative of Fijian history since 1879 was plotted by the colonizer the moment the Indian arrived. Postcolonial Fiji would replay its colonial past, though with far less panache and certainly less class. There was no Latin postscript appended to a colonial despatch by an ex-Balliol district officer.

It is the "moment" of the Fijian rebellion that takes me back to essays on Fiji Indian literature and culture I wrote between 1977 and 1980 (V. Mishra 1977; 1979; 1980). As a contribution to this volume on the Indian diaspora, the schism occasioned by the events of May 14, 1987, necessitates a reexamination of the theses advanced in my earlier studies. The chapter will therefore be a critique of my earlier positions and, on the whole, a contribution to the relationship between theory and practice.

"Indo-Fijian Fiction: Towards an Interpretation" (V. Mishra 1977), subsequently reprinted as "Indo-Fijian Fiction and the Girmit Ideology" (in Tiffin 1978 and Subramani 1979), connected an identifiable Indian indenture consciousness with failed millenarian expectations. This consciousness, it was argued, arose out of the initial period of "servitude" which, cumulatively for this fragment, spanned some forty years, between 1879 and 1917. It was also argued that this millenarianism itself was a consequence of a cultural fossilization that necessitated a reading of history in terms of an unfulfilled past subsequently endowed with a fullness, a completion, which it never had. This explained the ambiguity of the *Rama-rajya* syndrome—the fact that in the Kingdom of Rama left behind the millenarian had found a complete, unproblematic expression. If this is the case, then the historical direction of the Fiji Indian is broadly akin to a failed millenarian quest, since the constant deferral of the real historical moment is continually displaced by the myth of a fulfillment in the future which, given the regression to Rama-rajya, would be a duplication of a past. The fossilized fragment seeks renewal through a paradoxical refossilization of itself.

The relationship between art and history is mediated, for the Fiji Indian, by a conception of the world that has for its ground a highly problematic reading of history. As K. L. Gillion (1962) demonstrates, Indian indentured laborers, when asked to explain the reasons for their quite pointless emigration, filled their narratives with decidedly "end-oriented" possibilities, confirming, in other words, the tyranny of the structure of millenarian thinking as well as the special nature of the genre of recollection itself. In these narratives one gets very little of the prevailing social conditions of the times, little indeed of those factors that force people out of their societies into newer ones. The fact that the laborers' vision of the past was distorted by their sense of disillusionment is vividly captured by Gillion, who states that the Indians called "their life on the plantations in Fiji '*narak*', which means 'hell' " (129). Herein, I believe, lies the clue to an understanding of Indian psychology in Fiji: no matter what positive virtues the system may have had (standards of living were better, there were fewer caste divisions, etc.), the bitterness of displacement and its consequent dehumanization in coolie lines, which Totaram Sanadhya called *bhut len* (haunted lines), must have had a deep psychological effect upon a group perhaps by culture more sensitive than most toward the evils of crossing the *kala pani*, the dark seas.

The typical indentured laborer was, however, ill-equipped to come to terms with an unfulfilled dream. Estranged from the village society, he had no one to tell him that this was not the hoped-for *moksha* (heaven). When the tenth incarnation did not eventuate, his village always had a learned Brahmin to make meaning of God's peculiar ways. Of men's deception in an alien land there was no consoling rationale or an omnipresent line from the *Gita*. But there were other "memories" that had a stark impact on that consciousness. The cholera, sickness, and deaths on the first ship, *Leonidas* (1879), were quickly transformed into all the evils of *kaliyuga* (an apocalyptic era that precedes the millennium); the wreck of the *Syria* on the evening of May 11, 1884—about which a contemporary wrote: "The scene was simply indescribable, and pictures of it haunt me still like a horrid dream that one is glad to escape from by waking. People falling, fainting, drowning all around one" (Gillion 1962, 64–65)—became a haunting memory of a journey whose validity is still to be established. The ghost in Satendra Nandan's verse, for instance, tells the listener:

> o my father's fathers
> what forgiveness is there in me?

o my children's children
listen to the voices from the *syria*
drowning the silence of the sea!

(Nandan 1985, 54)

Satendra Nandan, the Fiji Indian poet and short story writer, is, of course, troubled by that experience and attempts to make meaning of it. He returns again and again to this theme, as we shall see later.

Given the extremely powerful, even poetic, nature of the experience, the sad fact is that fiction has taken so long to establish itself in Fiji. Of course, there were Indian writers such as Totaram Sanadhya, Pandit Amichand (both Indian expatriates), Pandit Pratap Chandra Sharma, and Kamla Prasad (both local Fiji Indian writers) who have tried to capture something of the intensity of the indenture experience in their Hindi writings. Pandit Pratap Chandra Sharma's poem "Keni Peni" is especially important in that, though it deals with the lives of two Fijian boys during and after the *badi beemari*, the Great Plague of 1917–18, it is presented very much through an Indian sensitivity as a microcosmic rendering in fact of the dreams and expectations of the indentured laborers generally. In many ways Sharma's verse predates the more conscious search for meaning that one finds in the fiction of contemporary Indo-Fijian writers, particularly in the works of Nandan, Subramani, and Sudesh Mishra.

It was in such a context, the context, that is, of the Fiji-Indian past as a dynamic and valid creative background, that I considered Fiji's best-known writers, Satendra Nandan, Raymond Pillai, and Subramani. To this list I would now add the name of Sudesh Mishra. Nandan and Sudesh Mishra are the writers who have been most acutely conscious of the weight of the Girmit experience, its contradictions and its function as a defining source of indenture consciousness. Thus for them it is the *pastness* of the Girmit past and its relationship to the creative consciousness of the poet that require artistic organization. Thus Nandan's ghost continues:

youth i lost here, and grace
i gave to this island place.
what more than a man's age
can one give to history's outrage?
. . . .
i have lived this exile
more gloriously than rama
and built kingdoms, you may find,
nobler than ajodhya
in my ancient, eternal mind!

There is something pathetic, out of sorts in fact, about the claims of those who participated in the original journey. The comparison with Rama ("more gloriously") is a necessary overstatement given the need to affirm one's exile, but the achievement, the building of kingdoms, is a curious double take. The new kingdoms are certainly nobler, but they are also regressive and fictive: "in my ancient, eternal mind!" But oral history is also inauthentic, says Nandan. The claims of a superior experience, a finer, more solid achievement, are, after all, claims of the word, of oral history, which Nandan finds ironically inadmissible in "The Old Man and the Scholar":

> authentic history cannot be written
> with words from living mouths.

> (Nandan 1985, 61)

In Subramani's short stories—and notably in "Sautu," "Marigolds," and "Kala"—we find a much more ironic and detached "transformation" of the Girmit ideology (Subramani 1979; 1984). In "Sautu" the transformation is less mediated, since the relationship between the historical experience and Dhanpat the farmer's mental disintegration is given more directly. In subsequent work, Subramani has explored the minds of his Fiji Indian characters in ways that demonstrate the growth of a complex sensibility. Indeed, it can hardly be claimed that, in his representation of Kala, Subramani is self-consciously working out the massive social and cultural problems of the Indian fragment in Fiji. But she is being constructed as a particular totality whose relationship with her husband Sukhen and whose encounters with the metaphysics of love (both love-in-separation, *viraha*, and love-in-union, *sambhoga*) make her so susceptible to desire as she negotiates a silent conspiracy of love with a stranger in an ideal reenactment of viraha. The point, however, is that Kala's fragility arises out of the complex function of the experience of the Indian fragment as that fragment finds new ways of constructing meaning. The triumph of Subramani's "Kala" grows precisely out of the need of a new "construction" that requires for its completion the voice, the projection, the images of a woman, the silent, unwritten, "unpraised" Other of the Girmit ideology.

Yet in a peculiar way Subramani's short stories lay bare an intractable, deepseated schizophrenia or contradiction, one that Mudrooroo Narogin has found in Aboriginal literature as well (Hodge and Mishra 1990). This contradiction arises from the way in which the colonized is compromised by the generic expectations of the colonizer. The absent colonizer continues to manipulate the discourses of the colonized, imposing ghostly standards through an insistence upon the perfection of standard English and thus prohibiting (as aberrant) the emergence of a language that can speak with the authentic voices of the colonized. In a way Subramani is bonded to a kind of literary imprisonment which leads to a general mimicry of the colonizer's discourses. What this mimicry demonstrates is the degree to which the indentured Indian has become fossilized twice over: once as a frozen fragment of Mother India, and again as a "linguistic" fragment of the language left behind by the colonizer. Beneath this is the power of the colonizer's immense control over those apparatuses that control culture.

Thus the colonizer's estranged standard English, his selective Protestant ethic, and his dissemination of selected literary texts for colonial consumption (*Henry V*, Sheridan, Thomas Hardy, *The Golden Treasury of Verse*) meant that the colonized were never exposed to the great and complex texts of the metropolitan center. Nor were they exposed to those high modern texts that were experimental and that arose from a desire to foreground the uncanonized. Indentured Indian writing, like Aboriginal writing (Narogin 1990; V. Mishra 1988/89), was trapped in this generic and linguistic vacuum, since the Indians were taught no other: their own fantastic texts (which included the greatest text of mankind, the *Mahabharata*) were suppressed as texts without power and bereft of knowledge (V. Mishra 1988).

Thus, even at his best, Subramani's characters "translate" into standard English their innermost feelings. The need for an explosive polyphony through dialogism, for instance, is constantly held in check by the absent colonizer, whose discourses and modes of representation control the text. Like the classic ethnographic writer, there is a preferred, a controlled, mode of representation that Subramani adopts which, in James Clifford's words, is a "controlling discourse" (47), a preference for the Flaubertian *style indirect* over a Dickensian discursive heterogeneity.

Nowhere is this tendency toward control, and silent adulation of the colonizer's selection of texts for colonial consumption, more evident than in the works of Raymond Pillai. The generic form that Pillai appropriates—the fable, the ballad, hymnody, mimetic representation, linear narrative, and so on—demonstrates the strength of the control over literary culture the colonizer had over the colonized. Raymond Pillai's poems and short stories show how "scarred," how much of a "splinter" (in the side of a colonial culture) the Indian diaspora generally is. It is pointless to accuse Pillai of antiquated rhythmical patterns in "Labourer's Lament" and "To My Foster Mother" (Subramani 1979), which are, by the standards of the metropolitan center, effete and dated. What is significant is the political statement that underlies the mimicry. This statement speaks of linguistic slavery and conformism, of a cultural imperialism that triumphed in the colonies and was continued when a curriculum based upon Senior Cambridge was replaced by that of New Zealand University Entrance.

In my introduction and epilogue to *Rama's Banishment* I returned to the psychology of the indentured Indian through V. S. Naipaul's return to India. I have yet to complete my study of Naipaul in terms of the Girmit experience, but I would like to return to the issues I raised then, since I do believe that it is an extremely under-theorized aspect of both V. S. Naipaul and of the relationship between the fossil and its totality. Whilst the fossil remains uncomfortably situated between a center whose dynamism it can no longer duplicate and a context whose social formations it cannot totally adopt, it nevertheless cannot return to the center for either emotional sustenance or cultural capital. In other words, when the return does take place, the diaspora becomes hysterical: a hundred years of banishment has made any easy return to the totality of the center impossible. In this respect the diaspora, often unawares (since it continues to hanker after the totality left behind), has become a splinter in the side of the indigenous culture itself. Thus, like Rama, Naipaul's return to India can only lead to the diaspora's disavowal of India as the source of origin. In rejecting India, Naipaul repeats Rama's rejection of Sita upon his return: the fact of banishment is so complete that the fragment must reject its origins since that is the only way in which it can confirm or affirm its difference as superior to that which it left behind (V. Mishra 1978).

The third essay that I wish to refer to appeared in 1980 (V. Mishra 1980; Nandan 1983). In this paper I argued that the Girmit consciousness, which developed as a result of forty years of direct indenture, is a false consciousness or, at any rate, could be read as a false consciousness, an ideology which in Marxist theory is opposed to the *real*. Whilst it was a false consciousness, it was nevertheless necessary, and the Fiji Indians transformed this falsification into a highly sophisticated social construct. The Girmit ideology informed Indian social processes and formations to such an extent that it alone legitimated their existence. In this way the diasporic Indian excluded from his own interactive domains other Indians (notably merchant traders and other free Indian migrants) who could not possibly share this Girmit past. Furthermore, the Girmit ideology blinded the Fiji Indians to the facts of life in Fiji and the relationship that they ought to enter into with regard to native Fijians. But above all, it gave the Indians a false sense of security, a false reading of politics, and an insularity that could then be exploited by others (by the colonizers as well as by expatriate Indian politicians). It gave them, quite possibly, an inferiority complex, because the practical enactment of consciousness was not possible. For the literary theorist, then, it is only those literatures of the diaspora that struggle to get out of this distortion, that demonstrate the Girmit man's struggle to redefine this conscious-ness and triumph over it, and that explode the processes and compromises that led to their construction in the first instance, that require special attention.

It is in Subramani's short stories—and notably in "Marigolds"—that one detects a form of fiction that transcends this Girmit false consciousness by denoting through an intrinsic concentration on its central character, Chetram, actions that, while reflecting the crisis of a hundred years of banishment, dem-onstrate simultaneously an awareness of where the ideology has gone wrong. But more is at stake here, since a false consciousness, ultimately, necessitates an act of practical commitment, a drastic reorganization of the fundamental processes within the matrix that buttress and uphold that consciousness. This program, articulated variously by the left wing of the Fiji Labor Party, was preempted by the Fijian revolt of 1987. In the process, the fragment returned to its fossils, and the indigenous Fijians demonstrated once again their own equally false ideology, which was created for them by imperialism. Transformed into an "immemorial tradition" (France, 174), this ideology of orthodoxy and chiefly power paid no heed to the truth of history itself. In doing so it refossilized both the fragment and its own self, adopting and embracing in the process the structures of a colonialism which, finally, had time for neither the Girmitiyas nor the Fijians. To the metropolitan center, they were both the wretched of the earth: one to be denigrated for its ambitions, the other first to be projected as pre-Edenic characters and then patronized and exploited. Republican Fiji still parades its Knight Bachelors.

GIRMITIYA POLYPHONY: TWO EXEMPLARY VOICES

I would like to end my primarily theoretical contribution to this volume on the Indian diaspora with a reading of a poet whom I have mentioned in passing (Nandan 1985) and another who has not been an object of any sustained critical disquisition (Sudesh Mishra 1987). Satendra Nandan writes poetic narratives in the realist mode. These narratives have a unity that arises out of the experiences of the past, many of which occurred in and around the village of his birth. Both his recent collection of verses and its earlier prototype (1976) are therefore journeys back into a past left behind. What strikes me more emphatically upon rereading his poems is the polyphonic nature of his verse. This polyphony takes the form of a realist mode that is carved open or radically splintered by a specifically Girmitiya discourse generally referred to as Fiji Hindi by linguists. The discourse of Fiji Hindi is one way in which the language of the colonizer may be both ironized and deconstructed. Let me examine this further with reference to his poem "The Strange Death of Bisnath" (Nandan 1985, 63–65). The poem has a simple, straightforward narrative structure. An airport has been built around Bisnath's hut, and his hens as well as his cows have lost their freedom to graze. He complains to the colonial governor, but is rebuked for such audacity by the local district officer, a fellow Indian, who tells him that matters of this kind (complaints based upon a total ignorance of the pecking order) could be amicably handled between Indians. The gesture understood, "bisnath, ramnath's brightest son," offers him *nagona* (grog) that night but dies in the early hours of the morning as a result of a coronary thrombosis.

The simplicity of the structure belies an ideological statement that arises out of Nandan's destabilization of the natural "continuum" of the colonizer's language. In one way the colonizer assumes unproblematic "representationalism" through the English language: once the colonized have mastered its grammar, they too can mimic poetic forms for purposes of artistic representation. To an extent, Nandan is trapped in this borrowed linguistic garb. But the defining moments in the poem arise not when the signifiers can be grounded to their signifieds but when an alien discourse distorts and disorients the language of standard English. It is at moments like this—appropriation marked by linguistic rebelliousness—that another voice, a polyphony, emerges and requires, from the reader, an act of labor. In classic accounts of the reading process it is ambiguity or resistance to representation in the dominant language itself that leads to poetic "significance" and the construction of meaning. Here the resistances come from the manipulation of another language, which requires both a gloss and a radical shift in perspective. The critique comes from precisely the discourse of the Other, which colonial curricula had suppressed. And in the self-conscious appropriation of the discourse of the Other that was most suppressed (Fiji Hindi as opposed to High Standard Hindi, *Khari Boli*), we find a challenge to the nature of poetry itself. Let us look at just one particular phrase: *"ghar jao nagona pio"* (go home and drink *yagona*/grog), varied to *"sahib, au nagona pio"* (Sir, come in and drink *yagona*). Now, there can be nothing more ordinary than these utterances in Fiji Hindi. And nothing can be more removed from poetic discourse either, especially as the colonial overseers in the sugar plantations had included this in the list of phrases they memorized. Thus the Indian district officer's use of it (through the echo of its use by the ruling class) makes him an accomplice and gives him power over his own kinsmen. Similarly Bisnath's manipulation of the phrase (who understood the district officer's "cunning, coolie smile") through its repetition demonstrates the ways in which the colonized too had learned to play the game. Bisnath, an informant in classic ethnographic discourses, enters, as interpreter of his own culture, the world of the postcolonial.

The contradictory discourses that go into the making of "The Strange Death of Bisnath" may be found elsewhere in Nandan's verse, though unfortunately not in the gratuitous translations into Khari Boli of selected pieces at the end of the volume. There is, however, another kind of polyphony, arising out of non-realistic representations, which is directly related to my discussion so far. This kind of polyphony is best exemplified in the poems of a young Fiji Indian poet, Sudesh Mishra. Mishra's polyphony reworks the Indo-Fijian literary tradition exemplified in Nandan's realist texts into discourses which mingle into one another and which have a markedly "postmodern" resonance. The postmodernity I have in mind is the type that groups a certain "uncanonized" body of literature as the underside of a literary-cultural dominant. In this postmodernity, for which the postcolonial is remarkably well equipped, discourses of the Other threaten to blast open representation without marking their difference out, as Nandan's discourse, more cautiously, does. Thus Nandan's postmodern polyphony is anticipated, marked, and glossed in the texts themselves. Mishra's, on the other hand, invades the colonizer's language and substitutes, in strategic places, the language of the colonized for that of the colonizer. Here are two lines from the opening poem of his collection, "Confessions of a Poetaster from Fiji":

> forking visions of men in mire,
> maya in men. Deep in my *teeriteeri*
>
> (Mishra 1987, 1)

The hidden intertext here is obviously Yeats's "Byzantium" ("And all complexities of mire or blood"), but notice how "men in mire" (Mishra's version) is invaded by its chiasmic "maya in men." "Mire" (literally "swampy ground") is glossed by "maya" (the principle of illusion), which is closer to what Yeats had in mind in his own "And all complexities of mire and blood." But notice too how the base meaning of "mire" now gets repeated in the hidden, *sandhya bhasha* ("twilight language"), the cryptic language of the colonized as it appears in *teeriteeri*. This Fijian word (not a Fiji Hindi word), which is glossed as "mangrove swamp," has become part of Fiji Hindi and is therefore doubly contextualized. But it does a fillip on "mire," since that word finds its "representational" synonym in "territeeri" but its poetic meaning in "maya." This complex semiotic coding, on the basis of a play on a language that the language of the colonizer negates or occludes, is a characteristic feature of Mishra's verse and gives it a kind of polyphony—an Other voice—markedly different from the kind of polyphony (which is equally effective nevertheless) found in Nandan.

The definition of the Fiji Indian also undergoes a transformation that lacks the optimism and affirmation of Satendra Nandan. Mishra's "Indo-Fijian" (in a poem of that name) is all memory and maya, as he reconstructs out of "papier mâché" a self "gored" by "hysteria" and "panic," and suffocated by a "muffled scream." There is no redemption from "the panic of the cutting season," no escape from the original condition of indenture. It is this negative transformation that separates Mishra from Nandan as he constructs in the process a schizophrenia that is constitutive of the Fiji Indian. This schizophrenia of a fragment twice dislocated finds its discursive form in the multiplicity of languages and voices through which it is articulated.

With an eye to the past (the India left behind by the fragment) and another to the present (the future, for those who know the "grisly truth" of the wreck of the *Syria*, offers no consolation), Mishra mediates the Girmit ideology with poems that do not open up their secrets easily to the uninitiated. One of its central metaphors, and its primordial secret, is captured in the title poem of the collection, "Rahu," the name given to the decapitated demon whose immortal head (since he too had partaken of the eternal elixir during the churning of the ocean) intermittently plays havoc with Vishnu's conspirators, the Sun and the Moon, by swallowing them. The ambiguity of Rahu—forever lost in the cosmos and recognized only by his shadow as the solar and lunar eclipses—becomes Mishra's central metaphor both of the Girmit fragment and also of mankind generally. Mishra's discourse is thus "interlaced" with an account of a race who migrated "From the land of henna, vermilion" ("In Nadi [5]") only to find that, like Narcissus, their gaze merely unlocks the truth about themselves.

The Fijian revolt of May 14, 1987 (exactly 108 years since the arrival in Fijian waters of the sailing ship *Leonidas* with its cargo of 463 Indian indentured laborers), has shattered the Fijian Indian to such an extent that the Girmit ideology itself is in need of reexamination and a new archaeology. In this largely theoretical chapter I have tried to demonstrate the significance of the Girmit experience as an ideological dominant in Fiji Indian society. My own attempt to come to terms with this ideology once again has been occasioned by the "imperative" of the Fijian rebellion, since this "imperative," as I have argued, confuses and places in disarray the historical foundations of the fragment itself. The reflection on my earlier essays has also enabled me to meditate upon the larger issues of postcolonialism in the context of a multiracial society where the colonizer leaves intact structures which, transformed, would only play out a history always implicit in the structures themselves. The meditation, however, convinces me, nevertheless, of the structural necessity of the Girmit ideology: such indeed is the nature of a fragment society so rudely wrenched from its metropolitan center that "every mimosa that infolds within, infolds / A part of the racial memory" (Mishra 1987, 23).

WORKS CITED

Clifford, James. *The Predicament of Culture: Twentieth-Century Ethnography, Literature, and Art*. Cambridge, Mass.: Harvard University Press, 1988.

France, Peter. *The Charter of the Land*. Melbourne: Oxford University Press, 1969.

Gillion, K. L. *Fiji's Indian Migrants*. Melbourne: Oxford University Press, 1962.

Hodge, Robert, and Vijay Mishra. Review of *Writing from the Fringe*, by Mudrooroo Narogin. *Westerly* 3 (1990): 91–93.

———. *The Dark Side of the Dream: Australian Literature and the Postcolonial Mind*. Sydney: George Allen and Unwin, 1991.

Lal, Brij V. *The Girmitiyas: The Origins of the Fiji Indians*. Canberra: Journal of Pacific History, 1983.

Mishra, Sudesh. *Rahu*. Suva: Vision International, 1987.

Mishra, Vijay. "Indo-Fijian Fiction: Towards an Interpretation." *World Literature Written in English* 16 (1977): 395–408.

———. "Mythic Fabulation: Naipaul's India." *New Literature Review* 4 (1978): 59–65.

———, ed. *Rama's Banishment: A Centenary Tribute to the Fiji Indians*. Auckland: Heinemann, 1979.

———. "Rama's Banishment: A Theoretical Footnote to Indo-Fijian Writing." *World Literature Written in English* 19 (1980): 242–56.

———. "The Quiet Coup." *Arena* 80 (1987): 29–35.

———. "Aboriginal Representations in Australian Texts." *Continuum* 2 (1988/89): 165–88.

Nandan, Satendra, ed. *Language and Literature. ACLALS Proceedings*. Suva: University of the South Pacific, 1983.

———. *Voices in the River*. Suva: Vision International, 1985.

Narogin, Mudrooroo. *Writing from the Fringe: A Study of Modern Aboriginal Literature*. Melbourne: Hyland House, 1990.

Said, Edward W. *Orientalism*. London: Routledge and Kegan Paul, 1978.

Subramani, ed. *The Indo-Fijian Experience*. St. Lucia: University of Queensland Press, 1979.

———. "Kala." *Span* 18 (1984): 2–19.

Tiffin, Chris, ed. *South Pacific Images*. Brisbane: SPACLALS, 1978.

Tinker, Hugh. *A New System of Slavery: The Export of Indian Labour Overseas 1830–1920*. Oxford: Oxford University Press, 1974.

Wolf, Eric R. *Europe and the People Without History*. Berkeley: University of California Press, 1982.

2

V. S. Naipaul: History as Cosmic Irony

P. S. Chauhan

No English writer since D. H. Lawrence has been the center of such a bitter controversy as has raged around the work of V. S. Naipaul. To cite but a few contrary opinions about his achievement, Irving Howe regards him as "the world's writer" who, with Octavio Paz, Milan Kundera, and George Konrad, would suitably constitute the finest quartet of contemporary literary luminaries (350). But one Patrice Johnson can find in him nothing finer than a servile authority, ready "to serve up a view of Third World politics palatable only to a colonialist sensibility" (14). And yet there is J. J. Healy, who discovers in Naipaul's work not a trace of opportunism, but an irrefutable proof of something valiantly executed "with great risk over the last twenty-five years" (51–52). On the issue of authenticity, if Murray S. Martin thinks that Naipaul's work is "affected by the history of his own island home and by its place in the world scheme of things" (33), Helen Pyne-Timothy believes that "V. S. Naipaul is an anachronism in Third World writing" (247). Clearly, the gulf between Naipaul's admirers and his critics calls for an explanation that may help his readers negotiate the enigma that his work has been made out to be.

The debate about the nature and status of Naipaul's work—in Cudjoe's terms "the battle of readings" (226)—partisan even when it is passionate, often suffers from limitations of the critical assumptions that are unable to accommodate his philosophical outlook. Indeed, much to its embarrassment, the criticism of Naipaul begins with a litany of his Trinidadian origins, glosses over his Indian parentage, and insists upon his British education, as if the key that would unlock the author's mind might ultimately lie in the accidents of his life. His critics, confining themselves to a biographical perspective or to occasional ideological

forays, get into high dudgeon because Naipaul would not engage in either formulaic denunciations of the colonial masters or the self-righteous praise of the
land of his ancestors, the two favorite tacks of colonial writers. An open reading
of Naipaul's work would suggest that if his critics, instead of imposing their
expectations upon it, related his individual statements to the unifying philosophic
outlook that underlies his writing, they might recognize that his work carries a
more devastating judgment upon the dreams and the deeds of the colonizer than
would any wholesale ritualistic denunciation. They might see, too, why his work
has come to be part of the modern consciousness that it embodies evenly, without
any fear or favor.

The purpose of this chapter is to look at the recurring rhetorical devices that
not only advance the plots of his novels but also hold the threads of his historical
narratives together. Embedded in the interstices between the narrative blocks
may lie the evidence, it is assumed, that could well explain the movement of
the narrator's mind from one detail to another, till the entire curve of the text
gets plotted. And the repetitive pattern of the narrative can alone illuminate the
nature of the writer's consciousness and explain the basis of his judgments.

Now it is commonly agreed that the first four works of Naipaul, from *The
Mystic Masseur* (1957) through *A House for Mr. Biswas* (1961), form a category
by themselves, even though the latter sounds a note slightly different from those
of the rest. The author's imagination, reveling in *la comédie humaine* of the
East Indian community, populates the fiction with characters—now comic, now
pathetic—who dodge in and out of the streets, villages, and villas, till the curtain
comes down upon their antics and shuts out their play. For all its irony and
irreverence, theirs is a solid world of realistic details, one not much different
from what we have come to identify as the literary preserve of a Balzac or a
Dickens. The author's gaze, occupied by the here and the now, does not stray
into the heretofore and the hereafter. The present shall suffice for the moment.
The young author seems content reflecting upon the pageant of the people whom,
as he says in *The Overcrowded Barracoon*, he can unerringly "place almost as
soon as [he sees] them" (15).

By the time we reach his next novel, *The Mimic Men* (1967), however,
something seems to have shifted. The narrative is no longer linear, the tone far
from comic, and the scene anything but stable. The story straddles two islands,
England and Isabella, as the hero vacillates between the orderly existence of the
former and the chaotic life of the latter. Everything is adrift in the story, where
all well-laid plans go awry. The world the novel delivers is found caught in a
vortex of contemporary history, spinning beyond men's calculation, indeed beyond human control. The men who planned to change the face of Isabella,
broken and discarded in the attempt, are shoved to the sidelines and left to
reminisce about their past. The story registers a change not only in Naipaul's
perception and understanding of the human situation but also in his art. The
chronology of events is broken up and time is telescoped, and this is done to
subject the narrative to a dominant idea: that of the vanity of human wishes.

The fiction, the history, and the travelogue that follow rehearse the same theme, although in different costumes.

Between Naipaul's earlier fiction and *The Mimic Men* lies, it must be observed, *An Area of Darkness* (1964), containing the author's appalling discovery, like Kurtz's before him, of the darkness within, and containing, too, his meditation on how the ancient Indian civilization, once vital, pathetically comes to be engulfed in greater darkness. In people's ignorance of their own history lies, Naipaul concludes, their inability to comprehend their place in the world and the meaning of their fate. Their lives, oblivious of the general direction of their movement, must remain a constant skip and shuffle. Hence, perhaps, the tenacious need in the writer to impose a historical perspective on every bit of human existence. It is as if, confronted by the ruins of a great civilization and baffled by the historical amnesia of its survivors, Naipaul returns to the West with a sharper awareness of the transitoriness of all human enterprises and with an enhanced respect for a historical perspective.

In any case, after the publication of *An Area of Darkness*, Naipaul seems to have lost interest in factual representation, preferring, instead, to emphasize the historical contours of the collective lives of the people who happen to be the subject of his momentary engagement. Empirical details, the ephemera of history, will henceforth be shunned in favor of the patterns of history his mind has begun to discern in the tangled stories of Arabs and Indians, Africans and Latin Americans. Microscopic mimesis, still admissible in small sections, is now to be replaced by grand, telling impressions that can lay bare the macroscopic hieroglyphics of time. If the earlier Naipaul, to use Aristotelian terms, was a historian of realism, relating "what has happened" to a certain community, the later Naipaul becomes a poet, writing of "what may happen" to the human kind, "of what is past, or passing, or to come." From now on, his writing will become analogic; every tale, the fable of a bitter truth that has happened once and will happen again, the human race being what it is—greedy, petty, blind, and stupid— unwilling to learn and unable to change.

The Mimic Men, the novel that ushers in the second stage in Naipaul's development, carries several clues to the new orientation of the author. "My first instinct," says Ralph Singh, the hero, "was towards the writing of history," the instinct beginning to stir within him the moment he begins to think of himself "as a performer" (81), a writer. The narrator becomes both the participant and the observer of his own acts, at once the subject and the object of his musings, a dispassionate intellect. The sensation confers upon him "the shock of the first historian's vision" (81), ushering in a religious moment that brings about a vision of disorder. In successive fictions, the reader will be called upon to share such vision, if only in bits and pieces. It is not the episodes but their design that will henceforward be important, be the text a novel or a travelogue.

Once Ralph Singh, driving with his father, comes across old Carib areas where the populace was more Negro than Carib. Yet there had been a time, he recalls, when the Caribs were the Negroes' implacable tormentors. But decimated and assimilated, the Caribs "had simply ceased to be" (121). Here Singh confronts, then, a discovery of great import, a concrete proof of "the rise and fall and extinction of peoples." And when he realizes that history has dealt evenly with everyone, with trackers and runaways, with the hunter and the hunted, Ralph Singh, like a Buddhist, reaches the conclusion "that nothing [is] secure" (121).

Whereas another narrator would have noted only the villages of a people who "were a baked copper color" and "had big light eyes," Ralph Singh's mind, tunneling through history, tumbles upon the brutal past of the island writ large upon the depleted stock of the people, disfigured by disease. The scene, ominously devoid of the original inhabitants of the island, brings to the narrator's mind the philosophic truth the Indian thinkers had known too well—"that nothing was secure," that what looked stable was but an illusion of permanence. Following the train of the protagonist's thought, the reader has gone through a moment of epiphany such as is sparked only by a great piece of literature.

The enlightening vision of history, always the privilege of the Naipaul narrator, repeatedly illuminates the reader's way through the author's maturer fiction. Salim, our young guide through *A Bend in the River* (1979), senses some restlessness in his locality, "an Arab-Indian-Persian-Portuguese place," which, though located on the east coast of Africa, was not really African (10). He looks at a stockade on the beach and realizes that "it was in this stockade that the slaves were kept after they had been marched down from the interior in the caravans" (12) and that it was there that they waited for the dhows to take them to the Arabian peninsula. Later on, driving into the heart of Africa, he would discover the irony of his own situation. He was making the same journey that the enslaved had done centuries ago, but in the opposite direction. He was trudging from the coast to the interior, while they were driven from the interior to the coast. He would even relive the emotions of the slaves of generations gone by, becoming anxious only to arrive. Salim's harsh situation, when linked with the African past, becomes bearable if only because, subsumed as part of a historical pattern, it has become intelligible. History does have its consolations, after all.

It is not only Salim, an individual, who rehearses the journey of individual slaves. The entire slave-owning communities have been condemned, with the passage of time, to relive the fate of their former slaves. Initially, for instance, it had been the Arabs, who, taking African women into their harems, had transferred "blood from master to slave." But, lately, the process had become reversed. The slaves had so successfully swamped the masters that "the Arabian race of the master had virtually disappeared" (14). History, the novel insists, inexorably reenacts scenes from the past; only the roles get reversed in the restaging. Whether it is the Caribs or the Arabs, the persecutor finally feels the vengeance of the persecuted; the oppressor yields the stage to the oppressed. The colonizer exchanges places with the colonized.

The panoramic view of history that the Naipaul novel invariably sketches reminds us that, down the ages, most human enterprises have foundered in a sea of irony. What the long perspective of human conduct brings home to us is not the heroism, but the blindness, of the human race, of a breed incapable of visualizing what tomorrow will deal out to the enthusiasts of today. Viewed in a historical perspective, all human endeavors seem to have an ironic ending.

It is, however, not in its grand sweeps alone that history works out perversely, forever stranding posterity as an embarrassing testimony to the great ancestors' folly. The personal careers of Naipaul's creatures trace a similar curve—from dream to disillusionment. The seared Ralph Singh, all passions spent, concludes: "From playacting to disorder: it is the pattern" (*Mimic Men*, 184). He had, like many an American expatriate before him, left the Caribbean island for London, the heartbeat of the world, hoping to find culture and "the beginning of order" in the great metropolis of the empire (18). Finding neither, he returns to his island home, planning to install himself in a paternalistic "old timber estate house . . . hung with cooling ferns, the floors dark and worn and shining." As to his lifestyle on the estate, he dreamt he "would have gone riding in the early morning. The labourers would have been at their undemanding tasks. . . . Words would have been exchanged, about their jobs, their families, the progress of their sons at school" (33–34).

The use of the wishful subjunctive, "I would have," comes as a pathetic commentary on the futility of his dreams. For Ralph Singh ends up, finally, in a cramped and narrow attic of a seedy hotel in London. "I write," he reports like a Gerontion, "in circumstances so different," in a room whose "skirting board has shrunk, with all the woodwork" (34). And beyond his room "there is a ceaseless roar of traffic." Here, alas, there are "no cocoa trees! No orange-and-yellow *immortelle* flowers! No woodland springs. . . . No morning rides" (35). Ultimately, he is left with nothing that he had hoped for and striven for. Whereas he had looked forward to a pastoral paradise, he ends up in an urban purgatory.

His lifelong quest for "order" ends, too, in a spiritual morass. He had escaped from Isabella because he used to believe that to belong to an obscure, barbarous New World transplantation was "to be born to disorder" (118). In the colonizer's capital, he would find, he had believed, an implacable order—an unambiguous, firm, and predictable set-up. Once there, though, he discovers that that world is not his. "It goes beyond my dream" (36). As a consequence, he ends up with the bitter knowledge that "disorder has its own logic and permanence" (118). Unexpected twists and turns, he must painfully learn, are an integral part of the universal history. But if "a man . . . fights only when he hopes, when he has a vision of order," then a paralysis of will must strike Ralph Singh, as indeed it does. For, as the narrator acknowledges, at the end "there was my vision of a disorder which it was beyond any one man to right" (207). The uncompromising seeker has made a compromise.

If the exemplary medieval mind had managed to stay "unassailable," it was because, as Naipaul says in *An Area of Darkness*, "it existed in a world which, with all its ups and downs, remained harmoniously ordered and could be taken for granted.'' The reason why the medieval mind, as opposed to the modern, had escaped an ontological despair was that "it had not developed a sense of history, which is a sense of loss" (152). Naipaul's despair about the future of various peoples, it is fair to surmise, proceeds from his perception of the recurrence of an ironic pattern in modern human history.

Should we conclude that Singh was foiled by the peculiar nature of his island society, we shall be warned that Salim's fortune in the continent of Africa turns out no differently. Renouncing his home and connections on the east coast, he plunges into the heart of the continent in search of a fortune. But as the novel draws to a close, we find him in jail, deprived of his shop and stripped of his property, escaping only with the help of Ferdinand, the lycée boy to whom he was once a mentor. Their roles now reversed, Ferdinand can let his patron escape with his hide intact. Salim lives to see the reversal of his fortune.

The times changed for the Domain as well, the "showplace" colony of artists, intellectuals, and university teachers. What the Big Man had created as a tribute to his modernizing vision was finally reverting to the bush. The land in front of the house where Raymond, the one time advisor to the President, used to live was now beng forked up by "the new man, barebacked," who "was going to grow maize and cassava" (259), dragging into the prestigious development a bit of the forest from which he had emerged. Hence the symbolic appropriateness of the water hyacinths, the hardy plants of the mighty basin that weave in and out of *A Bend in the River*, till we fully grasp that the tenacious tentacles of African nature will alone abide when the past reclaims the land, as it must. The bold, almost quixotic, attempt at the development of Africa is nullified by the brooding spirit of the land. A modern township, an alien import nurtured for a while, is foiled by what has been natural to the native grounds. The rush to modernity is stalled, yielding place to the old order.

The figure the plot makes is, thus, reinforced by the reflections of Salim that dot the narrative. At the outset of the novel, Salim, looking upon his environment, observes: "Once the Arabs had ruled here; then the Europeans had come; now the Europeans were about to go away" (12). And toward the close of the novel, watching the barebacked man "from somewhere down river" forking the soil in the new development, he marvels at the changes time has rung upon the African world: "This piece of earth. . . . Forest at a bend in the river, a meeting place, an Arab settlement, a European outpost, a European suburb, a ruin . . . of a dead civilization, the glittering Domain of new Africa, and now this" (260). Nothing stands still; everything meets its end.

But did the Arabs, expelled from Africa, stay put? They have taken over London—indeed, the world, he tells himself. If previously they were in Africa, now they are in Europe, "pumping the oil in and sucking the money out. Pumping the oil in to keep the system going, sucking the money out to send it crashing down" (234). Implicit in the same act are the inevitable dialectics of change.

Nor can the radical expulsion of Europeans from Africa be considered final in any way. They have to be invited back as engineers, technicians, financiers, and mercenaries. The Big Man may denounce them now and then to win the support of his "Liberation Army," but he can't do without the goods, the services, and the technology of Europe. The colonizer in the riding boots is replaced by the technocrat in a three-piece business suit. What the revolution once expelled, the urge for development now invites back. The unfolding tale of another continent but unravels a vast, nay, a universal irony.

The critics who condemn Naipaul for lack of sympathy with the colonized forget that, in his view, it is not only the disenfranchised and the marginalized that end up as dupes of history. The mighty empires of the world have fared no differently, if only because their powerful agents have not been impervious to the depredations of history. To discover the cosmic operation of the historic irony, one need only look at the fates of two modern empires: the sixteenth-century Spanish and the nineteenth-century British. The destiny of the former finds a poetic expression in *The Loss of El Dorado* (1969); of the latter, in the brooding narrative of *The Enigma of Arrival* (1987). Neither the difference in the sitings of the two narratives nor the gap of nearly twenty years in the publication of the pieces seems to have altered Naipaul's worldview.

Incidentally, despite the variation in the subject, the two books are not totally unconnected. The former begins with a discussion of Chaguanas, "a small country town . . . a mile or two inland from the Gulf of Paria" (13), where, "more than four hundred years after Columbus," the author's ancestors had arrived from India. It is, at one level, an attempt to recover the past of the Caribbean that had become his home. The latter book, by the same token, is an attempt to understand his arrival in another island, England, the home of his choice. Retracing the imperial histories, the narrator seeks not only to visualize the paths the empires had travelled, but also to comprehend his age and his own position therein. The reader is surprised by the tremendous similarity in the curves described by the histories of two peoples temperamentally so far apart as the Spanish and the English.

Antonio de Berrio comes out to the Indies in 1580 to claim his inheritance in the Spanish kingdom of New Granada, "in what is roughly Colombia" (*Loss of El Dorado*, 25). Enjoined by his father-in-law Quesada's will to search for El Dorado, he declares himself the general of the King, desiring to be appointed "the third marquis of the New World, after Cortés and Pizzaro" (25). The tenacious soldier of fortune keeps mounting expeditions in search of El Dorado, till he is totally broken, left to spend his last days as Raleigh's captive, "almost certainly lunatic now," on "an island in the Orinoco river" (21). Defeated and disappointed, he is totally cast aside when Raleigh takes over the stage. "Time, the discoverer of truth," we are informed by the narrator, "swallowed Berrio up. No portrait remains of the man who sought the third marquisate of the Spanish New World" (77). History holds the mirror to the ultimate human truth.

And what about Berrio's son, Fernando, whom the father had commended to the attention of the King? Suffering from syphilis, Fernando, a "lifelong dealer in slaves, has found himself taken, at the age of forty-four, to the busy slave market in Algiers'' (108). The wheel has come full circle. The mighty of a few decades ago end up as pitiable subjects of ill fortune.

At the end of the eighteenth century, people would point out "a ragged shepherd . . . a descendant of the conquistador Gonzales Ximenes de Quesada,'' of the man "who had won for Spain the wealth of the Chibchas, had founded the Kingdom of New Granada and had bequeathed to the husband of his niece the quest for El Dorado and the dream of the New World's third marquisate'' (109). Such a fate for his descendant was surely not foreseen by the ambitious ancestor. The comment with which the life story of Berrio is brought to a close gives away the narrative's intent. Says the narrator: "So the great names of the conquistadores disappeared in the lands of the conquest'' (109). The author attends to the lesson that history usually wipes out all that valor, cunning, and cruelty carve out and wish to hold forever. What the imperious will to empire proposes, time smoothly disposes—and, not infrequently, in abrupt and violently unsympathetic ways.

In another land, the course of the lives of the English aristocracy repeats but another version of the tale of the conquistadores. The narrator of *The Enigma of Arrival*, a tenant of the lord of a manor now ensconced among decaying trees and moral disorder, gradually realizes that "the cottage where [he] lived had once been the garden office'' and that "in the great days of the manor sixteen gardeners looked after the grounds and the orchard and the walled vegetable garden'' (61). But gone was that glory now. The "history had repeated, had radiated outwards, as it were.'' The glamour and the grandeur of the Victorian-Edwardian manor and the life and activity of its gardens and ancillary buildings "had come from the empire. . . . But its glory had lasted one generation.'' With the empire gone, then, everything was falling apart. "The family had moved elsewhere; the estate had become the manor and grounds alone; it had shed its farms and land'' (92). Even the aesthetic impulse of the lord, derived from the empire, was expiring. He sent his poems on Krishna and Shiva for the tenant's approval, who concludes that his lord's "Indian romance was . . . something he had inherited.'' It was "something from the days of imperial glory, when . . . it had been ordered for a whole century and more.'' But now the "power and glory had begun to undo themselves from within'' (212). Even creative vitality is a slave to inexorable laws of history.

Each culture, every scheme, is invested with a certain amount of energy; when that is used up, the effort collapses. In the end, everything collapses. In the name of efficiency, the old cowsheds and dairy buildings are pulled down and replaced by "a wide prefabricated shed with slatted timber walls.'' The place of the old manager, who was part of the landscape and in tune with the changing seasons, is taken by "the tense young men, conscious of their style, their jeans and shirts, their mustaches and cars . . . all aspects of the new, exaggerated thing that had come upon us'' (55). A new order was determined to replace the old.

And yet "the parlor hissed mechanically, electrically,'' only for a couple of years; then the whole mechanical dairy farm was gone from the scene, gone as abruptly as it had barged into the estate. "The venture failed. And even this failure—large as it was—seemed to happen quietly. . . . But then gradually the failure, the withdrawal at the center, began to show" (83). The new business went the way the farmers' flint cottages and the black and rusty barns had gone— to seed. "Swiss rolls of hay still stacked in the space between the wood . . . and the hill of larks . . . had indeed, below their tattered plastic sheeting, turned to earth. Grass to hay to earth" (87). Things of men and nature, the reader learns from the discourse, are alike subject to a cyclical change. Nothing resists the march of time, which turns everything upside down. Only men, engrossed in the thrill of the moment, fail to notice what had always been in the offing.

That for Naipaul it is the shape of what is always in the offing that is more important than a single incident or person is borne out by several aspects of his fiction. Ultimately, his stories are not about individuals; they are narratives about peoples, where individuals function but as straws revealing the general direction of the wind. The deliberate action of a human agent carries the lowest premium there, if only because Naipaul's stories are not about the plans of a Darcy, the vendetta of an Ahab, or the expedition of a Marlow; certainly, seldom about the misadventures of a Moll Flanders, the regeneration of a Hester-Prynne, or the hospitality of a Mrs. Ramsay. If the individuals turn out to be interesting, it is seldom because of personal merit or because they are diverting in their own right. Their value derives, instead, from their reflectivity, from the degree of the unconscious metaphysics of the group they can radiate.

The chain of action in Naipaul's drama is, similarly, fashioned to reveal not the character, but some hidden design, which turns and turns around the entire menagerie, often to its unexpected ends. The narrator, therefore, looks for the word that will betray the person, the gesture that will reveal the culture, the act that will manifest, say, the Zeitgeist. Words, acts, and gestures—in traditional fiction interesting in themselves—in Naipaul's fiction are valuable merely as reflectors, as prismatic devices, important because they reveal something beyond themselves. There is strong reason to suspect that their author, in using them, probes beyond them for something vaster, something unifying, something that predetermines and, hence, can explain their slant.

Unlike the realist, who is constantly being detained by the minutiae of the present, Naipaul would cross from the present to the past in an effort to see and to explain how things got to be what they are. His fiction, in seeking to grasp the inception of an event along with the final outcome, carries a double exposure, one contrasting with the other. Hence his narrative is pervaded with the rhetoric of "then" and "now." What this contrastive strategy often invokes is what Camus, in *The Myth of Sisyphus*, calls "the feeling of absurdity," which "lies in neither of the elements compared; it is born of their confrontation" (30). For to juxtapose man's intent against his achievement is to discover the unbridgeable gap between the two, is to be aware of the terrible irony that presides over human affairs. But the irony is not only that the best of people keep hitting the opposite of what they had aimed at. It resides, too, in the terrible difference between appearance and reality. The literal significance of the present constitutes the appearance. The lurking design behind the show, the meaning of the present, is the reality. The narratives of Naipaul, weaving the web of events, constantly display the hidden pattern of history, one forever shot with ironies. And his view of history is what William R. Smith calls a mode of argument (173–204), a view that interprets what it describes.

The brutal reality of the past human record that emerges from Naipaul's writing, unsettling to some and unpalatable to most, provokes two kinds of reactions among his readers and critics. Unable to appreciate that a historic vision undergirds his utterances as well as his art, some, like Thieme, seek to dismiss him as a victim of ''the colonial mentality . . . [of] the abnegation of freedom of choice'' (13) or, worse, of a prejudice against the underdog. Others, like Healy, find in his work ''the pressure of a very lucid despair'' (46).

A close reading of Naipaul will suggest that he is, rather, of the tribe of Joseph Conrad and D. H. Lawrence, of James Joyce, T. S. Eliot, and Ezra Pound, who arrived at their respective critiques of the modern age through a similar personal understanding of Western history. Naipaul, like them, is posessed by what A. A. Mendilow calls ''the time-obsession of the twentieth century'' (69). If his view of human history differs from theirs, it is because, despite an Oxford education and his crossings and recrossings, he has carried within him the Hindu consciousness of the terrible fluidity of things human and nonhuman. Man, the Hindu scriptures say, dreams of permanence, yet time proves everything ephemeral. Visionaries believe they know the future, but the future belies their hope. The expectations of grandeur, of success, of fame are but illusions; only the complacent recognize not their nature. Such wisdom, for whatever it may be worth to the faint hearted, constitutes the cornerstone of Naipaul's courageous vision of the human panorama.

Luckily for the author, besides the ancient Hindu and Buddhist texts, a close reading of mankind's history will confirm the unerring truth of Naipaul's worldview. In mistaking his vision for a wilful trait of the author, therefore, as Chris Searle does in ''Naipaulicity: A Form of Cultural Imperialism'' (45–62), readers misread Naipaul, and, in identifying his view with the late colonizers' attitudes, they misidentify the source of his inspiration. The ancient Indian view of life shapes Naipaul's narratives as compulsively as, according to C. A. Patrides (70–98), the Christian view of history determines the shape of Renaissance works. Even authors are creatures of their cultural history.

Naipaul's ironic outlook unmistakably derives from the twin Hindu and Buddhist traditions, not from any Western cultural imperialism. And yet, neither his biography nor his genealogy can explain Naipaul's uncompromising vision of history. For Raja Rao and Kamala Markandaya, R. K. Narayan and Salman Rushdie are far more strongly immersed in the ethos of Indian culture. They choose, however, to take a different stand, to make different artistic choices. They prefer to dwell upon other bits of the human fabric, not on its pervasive design, the historical prospect. Because he takes a commanding perch and pitilessly commands a vast sweep, Naipaul's vision seems awesome, at moments truly sublime, one akin to Tolstoy's in its power. Its heartlessness is but the measure of Naipaul's honesty and of his artistic integrity. He deliberately refuses to hold out any sentimental salves. For, above all, it is the truth that must be served, the truth beneath surfaces, and in the way he sees it.

WORKS CITED

Camus, Albert. *The Myth of Sisyphus and Other Essays*. 1955. Trans. Justin O'Brien. New York: Knopf, 1964.

Cudjoe, Selwyn R. *V. S. Naipaul: A Materialist Reading*. Amherst: University of Massachusetts Press, 1988.

Healy, J. J. "Fiction, Voice, and the Rough Ground of Feeling: V. S. Naipaul After Twenty-Five Years." *University of Toronto Quarterly* 55, no. 1 (Fall 1985): 45–63.

Howe, Irving. *A Margin of Hope: An Intellectual Autobiography*. New York: Harcourt Brace Jovanovich, 1982.

Johnson, Patrice. "V. S. Naipaul." *Black Scholar* 15, no. 3 (May-June 1984): 12–14.

Martin, Murray S. "Order, Disorder, and Rage in the Islands: The Novels of V. S. Naipaul and Albert Wendt." *Perspectives on Contemporary Literature* 10 (1984): 33–39.

Mendilow, A. A. "The Time-Obsession of the Twentieth Century." In *Aspects of Time*. Ed. C. A. Patrides. Toronto: University of Toronto Press, 1976.

Naipaul, V. S. *An Area of Darkness*. 1964. New York: Vintage, 1981.

———. *A Bend in the River*. 1979. New York: Vingage, 1980.

———. *The Enigma of Arrival*. 1987. New York: Vintage, 1988.

———. *A House for Mr. Biswas*. 1961. Harmondsworth: Penguin, 1969.

———. *The Loss of El Dorado*. 1969. Harmondsworth: Penguin, 1978.

———. *The Mimic Men*. 1967. New York: Vintage, 1985.

———. *The Mystic Masseur*. 1957. Harmondsworth: Penguin, 1978.

———. *The Overcrowded Barracoon and Other Articles*. 1972. Harmondsworth: Penguin, 1976.

Patrides, C. A. *The Grand Design of God: The Literary Form of the Christian View of History*. London: Routledge, 1972.

Pyne-Timothy, Helen. "V. S. Naipaul and Politics: His View of Third World Societies in Africa and the Caribbean." *CLA Journal* 3 (1985): 247–62.

Searle, Chris. "Naipaulicity: A Form of Cultural Imperialism." *Race and Class* 2 (1984): 45–62.

Smith, William Raymond. *History as Argument*. The Hague: Mouton, 1966.

Thieme, John. "V. S. Naipaul's Third World: A Not So Free State." *Journal of Commonwealth Literature* 1 (1975): 10–22.

3

Voice in Exile: "Journey" in Raja Rao and V. S. Naipaul

K. Chellappan

Literatures of both the East and the West abound in images of journey and exile. In fact, these motifs often provide the basic metaphor for plot itself. In the East, in both the great epics of India, *The Ramayana* and *The Mahabharata*, the major event is the exile of good forces and their return home. In *The Ramayana*, the archetypal epic of journey in the East, Rama and Sita create a new home in the forest, and later the real exile is Sita's separation from Rama, which is the archetypal image for all others' separation from God, but they also seek and find union with Him. If Ravana's journey necessitates history or time, Rama's feet redeem them, and all other journeys find their fulfillment in the still point of Rama's feet still moving.

Parallel to this, in the West, *The Odyssey* and *The Aeneid* are built on the motifs of journey and separation, and in John Milton's *Paradise Lost* we find the culmination of this pattern. Parallel to the journeys of Ravana and Rama here, we have the journey of Satan and that of Christ, with God as the still point. Satan the explorer is always seen in antagonism with space because of the otherness within, and he cannot escape the categories of space he has himself invented; whichever way he flies is Hell. It is this map-consciousness that he imports into the stillness of the Garden, and his experience of Paradise is again seen as a spatial separation. Later to Adam and Eve also, fall is separation, which results in the journey from Paradise: "They hand in hand with wandering steps and slow / Through Eden took their solitary way" (*Paradise Lost*, XII: 648–49).

In fiction, which is the modern counterpart to epic, we have more of the map-consciousness, particularly from Joseph Conrad. Even though we find this theme in quite a few major modern novelists like Fyodor Dostoyevsky, Graham Greene, Somerset Maugham, Aldous Huxley, and Hermann Hesse, it is in Commonwealth writing that we find a more intensive exploration of it because of certain historical facts. The Commonwealth is the symbol of Western colonists' quest for new boundaries, and in Commonwealth writing we find not only the discovery and conquest of new continents, but also an encounter of the old and the new. The Commonwealth writer in the postcolonial era links his search for identity with the quest for or the conquest of the heart of the matter by the earlier settlers or conquerors. Writers like Patrick White deal with the journey into the heart of Australia in several phases of history. We find George Lamming and Wilson Harris also exploring the land and reenacting an archetypal journey into the land in order to discover their true identity. In writers like Naipaul, there is a double displacement: he is cut off from his Indian roots, and his experience as a colonial in the West Indies as an ''inside outsider'' is further intensified when he chooses to live as an exile in London.

Among Indian writers in English, in Raja Rao, born into an orthodox Brahmin family in South India and brought up in the intellectual climate of France, the diasporic experience seems to be most acutely felt. As Shiva Niranjan puts it, ''the long years of expatriation have made Raja Rao more Indian than an average Indian struggling desperately to make the two ends meet'' (27). He also refers to Raja Rao's being an heir to two worlds: ''India, the land of his birth and inheritance, and France, the land of his acquisition, where he has spent an almost equal number of years as in India'' (32). In his *The Serpent and the Rope*, we find the dilemma of an Indian Brahmin (both Raja Rao and Ramaswamy) in exile to whom journey becomes the very mode of life, but all journeys ultimately lead him to India. In the exploration of the theme of journey as enactment of the author's exilic/diasporic sensibility we can see significant similarities between Raja Rao's *The Serpent and the Rope* and Naipaul's *A Bend in the River*.

According to C. D. Narasimhaiah, the whole of *The Serpent and the Rope* is an evocation of this ''tradition of India and its vitality especially in its encounters with the West—India seen as an idea, not as an area on the map'' (79). But this evocation of the pervasive India is linked with the sense of an exile. Though the novel begins with the statement, ''I was born a brahmin,'' it also says immediately, ''I was born an orphan, and have remained one. I have wandered the world and have sobbed in hotel rooms and in trains, have looked at the cold mountains and sobbed, for I had no mother'' (7). Narasimhaiah rightly says that ''the homelessness which was personal and cosmic now takes on an acuteness with the death of the father'' (83), and earlier relates this awareness of home or homelessness as ''awareness of the human condition, his own condition and the aspiration to reach the point of no return'' (82). Ramaswamy's sense of alienation and his search for India are brought out in terms of consciousness of and a journey to India, though he has been a wanderer in other places too—a ''wanderer on earth'' or a ''holy vagabond.'' Space consciousness is the pivot on which the plot is woven, but at a deeper level the boundaries also collapse. It is a

European Brahmin's passage to and from India, and the story is so told that one feels that he has always been travelling to India or his true self in all his encounters in the West, though in one sense there has been no journey at all. The sociocultural boundaries provide the base for an epistemological enquiry into the problem of the near and the far, as well as the metaphysical question of appearance and reality or the self and the other.

Also, in this inverted Wasteland, all men are one man; all places are one place—multiplicity and dualism of places and persons suggest something real and one. The basic question of dualism versus oneness or appearance versus reality is presented through the Europe-India antithesis symbolized by Paris and Benares, Madeline and Ramaswamy, Catherine and Saroja. The novel begins with Ramaswamy's journey to Benares—a return to India. But then he thinks of Madeline and, strangely, he associates her with

the unearthed marble with which we built our winter palaces. Cool, with the lake about one, and the peacock strutting in the garden below. The seventh-hour of music would come, and all the palace would see itself lit. Seeing oneself is what we always seek; the world, as the great Sage Sankara said, is like a city seen in a mirror. Madeline was like the Palace of Amber seen in moonlight. There is such a luminous mystery—the deeper you go, the more you know yourself. (13–14)

There is a similar montaging of places. Paris is described as Benares turning outward. Benares is also said to be a surrealist city. As O. P. Mathur puts it, Rama's "coming into close contact with the characteristic aspects of Eastern and Western ways of life and thought gives him a 'double vision' which makes him understand one with the eyes of the other" (51). He sees Mother Rhone as the Ganges and the Cam as flowing outside of history. But when he experiences India after "alienation," even in the midst of death the world seems to be good. The smell of India was sweet, but Madeline was very far. For Madeline, geography, like death, was real. But because of a disinterested devotion to a cause, she could transcend geography, and through Rama she identified herself with a great people. She noted differences, but he,

however, being so different, never really noted any difference. . . . To me difference was self-created, and so I accepted that Madeline was different. That is why I loved her so. . . . In difference there is the acceptance of one's self as a reality—and the Perspective gives the space for love. (20)

And this nondualism is beautifully brought out in the juxtaposition of "Holiness is happiness. Happiness is holiness," with Pascal's "Le silence éternel des grands espaces infinis m'effraie." Ramaswamy becomes a pagan going down to the Ganges, but Madeline recalls her love for the child whose birth was the birth of a God, and she goes to the church thinking of him. She hates going to Saint Maximin without him. But she transcends that alienation by feeling his presence in absence. Love needs space, though finally in love and knowledge there is neither near nor far.

In a sense Madeline represents not only Europe, but the world experience at the first level as the Other; in his relationship with her Rama experiences India and the self as the Other. Whereas Madeline accepts the differences and finally chooses Buddhism as a link, Ramaswamy's Advaita makes him really transcend the world as well as the East-West dualism, and in this process he is helped by Savithri. Through Savithri, to whom "isness is the Truth, or truth was wherever one is," Ramaswamy comes to know the self fully, and in this knowledge there is no dualism. She herself became the awareness behind his awareness, the leap of his understanding. He lost the world and she became it. That is why she quotes Yagnavalaya:

The husband does not love the wife for the wife's sake, the husband loves the wife for the sake of the Self in her. . . . All the world is spread for woman to be, and in making us know the world woman knows what the world is already seen as the world of neither thou nor I—not one, not I Savithri know that Ramaswamy could be Ramaswamy. (170–71)

A little later there is a mystic union of the self and the Other where time and space are annihilated.

History and my mind vanished somewhere, and I put my arms round that little creature—she hardly came to my shoulder—and led her along alleyways and parkways, past bus stop, bridge and mews—to a taxi. "Will you come, Savithri?" "Take me with you my love, anywhere." "Come," I said; "this minute, now." (207)

The novel does not deny the phenomenal or the feminine principle, but it shows that no man can love a woman for her personal self, but for the self within her. Savithri says that Italy is true when Shivohanm is; but, "meanwhile I go back to Allahabad and become Mrs. Pratap Singh" (213). But though Ramaswamy says, "But how can anyone go anywhere, how can anyone go from oneself," there is a merging of places and selves—and even time. Georges says, "We must have been brothers in a past life," and Catherine says, "I must have been your wife; that is why Vera knows you" (400). And when others think of Benares, Ramaswamy says that they should go to Travancore—"I have been telling you and myself a lie, all these years. My real home is in Travancore. Benares is there, and there you have no crocodiles nor pyres"; and Catherine responds to it beautifully: "I will make chocolate for two in Travancore" (406).

It has been said that Raja Rao repudiates Rudyard Kipling's assertion and makes the East and the West meet in this novel at various points, though there is no complete merger, and that Ramaswamy and Madeline commute between these two worlds through the rope bridges (Srivastava, 151). But there is a difference. Madeline only stands on the serpent because of her entanglement in the dualities of this world, and she accepts her defeat in bridging the worlds at the cultural level, though she also transcends it through compassion. Rama can see only the rope, because of his perception of reality at a metaphysical level. Now, E. M. Forster's *A Passage to India* is completed by an Indian, to whom what matters is not the space, but the self. One can never transcend space in space. The novel's superficial involvement in movements in space shows the world, the serpent; its perception reveals the self, the rope. But according to the Advaita, the serpent and the rope are not opposites; they are only two levels of perceiving reality. In that sense the Europe-India antithesis is both real and unreal, and the double perspective of the novel's structure is a corollary to its Advaita, which is not simple monism, but only nondualism.

Raja Rao's (or Ramaswamy's) very attempt to transcend space is the result of his acute awareness of homelessness, and if the novel at one level is permeated with India as consciousness, it is because of his sense of exile all the time. That is why at one point he is unwilling to go to India—"Why go there any how, I thought; I was born an exile and I could continue to be one. My India I carried wherever I went" (376). This doubleness of perspective—of all the time being both in and away from India—is central to the diasporic vision of Raja Rao's art, though at the philosophic level the contradiction is unreal.

To Naipaul, again an Indian Brahmin but doubly distanced, "an expatriate in his birth-place, an alien in his ancestral land," space and boundaries are more real. Naipaul himself relates the deep division in his psyche to his first visit to India, where he desperately tried to reconcile his childhood experiences of India in Trinidad, "where a strong inviolate Hindu culture lives in the heart of several ethnic groups" (Rai, 12), with what he saw around him. He says, "It was a journey that ought not to have been made, it has broken my life in two" (Rai, 9). Commenting on this, Robert Towers says: "Naipaul must have initially approached the grandmother country with expectations that were horribly wounded by what he found. Apparently he cannot stay away; the subsequent visits seem to have been made to see if things could possibly be as bad as he remembered them" (Rai, 25). He also sees in Naipaul's predicament of root-lessness an image of the doomed modern man himself. "For his is an odyssey in which he feels doomed . . . to voyage perpetually in 'middle passage', torn away from the security of his ancient home and without hope of landfall" (Rai, 26). But this alienation made his inherited new worlds also unreal to him. "How could I explain, how could I admit as reasonable, even to myself, my distaste, my sense of the insubstantiality and wrongness of the new world to which I had been swiftly transported" (Rai, 10).

Naipaul's *A Bend in the River* deals with an "inside outsider," Salim, who comes to the town at the bend in the river symbolizing real Africa, from "the east coast, an Arab-Indian-Persian-Portuguese place" (16). In face he belongs to neither, and he is only negatively defined. Spatially he does not belong to true Africa; but "when we compared ourselves with these people, we felt like people of Africa'' (16). The novel begins with Salim's arrival here; symbolically linked with the slaves' journey from home, ''he became anxious only to arrive'' (10).

If Raja Rao sees the human problem through the perspective of the Absolute, Naipaul sees things from a relativist perspective. Throughout the novel differences do matter; even among Africans there are differences. Salim's first encounter with the others is started off by the postage stamps of his area—he begins to look at the Arab dhow as something peculiar to his region and something the foreigner would remark on—and it is contrasted with the liners and cargo ship. This develops in him an ability to detach himself from a familiar scene along with a sense of insecurity that is linked with his seeking to occupy the middle ground, between absorption in life and soaring above the cares of the earth.

He is first distinguished from Indar's family, and this distinction leads him to decide to break away from his family compound and community. Nazruddin is his model and guide in this regard, and he introduces him to the town at the bend in the river, where the Arab power vanished before the European. There he meets Zabeth, a retailer who travels up the river often, and she is also distinguished from him—she calls him ''mis,'' short for mister, meaning a foreigner, further distinguished from other foreigners, who are ''monsieur.'' She brings her son Ferdinand to be a boarder at the lycée so that he can acquire education, which only foreigners can give, even though to her only Africa is real. Salim right in the beginning feels the difference in him and sees his face as a mask. With him, and even with Metty, the boy from the coast who acquires a new name now, there is only a relationship of power, as there arises a secret understanding between Metty and Ferdinand even though there are differences between them. This is partly because the two boys acquire their own sense of worth and power. This life of alienation for Salim is seen in his reaction to the imported ornamental trees, which give a touch of the forest village to the residential area.

> I knew the trees from the coast. I suppose they had been imported there as well; but I associated them with the coast and home, another life. The same trees here looked artificial to me, like the town itself. They were familiar, but they reminded me where I was. (57)

Psychologically too he feels that a web is being spun around him—mainly because of Ferdinand's interpretation of their relationship and Ferdinand's idea of what Salim can be used for.

Father Huismans represents the Belgian past, and Salim feels that the priest's Africa of bush and river is different from his own. He seems to accept the colonial past, though he also sees beyond it, envisioning himself as part of an immense flow of history, starting from Virgil's epic. That is why when the violent anti-government rebellion erupts, he simply views it as yet another event in the inexorable flow of history. At his killing, Salim feels that an unusually comprehensive view of African civilization dies with him. This is also an indirect indictment of the new violence in the Africans. After the death of Father Huismans the era of Big Man begins, and now the contrast is between the town and the New Domain, which is built to symbolize modern Africa, bypassing the real Africa of bush and villages, of which the house of Raymond and Yvette is an image. Even the boom has only made Salim anxious, and Salim attributes it to the political changes in the place.

The Domain has changed everyone. Salim's affair with Yvette also reveals only the corruption in private life consequent on the overall degradation. It is the manifestation of a wish to win the possessor of that body, impelled by a wish to be taken up to the skies, to be removed from the dullness, the pointless tension in the country. But in that process he finds himself bound, though indirectly, to the fact of the President's power. Soon he finds himself empty—like Mahesh and Shoba—and decides to rejoin the world, to break out of the narrow geography of the town.

When he is in Europe, Salim realizes that it is not the Europe he had known, the Europe Indar had gone to when he left for the university. When he reaches London the picture is complete. London seems to be another Africa: here also there is an invasion of Arabs, and here also people are fleeing. Sometimes while in London he feels that the picture of his Africa was very real, but its associations made it dreamlike. Now in London the idea of going home, of leaving, the idea of the other place with which he lived for so many years, seems to be a deception.

In spite of the girls in the cigarette kiosks, that way of life no longer existed, in London or Africa. There could be no going back; there was nothing to go back to. We had become what the world outside had made us; we had to live in the world as it existed. (252)

This seems to be a refined version of the opening lines of the novel: ''The world is what it is; men who are nothing, who allow themselves to become nothing, have no place in it'' (9). The novel has been said to be an inversion of the myth of Africa in Conrad's *Heart of Darkness* in the sense that the man with ''the inconceivable mystery of a soul that knew no restraint, no faith and no fear, was black, not white'' (Prescott, 549). To be more specific, the novel mainly deals with Africans becoming aliens in Africa, and then makes that alienation almost a universal condition, which almost all the characters in the novel experience in different degrees. Probably this is what John King refers to as the ''genetic sense of rootlessness, shipwreck as an ontological condition'' (232) in Naipaul. But is the novel so pessimistic about the search for home? London becomes the home of the homeless in more than one sense; in that archetypal home of the aliens, Karesha offers Salim the link—and he too realizes the value of Africa; the novel ends with the steamer starting up again, away from the area of battle.

Though in *A Bend in the River* the autobiography is more veiled than in Rao's *The Serpent and the Rope*, it is still there, and we can relate Salim's adventures and sense of homelessness to Naipaul's own; and, as we said earlier, Naipaul's homelessness springs from his treatment of his own real experience of India as an illusion. In his own words:

It was only now, as my experience of India defined itself properly against my own homelessness, that I saw how close in the past year I had been to the total Indian negation, how much it had become the basis of thought and feeling. And already, with this awareness, in a world where illusion could only be a concept and not something felt in the bones, it was slipping away from me. I felt it as something true which I could never adequately express and never seize again. (Rai, 23)

It is significant that Naipaul refers to his experience of India as negation and illusion, and also as something true. Whereas Raja Rao equates India with Brahma, which somehow seems to be unreal, Naipaul sees it as a maya which strangely becomes true because of his deeper agony and artistic distancing. Naipaul's novels, in a way, enact the split more honestly, and are thereby more aesthetically convincing as well as giving a stronger sense of India inextricably interwoven with his sense of alienation. In his novel, unlike in Raja Rao's, there is a journey not only in space but through several layers of history, though in a sense in *A Bend in the River* all history is made contemporaneous. But this is not a simultaneous awareness of all time—as we have a sense of the past permeating the present. Lynda Prescott rightly relates this sense of history to his rootlessness:

His personal sense of rootlessness, derived from the experience of growing up in an immigrant community in Trinidad and then living as a rather restless exile in England, gives a sharp edge to his emphasis on the social necessity of history. In practically all his work he affirms, directly or indirectly, the need for individuals and whole societies to know and to understand their history in order to make sense of the present. (Prescott, 550)

To conclude, the archetype of journey is fundamental to both the novels, dealing with alienation and the search for roots and with the self through the Other. In both cases, the spatial journey is also a spiritual or psychic journey, though in Naipaul it is brought out in terms of an Indian in Africa. In Raja Rao, the insistent presence of India heightens a sense of absence and alienation, whereas in Naipaul the very absence seems to suggest a presence, the denial itself being a way of affirming his Indian roots. Exile is almost ontological in Naipaul; if Raja Rao seems to be encountering space as the Other, he also suggests a mystic possibility of transcending the boundaries. The encounter with the Other is seen more in cultural terms in Naipaul and in metaphysical terms in Raja Rao. But even in Naipaul's vision it is possible to see another version of the world as maya, as illusion. Rao's *The Serpent and the Rope* is an Indian response to Forster's *A Passage to India*; Naipaul's *A Bend in the River* is a twice-displaced Indian's response to Conrad's *Heart of Darkness*, but the response is also a recognition. In this process we also see the enactment of an endless literary journey across space and time just as all these novels of journey end—with the beginning of a new journey.

WORKS CITED

King, John. "A Curiously Colonial Performance: The Ec-centric Vision of V. S. Naipaul and J. L. Borges." *Yearbook of English Studies* 13 (1983): 228–43.

Mathur, O. P. "The Serpent Vanishes: A Study in Raja Rao's Treatment of the East-West Theme." In *Perspectives on Raja Rao*. Ed. K. K. Sharma. Ghaziabad: Vimal Prakashan, 1980.

Naipaul, V. S. *A Bend in the River*. London: Penguin, 1980.

———. *An Area of Darkness*. London: Deutsch, 1964.

Narasimhaiah, C. D. *Raja Rao*. New Delhi: Arnold Heinemann, n.d.

Niranjan, Shiva. *Raja Rao: Novelist as Sadhaka*. Ghaziabad: Vimal Prakashan, 1985.

Prescott, Lynda. "Past and Present Darkness: Sources for V. S. Naipaul's *A Bend in the River*." *Modern Fiction Studies* 30, no. 3 (Autumn 1984): 547–60.

Rai, Sudha. *V. S. Naipaul: A Study in Expatriate Sensibility*. New Delhi: Arnold-Heinemann, 1982.

Rao, Raja. *The Serpent and the Rope*. New Delhi: Orient Paperbacks, 1960.

Srivastava, Ramesh. "Structure and Theme in Raja Rao's Fiction." In *Perspectives on Raja Rao*. Ed. K. K. Sharma. Ghaziabad: Vimal Prakashan, 1980.

4

South Asia/North America: New Dwellings and the Past

Craig Tapping

We are like "chiffon saris"—a sort of cross-breed attempting to adjust to the pressures of a new world, while actually being from another older one.
—Jussawalla, 583

Like other ethnic literatures in North America, writing by immigrants from the Indian subcontinent is concerned with personal and communal identity, recollection of the homeland, and the active response to this "new" world. Its forms are multiple and in many traditional and some newly created genres; but an autobiographical impulse—the desire to name experience and to create identity, to emerge from the dominant language and gaze of "nonethnic" America— impels even the shortest fictions, despite frequent disclaimers by the writers.[1]

Indo-American and Indo-Canadian writing are also both postcolonial literatures. That these immigrants write in English—a linguistic choice which influences patterns of migration and affiliation among writers as disparate as Ved Mehta, Rohinton Mistry, Bharati Mukherjee, Suniti Namjoshi, Michael Ondaatje, Vikram Seth, and Sara Suleri—is a direct consequence of British imperialism. This historical situation unites all these writers, who variously emplot their relation to the partition of the Indian subcontinent in 1947, the consequent political histories of newly created nations and nationalities which they have variously left, and the construction once again of even newer identities in the countries to which they have immigrated.

In its postcolonial forms, writing from the Indian diaspora is frequently described in terms of the literary careers of V. S. Naipaul and Salman Rushdie.

A writer like Sara Suleri, for example, is scrupulous in her critical analysis of Naipaul's place and influence as a writer of decolonized literature.[2] Bharati Mukherjee, on the other hand, negotiates a transformative distance in her critical writings between these two models of an international school of Indian writing.[3] As neither Rushdie nor Naipaul writes from an American or Canadian perspective, however, North America's Indian writers must now create their own traditions.

These traditions are still young, and are often found in journals that collect and anthologize disparate writings from otherwise unpublished new writers of Indian background. Here, the reader is guided through the developing voice of community and individual creative artist. In her recent introduction to an issue of the *Literary Review* dedicated to writing from the Indian diaspora, Bharati Mukherjee explains that Indo-American literature is a new phenomenon and as yet only in process of becoming a tradition.[4] Her list of writers, as well as the explanations of their homeland and newly formed communities elsewhere, confirms this argument. In compiling her anthology of Indo-American writing, Mukherjee conflates the term to include a range of writers from across the Indian diaspora. The problematic result is only partially solved by editorial disclaimer.[5] Most of her North American writers have immigrated to Canada or the United States from already established Indian communities in Africa or the Caribbean. Some, she admits, are Indian only by marriage.

Such a dispersive flavor to the literary samplings thus anthologized can be puzzling. Many of the writers are more accessibly read in the contexts of Indo-Caribbean or other so-called Third World literary traditions. Ketu Katrak and R. Radhakrishnan, editors of the *Desh/Videsh* special issue of the *Massachusetts Review*, expand already vague horizons by including visual art, critical essays, poetry, and pieces from outside the North American locus.

What becomes clear from such a quick, and of necessity reductive, survey is, however, paradigmatic. Domicile and ethnicity do not alone determine Indo-American or Indo-Canadian identities: geographical, lexical, political, and cultural differences are the signifying tropes of Indo-American ethnic literatures. Sam Selvon, Cyril Dabydeen, and Neil Bissoondath of Canada—although they are racially classifiable as ''East Indian'' (to use Mukherjee's editorial naming, which she elsewhere rejects)[6]—have little in common beyond this with Mukherjee herself, and are better read in the context of Caribbean and Third World literatures. Mukherjee and other explicitly Indo-American writers belong to the Fifth World: that of the economically and politically displaced immigrants of the twentieth century, transposed into alien contexts from where they redefine and newly construct alternative identities and communities.[7]

For this chapter, then, I inflate the prefix ''Indo'' to mean the subcontinent, and have therefore included writers born in what are now Pakistan and Sri Lanka with those from what is now politically defined as India. This is not to deny the historic partitioning of a former empire, but rather to allow a more open field across which, I believe, several pertinent comparisons can be drawn and distinctions made. Further justification for such a seeming disregard for contemporary boundaries can be made of the fact that all the writers considered in this chapter are now North Americans: geography thus offers commonality in provenance and destination, without denying local and regional cultural differences.

However, the most interesting example of such inflationary slippage across territorial and national boundaries occurs in Sara Suleri's *Meatless Days*. In an aside about the architectural splendors and confusion of Lahore, Suleri names herself and fellow residents from this part of the subcontinent "we Indians" (152): more nationally defined labels are the result of European imperial history. There is perhaps even more obscurity of terms in the label "Indo-American," but—despite a personal nationalism which reads these and other writers with an eye and ear both alert for their notations of difference between Canada and America—such caution seems outright pedantry when one considers how theoretical terminologies proliferate once we move beyond canonical boundaries of literature, history, and territories. In the interests of examining autobiographical witness to the migrations between South Asia and North America, we must finally abandon such promiscuity among labels and classifications if we are to begin reading actual texts.

That reading must begin with Ved Mehta's autobiographical enquiry, which now extends through several volumes and which locates what may be the foundations of an Indo-American writing tradition. In form and breadth of vision, *Daddyji*, *Mamaji*, and *Vedi* are almost conventional, however, and contravene no readerly expectations that the genre, autobiography, arouses. They locate the Mehta family in the Punjab in the nineteenth century, suggest the transformations that placed the family there, and detail in a surprisingly sensual form the geographical and climatic terms of that landscape. The attention to specifics of contour, shape, density, and color is more than exotica in these reconstructions of the past. Mehta has been blind since preschool age, and these rich depictions are his transcribed records of conversations, research, and communal inquiry. The Mehta family becomes a representative gathering of clan and individuals: this is a history of India read through one family's tree.

The Ledge Between the Streams shifts ground somewhat. Having explained his parents' independent and then mutual lives and family lines, and having chronicled his own childhood and schooling, Mehta departs from idyllic representation halfway through this volume in the chapter titled "The Two Lahores." This and subsequent chapters move the writing from the merely personal and awkwardly old-fashioned kind of universalizing memoir into the postcolonial and nonrepresentative autobiography. Suddenly, the world of religious fanaticism, ethnic separatism, politics, and communal violence erupts, disrupting an otherwise quiet and—despite its intimacies—reticent chronicle. Now, Mehta explains his consternation, the family's unpreparedness for social and public confrontations with dogmatism and bigotry, and the intrusion of such assaults into the sitting rooms and kitchens of a formerly becalmed middle-class household.

In a configuration repeated by subsequent writers, Mehta links the bloodletting and trauma of partition to the emigration of a generation of trained professionals. Partition and its adherents—those who fought for separate ethnically and religiously defined states—introduce a dogmatic sense of purity and authenticity, both of which deny and exclude the plurality of India before independence. This, too, is a repeated figure and informs, for example, Salman Rushdie's three novels about postcolonial India and Pakistan while returning this chapter to its original confrontation with narrow national definitions of South Asian writers in North America.

Departure and exile during the riots that accompanied the creation of two, and later three, new countries are made synonymous with liberal tolerance of difference and bourgeois social aims and aspirations. For Mehta, however, the new place of settlement and career is not the subject. India—what it was, what it became, and what it might have become—remains the subject of his autobiographical explorations to date. The United States enters his writing only through acknowledgment pages and the unacknowledged presence of a calm study in an entirely other world from which he remembers and recreates a more turbulent epoch of personal, would-be universal history.

The reader is left with an image of the author akin to that of Jorge Luis Borges. Mehta, the blind archivist of an order destroyed by politically charged events which he literally failed to see and which socially his class was unprepared to admit or transform, continually recatalogues his library from memory, thumbing through various otherwise forgotten pages from the ever-receding past.

Feroza Jussawalla, in her article "Chiffon Saris: The Plight of Asian Immigrants in the New World," addresses a critical issue that is often read as problematic in much Indo-American writing. Admitting that the writers and critics of Indo-American literature are usually privileged by caste and economic class, she nonetheless avers that the literature must reflect the conflicts and social violence that are mundanities for the entire ethnic community.

Such criticism, despite its noble aspirations and humane motivations, is problematic. The call for a social realist mode of literary production is, at best, anachronistic and geographically selective. Such an approach damages both contemporary reading and writing. First, the critical sophistication used to argue against and to exclude "bourgeois" writers is at odds with an apparent straightforwardness of the newly privileged social realist texts, which subsequently read as simpler and even idyllic in the clarity of their values: a reflection perhaps of an uncomplicated model of postcolonial political history. Second, no one condemns or calls to task the "nonethnic" writer for his or her avoidances and transgressions. White American and Canadian writers, for example, have multiple worlds and social strata therein to write from and about. Few who uphold the politically correct line about "immigrant" literatures address this disparate postmodern condition. Once again, limitation is held to be the natural condition for those whose provenance is not the so-called developed world. Third, to read this literature for its universalizing representation of an already disparate ethnic community patronizes that community, denies individual differences, and ignores those textual features that readers use to privilege other, nonethnic writings as "literature." In short, it is what Henry Louis Gates, Jr., calls "the ruinous desire to be representative, to collectivize the first person" (38).

The writers discussed in this chapter all foreground and articulate their personal, familial identities and sociopolitical contexts, explaining how and why they came to be where they are and write what they do. This conscientious explication of the construction of their own identities is tied to the recognition that being a universal exemplar for an entire subclass is a logical and political impossibility, except one should deal in stereotype and blinkered vision. The problematic of class or caste origin, however, remains foregrounded in each writer herein discussed. The manner in which each attempts to define self and community is therefore a dialogic engagement with history, making apparent the political and economic forces that have operated to create nations and literatures since 1947.

For example, Sara Suleri, Michael Ondaatje, and Bharati Mukherjee all extend the autobiographical tradition of Mehta in quite different ways. Suleri describes *Meatless Days*, an impressionistic meditation on history, family, politics, gender, and race, as a condition of "quirky little tales" (156). Ondaatje's *Running in the Family* transgresses several generic boundaries. Ondaatje uses writing itself to disrupt previously cherished notions of truth, voice, and history. By the end of this memoir of Sri Lanka and his family during the 1930s and 1940s, the reader is both elated at the sheer exuberance of the many kinds of narratives in which Ondaatje revels (including the photographic) and confused by the denied outcomes and deferred truths which each genre promises but which the writer then withholds. Mukherjee's most explicitly autobiographical piece, the second part of *Days and Nights in Calcutta*, also confronts the veracity promised by personal witness as she cuts across the narrative truths delivered in the first part, which is written by her non-Indian husband, Clark Blaise.

If these writers are the heralds of a new North American literature in both subject matter and style, Suniti Namjoshi is its supreme ironist. Her works never extend to the relatively full-blown autobiographical scale of these others. Namjoshi's use of revisionary fable and fragmented myth suggests a much wider range of imperializing discourses, including those of gender and sexuality, which are never geographically or culturally specific but which are always revealed in their local and regional idiosyncrasies. The prevalent power of such naturalized discourses has previously outlawed and silenced the kinds of writing and history that Namjoshi's subversively comic writing strategies now suggestively evoke. Not surprisingly, her prose writings are those of the provocative miniaturist.

All these writers use their personal histories to explore not only the self and the larger community but also to explore and subvert readerly expectations that adhere to variously personal modes of writing. Truth, presence, and verifiably witnessed history are all called into question by these would-be discreet confessionalists. In that process, postcolonial literature is born.

In *Meatless Days*, Sara Suleri probes language and the names we give—in English and in Urdu, in America and in Pakistan—to foodstuffs, loved ones and family members, rituals and social customs, political events and personal memories. The chapters weave through this labyrinth of languages and their usage, opening by turns into rooms of objective catalogue, historical account, subjective memoir, dream work, and oblique parable. Suleri uses analogies from Islamic and British Imperial architectural styles and habits of self-presentation, as well as recipes and folklore concerning various foodstuffs, to imply her own methodologies and to interrogate various introspective attempts to distinguish the national myths of present-day India from those of Pakistan.

There are meditations on the Third World, which she aptly describes as "locatable only as a discourse of convenience" (20), and accounts of life in Pakistan during and after independence. With her father editing and the family proofreading and helping to assemble the galleys of various daily newspapers throughout Pakistan's recent history, Suleri is well placed to record her own observations on this postcolonial history. Her descriptions of the 1947 partition as the "perpetual rewriting" of boundaries (87) lead to an ironic questioning of contemporary nationalisms as she considers

those bewildered streams of people pouring over one brand-new border into another, hurting as they ran. It was extravagant, history's wrenching price: farmers, villagers, living in some other world, one day awoke to find they no longer inhabited familiar homes but that most modern thing, a Muslim or a Hindu nation. There was death and panic in the cities when they rose up to flee, the Muslims traveling in one direction, the Hindus in the other. (116)

The proximity to this history entangles Suleri in a debate with her father about Pakistan, humanity, and writing. This last concern explicitly enmeshes her consideration of women in the chronicles of nationhood and independence.

Meatless Days begins, in one of its many paths through the maze of language and history, as an answer to an American student's question about equal representation on the syllabus of a literature course devoted to the Third World, and ends in fulfilling that question while undermining our perhaps ethnocentric hopes for a more satisfactorily definite answer. Suleri answers, "There are no women in the third world" (20), after explaining that

the concept of woman was not really part of an available vocabulary: we were too busy for that, just living, and conducting precise negotiations with what it meant to be a sister or a child or a wife or a mother or a servant. By this point admittedly I am damned by my own discourse, and doubly damned when I add yes, once in a while, we naturally thought of ourselves as women, but only in some perfunctory biological way that we happened on perchance. Or else it was a hugely practical joke, we thought, hidden somewhere among our clothes. (1)

From this perspective, Suleri's ruminations on her sisters and their mother, a woman who migrated from Wales via London into Pakistan after independence, is the extended answer to that question, just as her own departure for America is presented, in part, as the end of an argument with her father and a history made by generals and other men who engineered

Islam's departure from the land of Pakistan. The men would take it to the streets and make it vociferate, but the great romance between religion and the populace, the embrace that engendered Pakistan, was done. . . . God could now leave the home and soon would join the government. (15)

The leave-taking is never final, however. Suleri's book continues the dialogue long after the severance, and carries her sense of being "an otherness machine" (115) from these arguments with her brother and father into the heartland of New England. In America, she considers how to assemble the chronicle she now writes—"I have washed my hands of sequence" (76)—and how to convey the almost impossible, "to explain the lambent quality of the periphery, its curious sense of space" (106).

The curious sense of space and its lambent qualities at the margins of empire can be said to concern Michael Ondaatje's *Running in the Family* as well. Ondaatje interweaves photographs, musical notations and the lyrics of imported American dancehall recordings, historical accounts, a wide reading through European and American portrayals of Ceylon, his own diary's examination of a return with his children to Sri Lanka after twenty years in Canada (often in the form of poetry), family legends, gossip, and local rumors in his memoir of his parents and their halcyon days in pre-independence Ceylon.

The pervasive comedy of his text is never far, however, from the recognition of imperial history and Western literary erasure of cultures beyond the edges of canonical event, like his family's. For example, a seemingly insignificant epithet from Paul Bowles inspires an outpouring of inventive versifying that is both an *ars poetica* in its exploration and almost definitive exhaustion of the metaphor as device and, not incidentally, the reinvention of a non-Western culture's bardic invectives.[8] Similarly, the photographs that are interleaved with the writing offer an ironic commentary on the linearity and verisimilitude of Ondaatje's narrative.

Perhaps the most revealing moment of self-reflexivity in Ondaatje's chronicle, however, is also one of the more concealed. After the close of his book, and having brought his narrative to a tentative conclusion, Ondaatje—as is frequently customary with other writers—offers acknowledgments and explanations of his funding, times and places of writing, and gratitude for the help he received in reconstructing the "history" of his family. At this point, long after we have finished reading, and in the small print, as it were, we encounter a refusal of the genre's label and consequent readerly promises that is benignly non-Western in its broad sweep across all claims to "truth":

While all these names may give an air of authenticity, I must confess that the book is not a history but a portrait or "gesture." And if those listed above disapprove of the fictional air I apologize and can only say that in Sri Lanka a well-told lie is worth a thousand facts. (206)

More recently, Ondaatje has again written "ethnic" fiction in his novel *In the Skin of a Lion*. His characteristically cinematic cutting between images that hang in the consciousness as if they were feathers to imagination's airstream and his concern with writing between the official pages of history are here used to evoke what it meant to be "ethnic" and "immigrant" in Toronto at the beginning of this century. That city emerges as this novel's protagonist and is built by the snatches of conversation and sometimes intimate voices of several different communities (all of them "immigrant" and all engaged in constructing a new world) that the novel embodies.

In a like manner, Bharati Mukherjee is exuberantly polyphonic in her drive to assimilate and refashion the American dream—at least since leaving Canada both residentially and imaginatively. Mukherjee is not so widely known for her examinations of Canadian racism in different genres—investigative journalism, personal essay, literary review, autobiographical memoir, novel, and short story. Her many attempts to represent the Canadian establishment's oblique responses to its communities of ethnic Indians enmesh autobiography and fiction, and attest to the depth and range of what has not always been read as a constructive and ameliorative vision clearly *because* the life does enter the work at several points. Similar autobiographical fictions by American writers of color suggest that the interference of life-facts and other particularities of individual experience should instead by read as inter-reference as such writers attempt to translate two disparate cultural spaces—their and ours—into a third, intercultural or postcultural space. Euro-American conventions of reading frequently, however, overlook this new territory from where new literary genres, mostly ethnic, emerge.[9]

A major theme in Mukherjee's nonfiction is that Indians in Canada have been subjected to racist assaults, physically and psychologically. The government has failed its citizens. She writes that she identifies with these victims and has explained her own traumatic sense of entrapment and claustrophobia while living in Canada. The claims of identification are frequently couched in terms of class expectation, without apology:

Great privilege had been conferred upon me; my struggle was to work hard enough to deserve it. And I did. This bred confidence, but not conceit. . . . Calcutta equipped me to survive theft or even assault; it did not equip me to accept proof of my unworthiness. ("An Invisible Woman," 36, 38)

Even in the 1989 essay on Rushdie, Mukherjee does not demur from such contextualizing. This is the generation who "traded top-dog status in the home-land for the loss-of-face meltdown of immigration" ("Prophet and Loss," 12). Unfortunately, this knowledge of the life, foregrounded by the essayist in her readers' consciousnesses, limits the ability of some North American critics—

with their almost endemic but often vicarious interest in politically correct and socially austere lives—to read the fictions clearly.[10]

If she is right that she wants to embrace the new, the dilemma is that she also carries a lot of the old with her—which we then read as elitism and class-exclusive aspirations. Rejections on these grounds, however, suggests that only those who have suffered or continue to suffer explicit economic violence should testify against a bourgeois culture's insensitivities. These "others" have no voice or access to that discourse in the first place. And thus, in both instances, we use such rules to silence a community.

Read differently, this very privilege, this sense of having "traded top-dog status," is an inscribed Canadianism of Mukherjee's writing. Another immigrant, the nineteenth-century Susanna Moodie, suffers the same disillusion of class expectations when confronted with the great leveling effects of community in Canada.[11] And, in the historic moment of the 1960s and early 1970s described at some length in both Blaise's and Mukherjee's sections of *Days and Nights in Calcutta*, Toronto is again "bush" in comparison to the metropolitan cultures of London and the intellectual sophistication of Calcutta.

In Mukherjee's "Canadian" stories—"The World According to Hsü," "Isolated Incidents," and "Tamurlane" from *Darkness* and "The Management of Grief" from *The Middleman and Other Stories*—racist violence is not fictionalized. The attacks on Indians are not digested narratively, but emerge as factual news headlines, eruptions in the text not to be achieved or constructed as fiction, but rather to confront the reader. The inclusion of these violent facts makes extratextual appeal to the lived experiences of her non–Indo-Canadian readers. It reminds the reader of the daily newscasts on radio and television. It is a narrative strategy of confrontation that does not allow complacent reading. It does not allow the domestication and comfort of metaphor.

Why this does not happen in Mukherjee's American stories is another question, suggested by analyses of similar moves in other writings of immigration and violence. Perhaps a "yearning for sincere interlocutory speech"—the reforming anger directed at the Canadian body politic and her outrage at the betrayal of her silenced community—"gives way to a play on written substitutes"—the exuberance and polyvocality of the American stories, celebrating a newly found sense of inclusion.[12]

For the protagonists of *The Tiger's Daughter* and for many of the immigrant protagonists in her short stories, America is the way out of the cul-de-sac of upper-class existence in Calcutta. In *Wife* and *Jasmine*, America is a place of random and excessive violence, and her American characters are subject to the uncertainties of life in such a state. For Dimple Dasgupta, ill-fated heroine of *Wife*, who cannot adjust to her new rootlessness and the breakdown in community support and behavioral systems that immigration has meant, this violence breeds anomie and then further violence. Mukherjee argues that her target—despite the American geography in this novel—is Canada.[13] In her other fictions—especially *Jasmine*—America is celebrated as the mythic center of an emergent world characterized by its "romance . . . its infinitely possible geography, its licence, sexiness and violence."[14]

Mukherjee's nonfiction is central to the range of expression in her short fiction. For example, we cannot read "The World According to Hsü" without recognizing that it resonates with and extends the documentary evidence of both "An Invisible Woman" and *Days and Nights in Calcutta*. The disjunction of Canada's two metropolises is somewhat bizarre and the heroine's dread at the prospect of Toronto inexplicable until we read the nonfictions. The Montréal experience of the memoirs explains how the protagonist of the short story can recall her strangely comfortable existence there, a nostalgia produced by the irrelevance of her own position, cultures, and languages to the warring factions in either strife-torn city. In contrast, Toronto occasions only anxieties which are relentlessly critiqued in the essay. Fear of personally directed racist violence builds in the story as she recalls the incidents and newspaper headlines which the essay cites for its authority.

So, too, "The Management of Grief," recognizably something quite other than her graphs of American life in *The Middleman*, is a fictional extention of Mukherjee's nonfictional analysis of her Canadian experience. This story must be read in conjunction with *The Sorrow and the Terror*, a nonfiction collaboration with Clark Blaise recently described by her as a quite different variation on the opening of Rushdie's *Satanic Verses*.[15]

Mukherjee and Blaise describe the destruction of Air India Flight 182 as the explicitly violent, repressed other of Canada's fumbling, liberally misdirected multiculturalism, a series of blind negations of new immigrants, most of whom revealed "a determined responsiveness to Canada" but all of whom were classified as non–Anglo-Saxon or "visible minorities" (*The Sorrow and the Terror*, 124). Mukherjee deconstructs this last term to condemn its inscription of a racist metaphysics, a never-to-be-overcome difference. Canada's loss—a generation of immigrants—is the vitality and idealistic future which she now fictionally locates in America, most clearly in *Jasmine*.

This relation between the fictional and the nonfictional analyses of power and transformation is both autobiographical and tribal. Mukherjee's prolonged examination of Canada and her embrace of America are ethnographic in that both reveal how the misrepresented "other" responds, individually and communally, to the shame and defilement of an exclusion that is always more clearly understood and more fully recognized on the margins than it is by the practitioners of casual disregard at the centers of our national hegemonies. By the time she emerges from this harrowing exploration of Canada's institutionalized racism, India is no longer a geographical place that connotes "home" for Mukherjee, but rather a way of perceiving reality and adapting to the empirical world. As she explains in the introduction to *Darkness*:

Indianness is now a metaphor, a particular way of partially comprehending the world. Though the characters in these stories are, or were, "Indian," I see most of these as stories of broken identities and discarded languages, and the will to bond oneself to a new community against the ever-present fear of failure and betrayal. (3)

The immediate characteristic of Rohinton Mistry's approach to the issues of ethnicity in Canada is that he is much less vehement than Mukherjee, and even gently ironic. *Tales from Firozsha Baag* is an exemplary postmodern, postcolonial literary collection. It stages the translation of oral cultures into literature with a commentary on the traditional society from which such practices derive; it reflects on its textuality and on the growing consciousness and literary abilities of its protagonist-author; it mocks well-meaning Anglo-Saxon liberalism through satire; and it appropriates the inherited narratives of the imperial canon in parody which opens our understanding of such figural systems. And not insignificantly, Mistry's own voice as author, as citizen, as fellow Parsi and Indian, is only obliquely present in this collection of stories.

Mistry further distances himself from the engaged passion of Mukherjee's work by explaining that his autobiographical situation creates a different set of circumstances and contexts for his fictional encounters with Canada: "My characters are outside Hindu India. And because of the history of the Zoroastrian religion, it does not provide a solid anchor like Hinduism or Judaism or Islam" (Hancock, "Interview with Rohinton Mistry," 149). Mistry's "low" culture pursuits as a former folksinger—"Bombay's Bob Dylan"[16]—suggest further variant cultural and political expectations, as does his adoption of a suburban retreat in Brampton, Ontario, for his writing base in contrast to Mukherjee's choice of metropolitan New York for its "gradual Calcuttaization" (Hancock, "Interview with Bharati Mukherjee," 31).

"Squatter," one of Mistry's *Tales from Firozsha Baag*, is an almost archetypal contemporary postcolonial literary artifact. Exemplary of the collection, it mixes the sacred with the profane, the high with the low. Its author is self-effacing in the manner of other postmoderns: commenting on another's literary performance, he obliquely alerts us as to how we should be reading his own.

The story begins by asserting the humor and self-assurance of the immigrant who gives himself ten years to become a Canadian or return to Bombay. Compared to the hackneyed truism that Canadians don't know who they are, it is revelatory to read an "other's" confident summation of our national characteristic. The public display and reception of such a hero's encounter with life in Toronto, and his ensuing moral responsibilities in his community, constitute the tale and its performance by the guardian of the word, the uncle who stayed behind in India.

The tale, a communal Indian rehearsal of Canadian multiculturalism, conflates high and low art forms, deflates liberalism abroad, and celebrates outsider status in its travesty of immigrant desperation. To convey the bathos of not learning how to use toilets in Canada within his protagonist's self-imposed ten-year time limit, Mistry plunders eighteenth-century English satiric modes—the scatological visions of Jonathan Swift were never such unabashed fun—and that Renaissance classic of "otherness," *Othello*. In Mistry's tale, the canon of English literature is appropriated and revised: an empire of literature displaced by a text hilariously performing an oral event in a subject-culture's contemporary repertoire.

It is fitting to end this chapter here. In this and other Mistry tales, his chapters are most eager to join others in the latest wave of immigration, the newest tide of those who will reinvent Canada. His protagonists purchase shameless Western bathing suits and, quite literally, jump off the deep end. The imagery of bathing suits with their sudden exposures of otherwise hidden body parts, deep ends of swimming pools, the public humiliations of swimming classes and changing rooms, overwhelming tides (of migration) or waves (of immigrants) are all drawn, of course, from the concluding story of *Tales from Firozsha Baag*, "Swimming Lessons." Here, the immigrant is no longer the paranoid solitaire, but just one more citizen in this experiment in social construction called by some a "New World."

NOTES

I would like to thank Emmanuel Nelson for his advice in compiling the bibliography for this chapter, and Shirley Geok-Lim for encouraging me to participate in the program arranged by the Discussion Group on Asian American Literatures at the MLA 1989 Convention in Washington, D.C.

1. See, for example, Bharati Mukherjee's disclaimer: "I am not at all an autobiographical writer, but my obsessions reveal themselves in metaphor and language." Geoffrey Hancock, "An Interview with Bharati Mukherjee," *Canadian Fiction Magazine* 59 (1987): 36.

2. See "Naipaul's Arrival," *Yale Journal of Criticism* 2, no. 1 (1988): 25–50.

3. See especially her contrastive analysis of the two superstars in "'Prophet and Loss: Salman Rushdie's Migration of Souls," *Village Voice Literary Supplement* 72 (March 1989): 9–12.

4. "The literary commonwealth of Indian-origin authors is a comparatively recent phenomenon, still largely unremarked in this country. . . . In Canada, where the East Indian population is proportionally greater than in the U.S., more names leap readily to mind. . . . Since I'm a frequent visitor to writing classes in both the U.S. and Canada, I can't help noticing the number of young Americans and Canadians of my own general background who seem to be writing seriously and semi-professionally. . . . I'm moved and a little daunted; I know the immigrant world well enough to know that each young writer is a doctor, accountant, or engineer lost; a bright hope, a bitter disappointment. I left India for the freedom to write and make my own life; I can imagine people somewhat like myself, but . . . it will take another ten years for the Indo-American writers to start making their mark" ("Writers of the Indian Commonwealth," 400).

5. "My choices for this volume may appear whimsically eccentric" (ibid.).

6. "I have no country of origin. In polite company, I am an 'East Indian' (the opposite, presumably, of a 'West Indian'). The East Indies, in my school days, were Dutch possessions, later to become Indonesia. In impolite company I'm a 'Paki'. . . . For an Indian of my generation, to be called a 'Paki' is about as appealing as it is for an Israeli to be called a 'Syrian'" ("An Invisible Woman," 38).

7. I am indebted to Kateryna Arthur of Murdoch University, who writes that her aim in using "Fifth World" to describe late twentieth-century immigrant communities is to

"create a stronger communal identity for a vast world-scattered migrant population of disempowered people who have lost their cultural, linguistic and political base" and to "dislodge further the hierarchical scale and geographical basis of numbering worlds by showing *all* such worlds to be regrouping and changing with shifting patterns of power born of very specific historical circumstances." Arthur rejects the words "immigrant" and "migrant" because they "define people as *not* belonging where they are" ("Fifth World," paper delivered at 1990 conference on the history of Ukrainian settlement in Australia, Melbourne).

8. Bowles is quoted on page 76 as having declared: "The Sinhalese are beyond a doubt one of the least musical people in the world. It would be quite impossible to have less sense of pitch, line, or rhythm." Immediately under this quotation, Ondaatje launches into one of his more celebrated improvisational poems, "Sweet Like a Crow," demonstrating a pitch, line, and rhythm quite other than what Bowles would obviously appreciate and thus decentering the ethnocentric notion that there be but one standard for judging pitch, line, or rhythm.

9. Michael M. J. Fischer, "Ethnicity and the Post-Modern Arts of Memory," in *Writing Culture: The Poetics and Politics of Ethnography*, ed. James Clifford and George E. Marcus (Berkeley: University of California Press, 1986), 219.

10. Note the *ad feminem* attack of Gayatri Chakravorty Spivak, who dismisses Mukherjee's cultural criticism as almost worthless because it represents the privileged perspective of "liberal third worldist feminism" (*In Other Worlds: Essays in Cultural Politics* [New York: Methuen, 1987], 256). A similar criticism, grounded on an equally implied agenda of social realist priorities, underlies Feroza Jussawalla's contemptuous dismissal of Vikram Seth as "the totally assimilated yuppie of the Silicon Valley: no qualms, no hint of Indianness except the name and the baggage of Anglo-Indian education expressed in the various intellectual references—superficially acquired, possibly in an Indian mission school" ("Chiffon Saris," 585). Jussawalla has misplaced the geographies of Seth's previous education. Also, his sociological scrutiny of Californian life (returning the gaze that has always seen India and Indians as exotic, as it were) has been misread as the abandonment of his own prior identity: a good argument, if Seth were anything but the very minor anagrammed player he is in the poem/fiction.

11. I refer to Susanna Moodie, character in and author of *Roughing It in the Bush* (first published in 1852, now a "classic" founding text of Canadian literature), throughout which the author complains that immigrants to Canada and the United States have abandoned their European sense of class and a concomitant respect for their "betters."

12. Adapted from James Clifford, *The Predicament of Culture: Twentieth-Century Ethnography, Literature, and Art* (Cambridge, Mass.: Harvard University Press, 1988), 111.

13. "In case anyone finds a copy of *Wife*, it should be read in the following way: the nominal setting is Calcutta and New York City. But in the mind of the heroine, it is always Toronto" ("An Invisible Woman," 39).

14. Part of a review of *Middleman and Other Stories* that has been quoted extensively, here by Gillian MacKay in "On Stage: Bharati Mukherjee," *Domino* (May 1989): 46.

15. "Speaking as the coauthor of a book on the actual Canadian-Sikh bombing of an Air-India flight in which all 329 passengers were killed, I can't help wondering why, in Rushdie's version of the disaster, the women, children, and Sikhs are allowed to disembark before the plane takes off. In real life, they were not. Real life shouldn't be starker, more horrible, more unflinching than fiction" ("Prophet and Loss," 10).

16. Rosemary Sullivan, "Who Are the Immigrant Writers and What Have They Done?," *Globe and Mail*, October 17, 1987, natl. ed., E1. (I have been unable to trace further references to Mistry's former career as folksinger.)

WORKS CITED

Arthur, Kateryna. "Fifth World." Paper presented at conference on the history of Ukrainian settlement in Australia, Melbourne, 1990.

Fischer, Michael M. J. "Ethnicity and the Post-Modern Arts of Memory." In *Writing Culture: The Poetics and Politics of Ethnography*. Ed. James Clifford and George E. Marcus. Berkeley: University of California Press, 1986. 194–233.

Gates, Henry Louis, Jr. "Remembrance of Things Pakistani: Sara Suleri Makes History." *Village Voice Literary Supplement* 81 (December 1989): 37–38.

Hancock, Geoffrey. "Interview with Bharati Mukherjee." *Canadian Fiction Magazine* 59 (1987): 30–44.

———. "An Interview with Rohinton Mistry." *Canadian Fiction Magazine* 65 (1989): 143–50.

Jussawalla, Feroza. "Chiffon Saris: The Plight of Asian Immigrants in the New World." *Massachusetts Review* 29, no. 4 (1988): 583–95.

Katrak, Ketu H., and R. Radhakrishnan, eds. *Desh-Videsh: South Asian Expatriate Writers and Artists. Massachusetts Review* 29, no. 4 (1988). Special issue.

Mehta, Ved. *Daddji/Mamaji*. 1972/1979. London. Picador/Pan Books, 1984.

———. *The Ledge Between the Streams*. 1984. London: Picador/Pan Books, 1985.

———. *Vedi*. 1982. London: Picador/Pan Books, 1985.

Mistry, Rohinton. *Tales from Firozsha Baag*. Markham and Harmondsworth: Penguin Books, 1987.

Mukherjee, Bharati. *Darkness*. Markham and Harmondsworth: Penguin, 1985.

———. "An Invisible Woman." *Saturday Night* (March 1981): 36–40.

———. *Jasmine*. New York: Viking Penguin, 1989.

———. *The Middleman and Other Stories*. New York: Viking Penguin, 1988.

———. "Prophet and Loss: Salman Rushdie's Migration of Souls." *Village Voice Literary Supplement* 72 (March 1989): 9–12.

———. *The Tiger's Daughter*. 1971. New York: Penguin, 1987.

———. *Wife*. 1975. New York: Penguin, 1987.

———. "Writers of the Indian Commonwealth." *Writers of the Indian Commonwealth*. Ed. Bharati Mukherjee and Ranu Vanikar. *Literary Review* 29, no. 4 (1986): 400–401. Special issue.

Mukherjee, Bharati, with Clark Blaise. *Days and Nights in Calcutta*. 1977. New York: Penguin, 1986.

———. *The Sorrow and the Terror: The Haunting Legacy of the Air India Tragedy*. New York: Penguin, 1987.

Mukherjee, Bharati, and Ranu Vanikar, eds. *Writers of the Indian Commonwealth. Literary Review* 29, no. 4 (1986). Special issue.

Ondaatje, Michael. *In the Skin of a Lion*. Toronto: McClelland and Stewart, 1987.

———. *Running in the Family*. Toronto: McClelland and Stewart, 1982.

Rushdie, Salman. *The Satanic Verses*. New York: Penguin, 1988.

Spivak, Gayatri Chakravorty. *In Other Worlds: Essays in Cultural Politics*. New York: Methuen, 1987.
Suleri, Sara. *Meatless Days*. Chicago: University of Chicago Press, 1989.
———. "Naipaul's Arrival." *Yale Journal of Criticism* 2, no. 1 (1988): 25–50.

5

Passages from India: Migrating to America in the Fiction of V. S. Naipaul and Bharati Mukherjee

C. L. Chua

Travel and migration have long played important roles in the history and consciousness of Commonwealth nations. In a sense, the fifteenth-century British search for a passage to India was responsible for opening up North America to Europe, sowing the seeds of Commonwealth there. Discovery of such an American passage then was a dream of fame and fortune, of egregious identity and material wealth. This dream of North America persists today, taking a reverse direction and appealing to individuals in Third World Commonwealth countries who conceive of migrating to North America as a passage to a better life, larger liberty, and swifter pursuit of happiness. Thus, in the United States in 1984, Asians alone made up 44 percent of the total influx of immigrants (Arnold et al., 111), and the Asian population was estimated as having grown 84 percent during the 1980s, with Indians accounting for 10 percent (Bouvier and Agresta, 291–92; Saran, 23; Gardner, et al., 7–8, 15); it was estimated that the number of Indian Americans would increase from 387,223 in 1980 to a projected 684,330 in 1990 (Bouvier and Agresta, 292). Similarly, the number of Asian Canadians more than doubled between 1971 and 1981, with South Asians numbering 130,625 in Canada in 1981 (Kubat, 238). Several fictions of V. S. Naipaul and Bharati Mukherjee have dealt poignantly with the experience of Indians making this passage from India, depicting the dreamers with realism and questioning the dream with irony.

Although Naipaul has examined America indulgently in his nonfiction *A Turn in the South* and glanced at it in his novel *The Enigma of Arrival*, his most intense fictional focus upon America is the story "One Out of Many," embedded in a book of five narratives of migration entitled *In a Free State*. Freedom, then, thematically unifies the book, freedom interacting between First World and Third, between empire and subject, distinguishing between what some sociopsychologists might call a passive "freedom from" and an active "freedom to" (Fromm, 35).

The story's title, "One Out of Many," already signals a rich ambiguity. As a generic indicator, for instance, it may designate the story and its protagonist as an exemplum, representative of the many who migrate to the United States. But it could indicate an exceptional case. It could signify belongingness—or displacement. It can also suggest links between First and Third worlds. For, on the one hand, as Bruce King has noted, it "alludes to the usual slogan of multiracial Third World nations: 'Out of many, one nation' " (King, 174). But it could also be noted that the title translates the Latin phrase *e pluribus unum*— the slogan of the United States, adopted by Franklin, Adams, and Jefferson in the eighteenth century when this country was defining its freedom and when it was a developing nation. Significantly, the origin of the phrase describes a Roman and an African slave preparing a salad or vegetable stew ("Moretum," attr. Virgil in Page, vol. 2) and startlingly anticipates the now commonplace "melting pot" image of Israel Zangwill's 1914 Jewish immigrant play. The motto denotes indeed the high ideal of a unified society and its plural ethnicity, a common ideology of freedom and individual rights. Ironically, this idealistic motto of the United States is most commonly found engraved upon money, upon five-, ten-, and twenty-five-cent coins, the small change of America. Naipaul's intricately meaningful title spins off this rich mix of idealism and materialism, of abstract idea and cold cash. It elegantly prepares for the irony that permeats and enlivens this tale.

Naipaul's sympathetic narrator-protagonist, Santosh, is a Bombay servant who chooses to migrate when his employer is seconded to Washington, D.C. It is an opportunity to participate in the American dream of betterment in life, liberty, and happiness.

These aspects of the American dream are examined under Naipaul's unsentimental gaze as he steers Santosh with ironic humor through three interrelated manifestations of the dream, terming these the three "worlds" of America: "The restaurant [where Santosh eventually works] is one world, the parks and green streets [of the hippies and Hare Krishnas] . . . are another, and . . . a third [is the black ghetto with] burnt-out homes, broken fences, and overgrown gardens" (57). The first American world, emblemized by Santosh's restaurant, whose owner repeatedly says "yemblems of the world" (42), is the materialistic and socioeconomic aspect of the American dream, the second world its pastoral aspect, and the third its minority-ethnic aspect.

Santosh gets a foretaste of the first American world the moment he enters the high-tech realm of transcontinental air travel. Everything there, including the toilet, is state of the art, but Santosh feels miserable, purging and vomiting an incompatible mixture of Western champagne and Indian betelnut. In a humorous but significantly foreshadowing image, Santosh sees his face in the mirror as having "the colour of a corpse" (25) and exaggeratedly wishes for death's release: "I hoped the plane would crash." Paradoxically, as several readers have noted (Boxill, 57–64), when Santosh arrives in the land of the free, he does not feel free. His Washington apartment, sealed in with labyrinthine corridors and incomprehensible elevators, makes him feel physically like a "prisoner" (27). Mentally, he is brainwashed by commercial TV's soapbox vision of an America comprising money and materialism.

But Santosh does glimpse America's second or pastoral world, imagistically a "green circle with the fountain" (52), a *locus amoenus*. There the hippies and flower children hang out. They represent the dream of America as a second Eden—innocent, pastoral, and Whitmanesque:

If the people in Hindu costumes in the circle were real, . . . I might have joined them. We would have taken to the road; at midday we would have halted in the shade of big trees; in the late afternoon the sinking sun would have turned the dust clouds to gold; and every evening at some village there would have been welcome, water, food, a fire in the night. But that was a dream of another life. (56)

However, Santosh is incapable of participating in this version of America. On the one hand, he is still captive to his old-country caste prejudices, which lead him to label a hippie as a "half-caste" and a "leper" (30). On the other hand, he has bought into the television soaps, not Whitman's poems, and he has been sold an America of cars and cash, materialism and money.

Simultaneously, Santosh is becoming aware of America's ethnic or "Third" World (57), an African American ghetto of "burnt-out brick houses, broken fences, overgrown gardens" (57). He enters this American Third World through the generous person of an African American maid in his apartment complex. She offers him the joys of sex, most of which escape him, again because he is captive to his Asian prejudice against blacks and aggressive females, which types the frolicsome woman as a superhuman man-eater: "I saw her as Kali, goddess of death and destruction, coal-black, with a red tongue and white eyeballs and many powerful arms" (38). Instead of reciprocating her affection, he exploits her by marrying her to gain American citizenship. Her community offers him soul brotherhood (57), but his prejudices prevent him from sharing it. However, this ethnic American world does provide Santosh a model and incentive for freedom because, as he watches a race riot of the sixties, he "share[s] their exhilaration" (41) and is empowered to free himself from his Old World employer: "The idea of escape was . . . simple, . . . but it hadn't occurred to me before" (41). He cannot refuse to accept the challenge to free himself at least from a parasitic or satellite identity: "I couldn't easily become part of someone else's presence again" (41).

Escaping his original Bombay employer, Santosh is able to reap the socio-economic harvest of the first American world. He becomes a chef in a Washington ethnic restaurant, not a servant; and although he is no yuppie, his wages do appreciate six times as he bargains in a free labor market (51). But though Santosh is *free from* the socioeconomic bonds of caste and servitude in America, he is not psychologically *free to* create a new individual self. He still does not know how to be responsible for himself; as a matter of fact, "it was worse . . . because now the responsibility was mine [since] I had decided to be free, to act for myself" (47). At one critical moment, when he is being driven to an Indian community meeting where he would have to assert his freedom as an American, Santosh yields to an angst-filled nostalgia for his past identity, which was "as part of my employer's presence" (37). He longs for the security of the old master-servant relationship and calls his new Washington employer, Priya, "sahib," begging him to turn the car around (48). With his old Bombay employer, "the word was not servile; it was . . . part of my employer's dignity and therefore part of mine" (48). But Priya's "dignity could never be mine. Priya I had always called Priya . . . the American way, man to man. With Priya the word was servile" (48). In this moment, Santosh loses his chance to become fully free— he has been *free from* but is unable to be *free to*. This Santosh seems to realize, saying, "I was a free man; I had lost my freedom" (49). Indeed, people like Santosh affirm the dominion of Dostoyevsky's Grand Inquisitor.

At the story's end, Naipaul's immigrant is a citizen of arguably the freest, richest country of the First World; he resides in Washington, D.C., "capital of the world" (21). But pathetically and ironically, Santosh has bought only into the meretricious and materialist aspect of the American Dream and is hampered by his baggage of Old World prejudices from accepting America's pastoral world or enjoying its ethnic multifariousness. Naipaul thus symbolically houses him in the American Third World of the minority ghetto, where he ironically regrets his lost past and anticipates only the future certitude of death.

It was Naipaul's irony that attracted Bharati Mukherjee. "Like V. S. Naipaul," she says, "I used a . . . self-protective irony" (*Darkness*, 2) for writing about migration, expatriation, and assimilation or, as she phrased it in an interview, "unhousement, . . . remaining unhoused, . . . and rehousement" (Mukherjee and Boyers, 5; Carb, 650).

Mukherjee, who describes herself as having been born "a Hindu Bengali Brahmin" (Carb, 651) in Calcutta in 1940, has lived mostly in Canada or the United States since 1961, earning degrees, raising sons, lecturing at universities, and writing numerous articles, two nonfiction books, three novels, and two short story collections. Her later works, comprising the novel *Jasmine* (1989) and the stories in *Darkness* (1985) and *The Middleman* (winner of the 1988 National Book Award), are her most rewarding. Almost all of them directly or indirectly deal with the disconcerting experience of migrating to North America. Although her first novel, *The Tiger's Daughter* (1972), is set in India, its protagonist is a passive young Bengali wife of an American, and it portrays her Chekhovian disillusion with India during a family visit. Mukherjee's second novel, *Wife* (1975), describes a weak-minded Bengali woman who migrates to New York with her engineer husband in search of a better life; but her sensibilities become so confounded by her changing cultural roles, the insidious television factitious-ness, and the tensions of feminism that, ironically, she goes mad and kills her husband.

Many of Mukherjee's later works expatiate upon this South Asian immigrant experience in North America, much of which is painful. Especially painful is the topic of racism; indeed, one possible reading of the title of her anthology *Darkness* is as a reference to racial prejudice, which is, after all, a darkness of the mind toward the darkness of another person's skin. Those works set in Canada, however, are more bitter than those set in the United States, especially on the topic of racism. In fact, Mukherjee goes so far as to account for the violence of the novel *Wife* by saying that New York was only its "nominal setting"; "in the mind of the heroine, it is always Toronto" (Mukherjee, "An Invisible Woman," 39). For Mukherjee, the Canadian Green Paper of 1975 gave "implied consent . . . to racism" to Canadians of the "founding races" (ibid., 38). She bitterly reports, "I was followed by detectives in department stores who assumed I was a shoplifter or treated like a prostitute in hotels. I was even physically roughed up in a Toronto subway station" (Carb, 652).

In *Darkness*, perhaps the most graphic story about Canadian racism, is "Ta-murlane," whose title derives from the Central Asian warrior-king, derisively nicknamed Timur the Lame (Nazareth, 185). It concerns an Indian Canadian cook who becomes so incensed when a Mountie mistakenly tries to arrest him as an illegal immigrant that he chops off the Mountie's hand, then ironically holds his Canadian passport in front of his face as he is shot (125). "The World According to Hsü" is a much less shocking, more ironic, and nonetheless de-spairing story. In it Ratna, a Eurasian woman of Indian descent, and her husband, a white Canadian professor, are vacationing on an island nation in the Indian Ocean off the African coast. The couple is trying to decide whether to move their home from French Montréal to Anglo Toronto in order to advance the husband's career. As if in concert with their decision making, a military coup breaks out on the island which may determine its future. The dispiriting uncer-tainty and irritable meanness of being uprooted and homeless is reflected in a backdrop of seedy caravanserais, uneasy politics, and directionless supporting characters. The wife is unwilling to move house because of her experience of "Toronto racists": "In Toronto, she was not a Canadian, not even Indian. She was something called, after the imported idiom of London, a Paki. And for Pakis, Toronto was hell" (41); she also recalls a Punjabi boy's having been struck there by a car sporting a bumper sticker reading "KEEP CANADA GREEN. PAINT A PAKI" (47). But conflict, Mukherjee implies bitterly, seems to be fundamental to the world, not just racial or marital; abrasiveness is embed-ded in the very structure of the planet. The trope for this lies in the story's title, which derives from an article (by a scientist, Hsü) that the husband is reading. The article is on plate tectonics and describes how continents have been formed by plates of the earth's surface smashing or grating against each other. Informed by this metaphor of fundamental and ubiquitous conflict, the apparently facile optimism of the story's ending is open to an ironical reading: "She poured herself another glass [of wine], feeling for the moment at home in that collection of Indians and Europeans babbling in English and remembered dialects. No matter where she lived, she would never feel so at home again" (56). But if being "at home" means feeling at ease, secure, and free from conflict, then she is only deluding herself. The inescapable fact remains that Ratna is shunned as a "white rat" in India (44) and scorned as a "Paki" in Canada; furthermore, she is clearly an alien on that island, surrounded by tourists (derogatorily described as "that collection") who are without homes there, "babbling" at each other without a common unifying language, in a country without political stability. Therefore, although the final sentence of the story appears to be too easily optimistic, as some readers take it to be, it could alternatively be read as an ironic and despairing assessment by Mukherjee that Ratna will never really be "at home" anywhere.

Mukherjee's U.S. stories may be intended to be kinder and gentler than her Canadian ones, but she is aware that America is "violent, mindlessly macho, conformist, lawless. . . . No dark-skinned person has the right to feel comfortable inside American history. Yet I do" ("An Invisible Woman," 38). And she prefers America's "melting pot," girded by its "human rights laws," to Canada's discrete "mosaic" (Carb, 652). Immigrants unwary or unable to adapt are victims or contributors to America's mindless violence. In "Loose Ends," for instance, the unwary daughter of an Indian motel owner is raped by a psychopathic Vietnam veteran (*Middleman*, 54). In "A Father," an Indian father in Detroit, incidentally a devotee of Kali, pounds the belly of his liberated unmarried daughter with a rolling pin (an imagistic equivalent of the traditional Indian club) when he cannot accept her pregnancy by artificial insemination (*Darkness*, 73). Some of Mukherjee's best stories show how immigrants who should support actually exploit each other. In "Nostalgia," for example, a powerful and well-to-do Indian psychiatrist, with a red Porsche, a white wife, and a preppy son at Andover (the American Eton), decides to sexually exploit an Indian salesgirl in New York—only to discover that she is really a prostitute and that he is being blackmailed. In a primal revenge, he reverts to his origins, and, "squatting like a villager," defecates into the sink of the hotel room owned by her uncle pimp "and with handfuls of his own shit—it felt hot, light, porous, an artist's medium—he wrote WHORE on the mirror and floor" (*Darkness*, 113). Perhaps the most subtle of the stories of exploitation is "Angela." The protagonist-narrator is an orphan adopted from the hell of Bangladesh (replete with "rapes, dogs chewing on dead bodies, soldiers" [13] cutting off her nipples [10]) into the heaven of a midwestern American family where she leads cheers in high school. But Angela is an angel trailing dark memories—the orphanage cook used to chop off crows' wings for her to sew angel wings. She visualizes "grace as a black . . . bat . . . on blunt . . . wings" (*Darkness*, 11). And her fate is to be courted by an unattractive middle-aged Goanese doctor to whom her adoptive family is obliged. She therefore feels guilty for wanting to go to college instead of accepting his "tempt[ation of] domesticity, . . . duplexes, babies" (19), and she goes to sleep to dream in a sensuously ambiguous image, of "leeches, I can feel leeches gorging on the blood of my breasts" (20)—a richly ironic conflation of the repulsive and the medicinal, of suffering and nurturing, of the appearance of grace and the reality of exploitation.

In Mukherjee's violent, exploitative, and frequently benighted North America, there can be instances when love may possibly be a saving grace. Thus a gentler love story than "Angela" is "Orbiting" in *Middleman*. Its male protagonist is an Afghan refugee who was forced to orbit the world, camping in airport transit lounges, until admitted to New York. His lover is a second-generation Italian-American woman who has herself orbited through several liberated DINK relationships (i.e., double-income-no-kids). She has invited him to her family's Thanksgiving dinner, a feast day celebrating the way Native Americans welcomed the Pilgrims of 1621 (who had done some orbiting of their own). As she watches him carve the turkey flesh with his Afghan dagger, she realizes "all in a rush how much I love this man with his blemished, tortured body. I will give him citizenship if he asks. . . . He . . . is a scarred hero and survivor. Dad and Brent [her brother-in-law] are children. I realize [he's] the only circumcised man I've slept with" (*Middleman*, 76). This richly sensuous closing image, like the leeches of "Angela," is ironically and ambiguously expressive of the interrelationship of pleasure and pain, sacrament and violence, but its context is a more positive one than that of the earlier *Darkness* story, and worthy of a Crazy Jane.

In Mukherjee's fictions of the South Asian experience in North America, especially in the United States, a few may actually be optimistic, though not painless. The *Middleman* tale "A Wife's Story," for instance, tells the positive variant of the novel *Wife*: the short story's protagonist is an Indian woman who absents herself from her husband to do graduate study in New York, and although she encounters racial prejudice and sees her women friends being sexually exploited, she is able through her liberating camaraderie with both men and women to discover in herself a power, confidence, and sexuality which she did not realize she was capable of. But it is Mukherjee's novel *Jasmine* (1989) that contains her most optimistic depiction of the South Asian experience in North America.

The novel *Jasmine* actually grew out of one of the *Middleman* stories, also entitled "Jasmine," whose protagonist "wouldn't die" from the author's imagination, demanding to be reincarnated in a lengthier genre (Steinberg, 47). Survival and reincarnation are indeed integral elements of this novel, for the protagonist is known by different names at different stages of the narrative, signifying her acquisition of different identities, different lives. But in more than that sense is *Jasmine* a novel about survival; it is also the account of an immigrant South Asian woman's metamorphosis, self-invention, and self-empowerment.

Jasmine's career begins in a village in the Punjab, India, where she is handicapped by gender and by fate. Born her family's fifth daughter into a society that considers "daughters . . . curses," Jasmine is almost strangled by her mother

(39–40). Then, when Jasmine is seven, an astrologer prophesies widowhood and exile for her (3). Rather than submit to these handicaps, however, Jasmine struggles against them. For instance, she resists the astrologer, falls down, bites her tongue, and scars her forehead (as Mukherjee did [Steinberg, 47]); but instead of succumbing to these wounds Jasmine resolutely metamorphoses them into advantages: she imagines the wound in her forehead to be a sage's third eye to scan invisible worlds (5), and the bloody tongue is an attribute of the powerful destructor goddess Kali, an image that reappears later in the novel when Jasmine knifes her rapist (118–19). The astrologer episode then closes on two unforgettable images: as Jasmine swims wrathfully in the river as though to cleanse herself, she bumps into the carcass of a drowned dog and tastes the stench of the water (5). Both these images affect her like curses then, but she is to exorcise them dramatically later in the novel: a few years later, she smashes in the skull of a dog who attacks the village women during their morning toilet, feeling "a buzz of power" during the incident (54–57), and again, before she kills her rapist, she drinks a glass of brownish water (116).

The astrologer's prophecy of widowhood, however, comes true. Jasmine, who is named Jyoti by her parents, marries at age fourteen an enlightened engineering student who educates her and renames her Jasmine. He wishes to emigrate to the United States, but before that can happen, he is blown up by a Sikh terrorist bomb. (It is perhaps significant to note that, in India, the protagonist has two names suggestive of the two conflicting cultures of the subcontinent: Jyoti is a Hindi and Hindu name, whereas Jasmine is a Persian-Arabic and Moslem name; respectively the names mean "light" and "sweetness," the two elements Matthew Arnold thought could save culture from anarchy. Needless to say, Mukherjee is well acquainted with Arnold, having quoted "Dover Beach" in *Darkness* [190] and borrowed a short story title from him in *Middleman* [146].)

Jasmine then sets out for the United States to realize her husband's immigration dream by proxy and also, like a virtuous Hindu widow, to commit suttee by cremating his suit (in lieu of his mangled corpse) and immolating herself in the flames. Paradoxically, during her odyssey to achieve this, Jasmine has to sell herself unvirtuously for food and passage. However, when a Vietnam veteran turned smuggler rapes her and makes fun of her husband's suit, she strikes back and kills him (instead of stabbing herself). In seeking virtue and death, Jasmine ironically stumbles into criminality and a desire to live: on the far side of one's Inferno begins Purgatorio. She is helped by a kind woman who illegally aids refugees and who renames her Jazzy (133), another reincarnation. Through her, Jasmine becomes an au pair, a "care-giver" (175), to an academic couple at Columbia University; when the couple's marriage breaks up, the husband, Taylor, becomes Jasmine's lover. He nicknames her Jase (176), yet another reincarnation.

A final reincarnation occurs when Jasmine relocates to the Midwest. She flees New York in terror and leaves Taylor when she recognizes a neighborhood hotdog vendor as her husband's assassin. By chance she ends up in Iowa as the common-law wife of Bud Ripplemeyer, a prominent small-town banker, and becomes known as Jane Ripplemeyer. Jasmine refuses to marry him for fear of her astrologer's prophecy of widowhood, and indeed Bud is shot by a distraught farmer facing foreclosure soon after he and Jasmine begin living together (198). Although Bud does not die, he becomes a paraplegic. Thus Jasmine has to take increasing charge of their relationship; in sex, for instance, she becomes the active partner, even deciding whether Bud should ejaculate (37). (This situation echoes that of the *Middleman* story "The Tenant," in which the woman protagonist has an affair with her armless landlord [113].) Thus, when Jasmine becomes pregnant, it is an event over which she has more control than most women, and it is an indicator of how much Jasmine is now in charge of her self and her life, of how much empowerment she has gained.

If Mukherjee had ended her novel at this point, she would have established Jasmine largely within the archetype of woman as a powerful and supportive care-giver, very much where Charlotte Brontë ended *Jane Eyre*. Indeed, as Jasmine comments at one point, "I am Jane with my very own Rochester" (236). Aside from Jasmine's situation and her being renamed Jane, there is an early illusion to *Jane Eyre* in the novel (41), not to mention that *Jane Eyre* has a wife burnt to death, a fate Jasmine once contemplated for herself. Clearly Mukherjee's heroine is intended to look back at Brontë's, but she also looks beyond her. Mukherjee, therefore, ends her novel by endowing her protagonist not only with power but also with the free will to exercise it. Thus Jasmine, who genuinely loves and cares for Bud, refuses to be bound to his wheelchair (as Jane Eyre is to her blinded Rochester). Instead, although she is ripely pregnant, she deserts Bud when her former lover, Taylor, tracks her down and proposes that she flee with him to pursue happiness in Berkeley, California. This ending has been judged to be "ambiguous" (Koenig, 132) if not a downright "abandonment . . . of responsibilities" (Gorra, 9). It may in fact symptomize a flaw in Mukherjee's plotting and characterization. However, it could be argued that Mukherjee is primarily interested in illustrating her theme at this point and that she is realistically showing that liberation has a cost that may not be to everyone's liking; furthermore, when Jasmine moves westward to a greater freedom and self-actualization, she is merely acting in the time-honored American tradition of lighting out for the territory ahead, a tradition hallowed by Horace Greeley and Twain's *Huckleberry Finn*. Mukherjee's Jasmine, therefore, emerges as a woman who has decidedly overcome her gender handicap, repositioned the stars in her astrological chart, and dared to be free. Unlike Naipaul's Santosh, who is only *free from*, Mukherjee's Jasmine is *free to*. Though not without pain and ambiguity, Jasmine's experience forms, on the whole, a positive and optimistic pattern for South Asians in the New World; for Jasmine has indeed come a long way, not only from the Punjab to California, but also from believing that a wife's virtue entails self-immolation to believing that a pregnant woman's happiness justifies her deserting the crippled father of her unborn child for the arms of a lover.

As Mukherjee has explored her immigrant world, her scope and language have evolved appreciably. Her early works are limited to the minds of young women, sensitive, educated, middle class. In her recent works, she empowers herself to appropriate the mentalities of men as well, of whites, of soldiers of fortune. Her narrative voices also have increased many fold. *Wife* begins with the archness of a South Asian Jane Austen: "Dimple Dasgupta had set her heart on marrying a neurosurgeon, but her father was looking for engineers in the matrimonial ads." And *The Tiger's Daughter* echoes the opening paragraph from E. M. Forster's *A Passage to India*: "The Catelli-Continental Hotel on Chowringhee Avenue, Calcutta, is the navel of the universe. . . . There is, of course, no escape from Calcutta. . . . Family after family moves from the provinces to its brutish center, and the center quivers a little, absorbs the bodies, digests them, and waits" (*Tiger's Daughter*, 3–4). But the narrative energy that infuses her recent works is neither British nor Indian. The beginning of "Angela" is a far cry from Austen: "Edith was here [in this hospital] to have her baby last November. The baby, if a girl, was supposed to be named Darlene after Mother. But Edith changed her mind at the last minute. She changed her mind while she was being shaved by the nurse" (*Darkness*, 7). And here is Mukherjee, speaking exuberantly through the throat of an Atlanta sports fan and financial consultant' "I'm in bed watching the Vanilla Gorilla stick it to the Abilene Christians on some really obscure cable channel when Blanquita comes through the door wearing lavender sweats, and over them a frilly see-through apron. . . . Okay, so maybe . . . she isn't a looker in the blondhair-smalltit-greatlegs way that Wendi was. Or Emilou for that matter. But beautiful is how she makes me feel. Wendi was slow growth. Emilou was strictly Chapter Eleven" ("Fighting for the Rebound," *Middleman*, 77, 80). With narratives like these, Bharati Mukherjee is firmly establishing herself in the American tradition of immigrant writers like Henry Roth, Isaac Bashevis Singer, and, above all, Bernard Malamud, to whom *Darkness* is dedicated. As she puts it, "The book I dream of updating is no longer *A Passage to India*—it's *Call it Sleep*" (*Darkness*, 3).

Both Naipaul and Mukherjee, one providing an example that the other has made into many, have written ironical and cautionary fictions about the uneasy passage of Asian Indians to participate in the American dream. Mukherjee evinces a somewhat more positive view than Naipaul of immigrant life in the United States, glimpsing occasionally the redeeming possibilities of love and the self-affirming opportunities for the pursuit of happiness—though neither love nor happiness is ever obtained without pain or without a price. More often, however, the American Dream is found to be meretricious, easily becoming a nightmare of violence, prejudice, and exploitation; sometimes the dreamer discovers that in dreams begin responsibilities of self-defining of which he or she is incapable. Frequently, therefore, the immigrant only ends up being exploited and victimized, deracinated and *dépaysé*, neither here nor there.

NOTE

A brief version of this chapter was presented at the meeting of ACLALS (Association for Commonwealth Language and Literature Studies) held at Canterbury, Kent, England, in August 1989. The author further acknowledges the support of a research award from the California State University, Fresno, which enabled the completion of this chapter.

WORKS CITED

Arnold, Fred, Urmil Minocha, and James T. Fawcett. "The Changing Face of Asian Immigration to the United States." In Fawcett and Cariño, 105–52.

Bouvier, Leon, and Anthony J. Agresta. "The Future Asian Population of the United States." In Fawcett and Carinño, 285–301.

Boxill, Anthony. *V. S. Naipaul's Fiction: In Quest of the Enemy*. Fredericton, N.B.: York Press, 1983.

Carb, Alison B. "An Interview with Bharati Mukherjee." *Massachusetts Review* 28 (Winter 1988): 645–54.

Fawcett, James T., and Benjamin Cariño, eds. *Pacific Bridges: The New Immigration from Asia and the Pacific Islands*. Staten Island, N.Y.: Center for Migration Studies, 1987.

Fromm, Erich, *Escape from Freedom*. 1941. New York: Holt, Rinehart, 1964.

Gardner, Robert, Bryant Robey, and Peter C. Smith. "Asian Americans: Growth, Change, and Diversity." *Population Bulletin* 40, no. 4 (October 1985): 3–44.

Gorra, Michael. "Call It Exile, Call It Immigration." Review of *Jasmine*, by Bharati Mukherjee. *New York Times Book Review*, September 10, 1989, 9.

King, Bruce, "V. S. Naipaul," In *West Indian Literature*. Ed. Bruce King. Hamden, Conn.: Archon, 1979. 161–78.

Koening, Rhoda. "Passage from India." Review of *Jasmine*, by Bharati Mukherjee. *New York*, September 25, 1989, 132.

Kubat, Daniel. "Asian Immigrants to Canada." Fawcett and Cariño, 229–45.

Mukherjee, Bharati. *Darkness*. Markham. Ont.: Penguin, 1985.

———. "An Invisible Woman." *Saturday Night* (March 1981): 36–40.

———. *The Middleman and Other Stories*. 1988. New York: Fawcett Crest, 1989.

———. *The Tiger's Daughter*. Boston: Houghton Mifflin, 1972.

———. *Wife*. Boston: Houghton Mifflin, 1975.

Mukherjee, Bharati, and Robert Boyers. "A Conversation with V. S. Naipaul." *Salmagundi* 54 (Fall 1981): 4–22.

Naipaul, V. S. *The Enigma of Arrival*. New York: Vintage, 1988.

———. *In a Free State*. 1971. New York: Penguin, 1982.

———. *A Turn in the South*. New York: Knopf, 1989.

Nazareth, Peter. "Total Vision." *Canadian Literature* 110 (Fall 1986): 184–91.

Page, T. E., ed. *Virgil: II*. 1918. London: Heinemann, 1930.

Saran, Parmatma. "Asian Indians in the United States." In *Dictionary of Asian American History*. Ed. Hyung-Chan Kim. Westport, Conn.: Greenwood Press, 1986. 23–27.

Steinberg, Sybil. "Bharati Mukherjee: PW Interviews." *Publishers' Weekly*, August 25, 1989, 46–47.

6

"The Sorrows of a Broken Time": Agha Shahid Ali and the Poetry of Loss and Recovery

Lawrence Needham

In "Beyond the Ash Rains," Agha Shahid Ali frames his text with an epigraph from *Gilgamesh*: "What have you known of loss / That makes you different from other men?" Rephrased, it is a fair question to ask about the poet himself: What is it about Agha Shahid Ali that makes him different from other contemporary poets, particularly other poets of the Indian diaspora? The simple answer, which returns to the epigraph and requires substantiation (the burden of this piece), is that Agha Shahid Ali has known loss, intimately and deeply. Of course, loss is a basic condition for poetry, and poets of the Indian diaspora certainly have thematized separation, absence, exile, and loss. But with Agha, it is in the blood. Loss is his Beloved, the interior paramour he has willingly embraced and kept faith with through four volumes of poetry—*Bone-Sculpture, In Memory of Begum Akhtar, The Half-Inch Himalayas, A Walk Through the Yellow Pages*— and manuscripts in circulation. In other respects he charts in his poetic career a recognizable course for many poets of the Indian diaspora: initially under the spell of English verse, the poet falls increasingly under the sway of native poetry, the tension between traditions resulting in a unique hybrid, a new kind of poetry. But in thematizing loss and charting the distinctions between one experience of loss and another, Agha emerges as a singular poetic voice. His distinct gift— won at great cost and effort—is his ability to look into the heart of loss and not flinch; he resists the temptation to retreat to an idealized "authentic" past or to lose himself in a continuous present as an antidote to separation and loss. He resides, instead, somewhere between the past and present, or in a time when both merge, in a space where he can see beyond the ash rains.

Being in-between comes naturally to Agha Shahid Ali, who is, in his own words, a "triple exile." Born in New Delhi, India, he grew up in Kashmir, returning to Delhi to complete an M.A. in English and teach at the University of Delhi. He subsequently received a Ph.D. in English literature from the Pennsylvania State University and an M.F.A. in poetry writing from the University of Arizona before moving to upstate New York, where currently he teaches creative writing and English literature at Hamilton College. His work bears the imprint of diverse places, influences, and audiences. Published in North America, Europe, Australia, and the subcontinent, Agha's poetry has appeared in numerous prestigious journals—*Grand Street*, *Poetry*, *Paris Review*, and *Antioch Review* among them—and significant new anthologies. In addition, he has written on T. S. Eliot, Salman Rushdie, and Faiz Ahmed Faiz, and, through translations of Faiz, has brought the ghazal and the Urdu poetic tradition to Western audiences. Yet Agha is most noted for his poetry, and, in the end, it is the poetry that best reflects his struggle to recover from multiple legacies of loss and gain something of value.

Agha first published in India two slim volumes of verse, *Bone-Sculpture* and *In Memory of Begum Akhtar*. They constitute "apprentice-work" and record Agha's struggle to come to voice as he wrestles with his "alien language," English, and the English poetic tradition. It is fair to say that, in these early works, he is overmatched in his efforts; the influence of his literary ancestors, Shelley and especially Eliot, predominates, as Agha speaks through their strong voices. The influence of Eliot, in particular, is most strongly felt in *Bone-Sculpture*. "Bones," for example, evokes the modern wasteland, echoing in phrase, in tone, and in image its famous literary predecessor:

> The years are dead. I'm
> twenty, a mourner in the Mohorrum
> Procession, mixing blood with
> mud, memory with memory. I'm
> still alone.
> . . . .
>   In this mosaic-world of silent
> graveyards the difference lies between
> death and dying.
>
> It's futile to light oil-lamps here
> and search for grandfather or
> forgotten ancestors. Their
> flesh must have turned soft as dust
> and how can one complain to bones?

                                                              (1–5, 8–15)

A late autumnal mood pervades *Bone-Sculpture*, which depicts a world beyond redemption, resigned to material corruption and a legacy of bones and dust. Like Sybil suspended in a jar or Gerontion seated on the garbage heap, the poet in *Bone-Sculpture* consistently strikes an attitude in which he is, to quote from

"Autumn in Srinigar," "waiting for death." For a young poet, this Gerontion-like posture is surprising, even disconcerting. It is all, of course, only a mask, as Agha later reveals in "Introducing," a poem from *In Memory of Begum Akhtar*:

> I tried being clever,
> white-washed the day,
> exchanged it for the night,
> Bones my masks, Death
> the adolescent password.
>
> (25–29)

Though self-confessedly "adolescent" (perhaps an overstrong, though understandable, assessment from a poet looking back at juvenilia), this posing is perhaps expected, even necessary. For an Indo-Anglian poet of his particular generation, it is foremost part of what one critic has called the writer's "dutiful genuflection to the post-war European gods" (Kulshrestha, 35). It is also, in the poet's words, a "dream ritual of dead men," an obligatory initiation rite at the beginning of *Bone-Sculpture*, certainly, but a necessary exorcism at its end, when, in the last poem of the collection the speaker is revealed "in the white sun outside / erasing language from / dead stones" ("notes for the unabandoned stranger," 2–3, 22–24). Finally, the masking is a self-protective device, allowing the poet to speak of loss and separation without revealing to himself and others the particulars of his history and the springs of his feelings. The alternative—a complete inventory of loss—is the painful project pursued in his subsequent poems, marking them as stronger, more authentic creations.

Before looking closely at later work, however, it is worth mentioning his other influence, Shelley, whom he singles out for attention in "Introducing," as someone he has left behind:

> At fifteen it was easy
> to write poetry: Shelley
> the prophet, Winter here
> and Spring round the corner.
> And when the narcissi
> came, Truth was Beauty, and I,
> sitting by the river.
>
> (1–8)

The irony directed at himself and his literary precursors bespeaks an increasing self-consciousness about his art and a growing confidence in his own poetic powers. Agha is able, by the time he publishes his second volume, to look back and dismiss both Shelley and Eliot, as well as his own juvenilia. The casting out of spirits is not so easily achieved, however, and an internecine warfare between Shelley and Eliot in his earlier work survives in later work as the collision between a Romantic temperament (of whatever provenance) and a modernist mood. Stylistically, the conflict often manifests itself in the juxtaposition of a startling, evocative image with a pared down, understated line, one of the brilliancies he exploits effectively in his maturer work. Thematically, the two opposing attitudes counterbalance any tendency in his verse to inertia or arrest (a real danger in poems on separation, loss, and death), providing the dynamic which drives his poetry beyond any fixed, dead center.

With *In Memory of Begum Akhtar*, Agha exposes himself to the terrors of history, coming to grips with real loss and the inescapable violence of change. In this collection, the poet, who in the last poem of *Bone-Sculpture* claims to have unmasked himself before the "unabandoned stranger," now reveals to his audience glimpses of a past that explain, in part, his preoccupation with death, separation, and loss. Modernist brooding takes on local flavor and actuality when, in "Note Autobiographical—1" and "Note Autobiographical—2," he provides his own version of the Death of God and Tradition in describing how "Dreams of Islam crumbled . . . / when our servant, his shoes / stolen at the mosque / turned deaf to the muezzin's call" (1–4). The theft of shoes at the mosque is, of course, only the convenient occasion for the poet's apostasy; it crystallizes for him a growing sense of the irrelevance of God, His unwillingness or inability to intervene in an increasingly secularized world. The real occasion for the poet's loss of faith is the death of a grandfather whom God might have saved and whose loss triggers a series of questions for which no one has answers, until the speaker "had nothing left to ask" ("Note Autobiographical—1," 23). His response to events is rendered movingly in "Note Autobiographical—2":

> The calligraphed dome gave way to the sky:
> Autumn caved into me
> with its script of flames,
> and ignited my dry garbage of God.
>
> I varnished my face with the sun.
> Dadi said,
> "My grandson is lost to us."
>
> My voice cracked on Ghalib
> and my tongue forgot the texture of prayer.
>
> (5–13)

The turn from God marks a turn to poetry; *In Memory of Begum Akhtar* records the poet's encounter with, and immersion in, the Urdu poetic tradition, specifically the ghazals of Ghalib, Mir, and Faiz, circulated as life-blood through the performances of Begum Akhtar. It can be imagined—as the above poem seems to indicate—that Ghalib was a particularly strong influence on the young poet; to quote Aijaz Ahmad, Ghalib's poetry, emerging in a time when "a whole civilization seemed to be breaking up, and nothing of equal strength was taking its place," possessed moral grandeur, certainly, "but also an intense moral loneliness, a longing for relations which were no longer possible, and a sense of utter waste" ("Introduction," xxi–xxii). Ghalib, then, as much as Eliot, is an inspiration for Agha's early poems of desolation; the English tradition recedes farther behind as the poet cracks his tongue on the Urdu language. Thus there appear, in *In Memory of Begum Akhtar*, two poems on learning Urdu, an original and a revision. At the same time, *In Memory* records the poet's growing discomfiture with the English language, in "Introducing" and especially in the following poem, "The Editor Revisited":

> I began with a laugh, stirred my tea with English,
> drank India down with a faint British accent,
> temples, beggars, and dust
> spread like marmalade on my toast:
>
> A bitter taste: On Parliament Street
> a policeman beat a child on the head.
> . . . .
>   The Marxists said, "In Delhi English sounds obscene.
> Return to Hindi or Bengali, each word will burn
> like hunger.
>
> A language must measure up to one's native dust."
> Divided between two cultures, I spoke a language
> foreign even to my ears;
> I diluted it in a glass of Scotch.
>
> (5–10, 13–19)

A comparison with the earlier "Dear Editor" from *Bone-Sculpture* shows how far the poet has come with his second volume. Though both poems draw upon the familiar Indo-Anglian topos of English as the language of alienation, "Dear Editor" causally and facilely presents the thematic ("i am a dealer in words / that mix cultures / and leave me rootless"; 4–6), whereas "The Editor Revisited" shows the poet's location between two cultures, recognizes the political implications of that position, and registers the lived consequences of alienation. To the extent that the poet emerges as a living presence, or voice, in *In Memory*, he certainly is right to introduce himself (in "Introducing") for the first time as a poet. Unmasked, he establishes a poetic identity, and, in confronting the power of time and the force of history, he discovers a poetic vocation: to memorialize. However, a great irony of *In Memory* is that just as he finds something to hold on to and claim as his own—a native poetic tradition embodied in Begum Akhtar—he is faced with the prospect of losing it, and, in attempting to redeem it through poetry, finds he carries a voice attuned to loss, unable to sustain the moment of memory:

> I wish to summon you in defence.
> But the grave's damp and cold, now when
> Malhar longs to stitch the rain,

wrap you in its notes: you elude
completely. The rain doesn't speak,
and life, once again, closes in,

reasserting this earth where the air
meets in a season of grief.

("In Memory of Begum Akhtar," 33–40)

What is experienced as lost—the dead, poetic power, tradition—merely goes underground to resurface in *The Half-Inch Himalayas*, a remarkable volume concerning nothing so much as the haunting of Agha Shahid Ali by history and the past. It is telling that the title poem of *In Memory of Begum Akhtar* reappears in this volume, strategically placed beside "Homage to Faiz Ahmed Faiz"; singer and poet are reclaimed and brought together again, and, instead of the silence of the departed, the poet hears "some song" by Faiz, recovering a "memory of musk, the rebel face of hope" ("Homage to Faiz Ahmed Faiz," 76).

In his encounter with the past, Agha also recovers particulars missing from his earlier work. Of the books he has published, *The Half-Inch Himalayas* is the most specifically situated; loss has a local habitation and a name—India, Kashmir, the Agha Clan—and there seems to be some urgency that the poet come to terms with it. The condition creating this urgency is exile, only this time, actual physical separation from the subcontinent. Separation from the beloved is both deprivation and opportunity in these poems; the poet suffers in exile, to be sure, but gains in self-knowledge and command as he inventories his loss.

The price of exile, reckoned in loneliness and anxiety, is set down in several moving poems. "A Call" records the speaker's isolation and emptiness, as well as his childlike fantasy that he will be supplanted in the affections of his parents by "the cold moon of Kashmir which breaks / into my house / and steals my parents' love" (2–4). "Houses" reverses the perspective; solicitous of his family's welfare back home, the speaker expresses the anxious concern of a parent worrying about absent children:

My parents sleep like children in the dark.
I am too far to hear them breathe

but I remember their house is safe
and I can sleep, the night's hair
black and thick in my hands. . . .

(5–9)

In its reversal of roles, the poem records both the need for attachment and the desire to change the terms of relationship and influence; exile is the necessary condition for both projects.

It is a truism to comment that in their absence, the members of the poet's family are most present to his memory; despite longing, however, he safeguards against nostalgia by refusing to sentimentalize the past. It is important that he do so, because nostalgia for an "authentic" time (the "real" past) or an "authentic" place (the "real" India or Kashmir) eventuates in a frame of mind that not only does violence to history, but ultimately diminishes the value and uses of memory, his primary resource and subject in *The Half-Inch Himalayas*. One of his chief objects in *The Half-Inch Himalayas* is, in fact, to avoid the frozen embrace of the past, the forgetful snows of winter (phenomenologically, Agha seeks the fluid, transforming condition of water, a recurrent symbol in his recent poetry), through exercising and emphasizing the re-creative powers of memory. His most stunning achievement in this regard is, perhaps, "A Lost Memory of Delhi," in which the poet places himself at the scene of his inception:

> I am not born
> it is 1948 and the bus turns
> onto a road without name
>
> There on his bicycle
> my father
> He is younger than I
> . . . .
> My mother is a recent bride
> her sari a blaze of brocade
> Silverdust parts her hair
> . . . .
> I want to tell them I am their son
> older much older than they are
> I knock keep knocking
>
> but for them the night is quiet
> this the night of my being
> They don't they won't
>
> hear me they won't hear
> my knocking drowning out
> the tongues of stars

(1–6, 10–12, 19–24)

Despite his failure to be heard, the speaker manages to make his presence in the past felt—at least to the reader. "A Lost Memory of Delhi" records a desire common to many poems in this collection: the need to intervene in history so as not to be bound or "frozen" by the fixed stare of its gaze. Agha's intervention is most evident in "Cracked Portraits"; he re-presents in his poetic medium the representations (photographs, paintings) of his ancestors, freeing himself from their paralyzing influence. The emphasis on re-presentation is consonant with the overall design of a book that presents itself not as an empirically accurate picture of the subcontinent, but as a simulacrum, an artifact, a half-inch postcard, partial and limited in scope. In this volume Agha seems to be looking not for the "real" past, but a "usable" past, perhaps the kind presented in "Snowmen":

> My ancestor, a man
> of Himalayan snow,
> came to Kashmir from Samarkand,
> carrying a bag
> of whale bones:
> heirlooms from sea funerals.
> His skeleton
> carved from glaciers, his breath
> arctic,
> he froze women in his embrace.
>
> . . . .
> This heirloom,
> his skeleton under my skin, passed
> from son to grandson,
> generations of snowmen on my back.
> They tap every year on my window,
> their voices hushed to ice.
>
> No, they won't let me out of winter,
> and I've promised myself,
> even if I'm the last snowman,
> that I'll ride into spring
> on their melting shoulders.

(1–10, 15–25)

Recognizing as his forbear the man of Himalayan snow, who brought with him, as his inheritance, " . . . whale bones: / heirlooms from sea funerals" (5–6), the poet claims a legacy of change and transition. Exile is in his bones, and the poem serves as a justification for his current exiled condition. Re-creating the past, providing his own version of it, is thus enabling, unburdening him of the generations of snowmen on his back who would press him into winter. At the same time, the past is the necessary ground for change; the poet can only "ride into spring / on their melting shoulders" (24–25). The failure to come to terms with the past results in arrest, as in *Bone-Sculpture*, when the poet flounders in a self-enclosed, repetitive dream world because of his refusal of history:

> In this mosaic-world of silent
> graveyards the difference lies between
> death and dying. It's
>
> futile to light oil-lamps here
> and search for grandfather or
> forgotten ancestors. Their

flesh must have turned soft as dust
and how can one complain to bones?

("Bones," 12–19)

Ancestors, he discovers, are not so easily consigned to oblivion, as is evident in "Cremation" from *The Half-Inch Himalayas*: "Your bones refused to burn / when we set fire to the flesh. / Who would have guessed / you'd be stubborn in death?" (1–4). They return, in fact, to haunt the mind as necessary ghosts, be they terrors of the night, conjuring painful visions of loss and desolation, or tutelary spirits, offering just the barest possibility of hope.

The spirit that happily haunts Agha's most recent poems, the ancestor he willingly embraces, is Faiz Ahmed Faiz, the Urdu poet whom Agha has translated extensively. The turn from Ghalib in earlier poems to Faiz in later poems is a telling shift, signaling Agha's growing historical and political consciousness. In *In Memory of Begum Akhtar*, there is the barest hint that Ghalib offered Agha a refuge from the ravages of time and historical change; yet even a master of Urdu "who knew Mir backwards, / and the whole Divan-e-Ghalib, / saw poetry dissolve into letters of blood" ("Learning Urdu," 11–13) when "History broke the back / of poetry" ("After the Partition of India," 12–13). Faiz, on the other hand, the poet who redefined the cruel Beloved as Revolution, stands inside history, "as always . . . witness to 'rain of stones' " ("Homage to Faiz Ahmed Faiz," 5). From Faiz, perhaps, Agha increasingly assumes in his poetry the role of witness, and in Faiz, perhaps, he discovers a model for employing tradition in startling and original ways.

Historical and/or political awareness infuse many poems in *The Half-Inch Himalayas*. "A Butcher," though not overtly political, discloses the inability of language to sustain a momentary bond between two strangers, who, though sharing a line from Ghalib, are irrevocably divided along class lines, and whose moment of connectedness is more commercial than cultural. "After Seeing Kozintsev's King Lear in Delhi" records one detail of the British legacy in India, finding parallels in the careers of Lear and Zafar, "poet and Emperor, / . . . led through this street / by British soldiers, his feet in chains, / to watch his sons hanged" by " 'men of stones' " (14–17). And finally, and perhaps most affectingly, "Dacca Gauzes" notes the passing of an art, the creation of gauzes "known as woven air, running / water, evening dew" (2–3). Production is halted when "the hands of weavers were amputated, / the looms of Bengal silenced, and the cotton shipped raw / by the British to England" (19–23). Like so much else in the world that Agha re-creates, the gauzes, first passed down as heirloom saris, then as cut handkerchiefs, are irretrievably lost, evanescing into the dew-starched air:

my grandmother just says
how the muslins of today
seem so coarse and that only

in autumn, should one wake up
at dawn to pray, can one
feel that same texture again.

One morning, she says, the
air was dew-starched: she pulled
it absently through her ring.

                                              (25–33)

    To a great extent, the poem's success is due to its use of contrast, specifically, the rich, poetic evocation of exquisite gauzes juxtaposed with the blunt description of horrific, violent acts. Contrast is an important rhetorical principle in Agha's poetry, as might be expected in a poet negotiating different cultural demands; it is particularly so in *The Half-Inch Himalayas* and later poems when the Urdu poetic tradition comes face to face with poetry in the American grain.

    The allusion to William Carlos Williams might seem misplaced; if anything, Agha is a poet of absence, not presence. And there are certainly more likely candidates for poetic affiliation: W. S. Merwin or James Merrill, perhaps, and surely Wallace Stevens. Yet in his later poetry Williams emerges not so much as an influence Agha is working with, as one he is working against. Agha meets up with Williams at 5 A.M. on Riverside Drive when describing the jogger he sees there:

     The dark scissors of his legs
     cut the moon's

     raw silk, highways of wind
     torn into lanes, his feet

     pushing down the shadow
     whose patterns he becomes

     while trucks, one by one,
     pass him by,

     headlights pouring
     from his face, his eyes

     cracked as the Hudson
     wraps street lamps

     in its rippled blue shells,
     the summer's thin, thin veins

     bursting with dawn,
     he, now suddenly free,

from the air, from himself,
his heart beating far, far

behind him.

(1–19)

Like Williams's "Danse Russe" (and, to a lesser extent, "Yachts"), "The Jogger on Riverside Drive, 5:00 A.M." is pure motion, unimpeded by full stopped lines, driven by its verbal phrases, and brought wonderfully to life by sudden transpositions and juxtapositions. It also is a poem of presence, insisting on the particulars of time and place and full embodiment until, suddenly, the jogger is "free, / from the air, from himself, / his heart beating far, far / behind him" (16–19). At that moment, the jogger absents himself, his transport outside the body placing him in an unspecified location. The result is startling; by working against the poetry of presence and location, Agha achieves a remarkable effect.

At other times, however, the principle of contrast is less successful, producing potentially unwanted effects. For example, the common, everday experience, the particularized event, often is not able to sustain the weight of Agha's resonant vocabulary of loss and desolation. In these cases, the rhetorical sublime leans toward the ridiculous, and pathos sinks downward. Consider, for example, the poet's description of a bar closing in "Philadelphia, 2:00 A.M.": "All routes to death / will open up, again, / as the bars close all over / Pennsylvania" (1–4). Unless the poet is alluding to driving and drinking in the first two lines, the opening is simply overstated. He continues in this vein: "I swallow / the melting rocks in my glass, / looking for shortcuts / by-passing death" (9–12). The language is melodramatic, the gestures broad and obvious. Perhaps too obvious, and it might be suspected that the poet is winking at his audience. But whether intentional or not in *The Half-Inch Himalayas*, the technique is consciously exploited in his next collection, *A Walk Through the Yellow Pages*, which lists in its table of contents a poem fittingly entitled "Language Games."

Much of the humor of *A Walk Through the Yellow Pages* derives from the mismatch of styles and registers. "Bell Telephone Hours," for example, joins the language of salvation and apocalyptic imagery to the discourse of the phone company with darkly humorous results: "I called Information Desk, Heaven, / and asked, 'When is Doomsday?' / I was put on hold" (59–61). Everyday, common experience indicates that the speaker will be endlessly deferred; the situation is mildly humorous until the reader sees in it his own postmodern condition. The poem ends with a chilling, anti-apocalyptic reply:

I prayed, "Angel of Love,
please pick up the phone."

But it was the Angel of Death.
I said, "Tell me, Tell me
when is Doomsday?"
He answered, "God is busy.

He never answers the living.
He has no answers for the dead.
Don't ever call again collect."

                                                                    (68–76)

"Bell Telephone Hours" depicts a world of failed connections and dead language, in short, the contemporary American wasteland. It presents itself as a challenge to the poet, who attempts its revitalization through his linguistic powers. Much of *A Walk Through the Yellow Pages* can be understood in this way; the poet discovers dead script—language processed mechanically and rendered insensible by dull repetition, language abandoned to the streets and bathroom stalls— and recovers it for vital use. He brings considerable linguistic talent to this project and, at the same time, discovers new resources, as high culture abuts popular culture in the form of advertising copy, bathroom graffiti, restaurant menus, and fairy tales. For a slim volume, *A Walk Through the Yellow Pages* possesses remarkable range; Agha experiments with the interview form, employs extended dialogue, takes up the found poem. However, as he explores the resources of language, he also meditates on its limitations and shortcomings. For example, "Bell Telephone Hours," structured around ad copy, demonstrates how fabricated language, circulated through mass media and processed for profit, walls off experience and obstructs genuine connectedness. "Language Games" holds out the promise of language as refuge, lifeboat, or asylum, but shows it as a vehicle of estrangement. And his fractured fairy tales—"An Interview with Red Riding Hood, Now No Longer Little"; "The Wolf's Postscript to Little Red Riding Hood"; and "Hansel's Game"—show the violence at the heart of language practice, how words are used to silence and exclude, masquerading under the guise of the "truth" when in fact operating as self-justification in the interest of preservation or power. As *The Half-Inch Himalayas* interrogates beginnings, these poems interrogate endings and closure, most simply by re-fashioning tales, making the "true" or "official" story one among many.

A Walk Through the Yellow Pages is charming, funny, clever—and meaningful—both in what it has to say and what it portends for the poetry Agha now is writing. His most recent poems continue his interest in telling the stories of history's victims—a Harappan servant girl, the Gypsies, the missing of Chile. Like Said Sultanpour, whom he memorializes in "Palm Reading," Agha is intent on remembering the earth's "vanished prisoners" (19) and "the names of those buried in unmarked graves" (21). He provides what he calls in one poem "a footnote to history," analogous to the wolf's postscript, but on a more serious level. Similarly, he uses the impersonation he employed so successfully in his fairy tales to give voice to those who have been silenced—Eurydice, Medusa, the youngest of the Graeae. Also, dialogue figures more importantly in his latest work. Yet in all of this, Agha is, as always, the chronicler of loss, and his most recent poetry insistently comes back to the source of Agha's poetic power. "A Nostalgist's Map of America," for example, traces "a route of evanescence'' as the speaker reacts to news that a friend is dying of AIDS. Playing off a poem of Emily Dickinson's, ''A Nostalgist's Map'' testifies to the limits of language, which fails to take the measure of suffering and is powerless, even false, before death. ''Crucifixion'' witnesses the death of religion, as a driver enters and leaves a timbered forest, oblivious to the futile attempts of the Penitentes to incarnate a God. But perhaps it is ''Snow on the Desert,'' a poem of contrast and surprise, and an example of successful hybridization, which best succeeds in its evocation of loss. In a context of change and transition, traced geologically in the desert's history and personally in his sister's hurried departure from Tucson, the poet suddenly experiences an epiphanic moment when the past and present collide in a moment of revelation:

As I drove back to the foothills, the fog

shut its doors behind me on Alveron,
and I breathed the dried seas

              the earth had lost,
their forsaken shores. And I remembered

another moment that refers only
to itself:

              in New Delhi one night as
Begum Akhtar sang, the lights went out. It

was perhaps during the Bangladesh War,
perhaps there were sirens,

              air-raid warnings.
But the audience, hushed, did not stir.

The microphone was dead, but she went on
singing, and her voice

              was coming from far
away, as if she had already died.

And just before the lights did flood her
again, melting the frost

              of her diamond
into rays, it was, like this turning dark

of fog, a moment when only a lost
sea can be heard, a time

              to recollect
every shadow, everything the earth was losing,

a time to think of everything the earth
and I had lost, of all

that I would lose,
of all that I was losing.

(53–81)

Lines like these exhibit the poet at his best, testifying to the power of his poetry of loss. In them, it is easy to see what Agha Shahid Ali has known and made of loss, which establishes him as such a singular poetic voice, so hauntingly different from other contemporary poets.

WORKS CITED

Ahmad, Aijaz, ed. *Ghazals of Ghalib*. New York: Columbia University Press, 1971.
Ali, Agha Shahid. *Bone-Sculpture*. Calcutta: Writers Workshop, 1972.
———. *The Half-Inch Himalayas*. Middletown, Conn.: Wesleyan University Press, 1987.
———. *In Memory of Begum Akhtar*. Calcutta: Writer's Workshop, 1979.
———. *A Nostalgist's Map of America*. New York: Norton, 1991.
———. *A Walk Through the Yellow Pages*. Tucson: SUN-gemini Press, 1987.
Kulshrestha, Chirantan, ed. Contemporary Indian English Verse. New Delhi: Arnold Heinemann, 1981.

7

Still Arriving: The Assimilationist Indo-Caribbean Experience of Marginality

Victor Ramraj

A prominent aspect of the early and current Indo-Caribbean experience as depicted by Caribbean writers of East Indian extraction is the Indo-Carribeans' sense of marginality in their adopted homes, be it the Caribbean itself or the European and North American countries to which they migrated. In the Caribbean, they are late arrivers, whose deeply rooted culture kept them apart from and prevented easy assimilation into the dominant British culture that was imposed on the colonies. Those who came to accept assimilation as an inevitable course are depicted as perpetual travellers in a constant state of arriving. Many Indo-Carribean assimilationists, like their black countrymen, migrated to Britain, perceiving London to be their capital and their journey there as a sort of homecoming, only to find, as Samuel Selvon and V. S. Naipaul relate, that they did not actually belong there and found themselves on the periphery of the society. In the 1960s, V. S. Naipaul, living in Britain, came to acknowledge that though the English language was his, the tradition was not (''Jasmine,'' 26), and later, in the 1980s, he observed that he was striving to find a ''centre'' (*Finding the Center*) and to grasp the ''enigma'' of his perpetual state of arrival (*The Enigma of Arrival*). Those who migrated to Canada, as Sonny Ladoo and Neil Bissoondath show, found themselves in a society in which the government's well-intentioned multicultural policy advocates the concept of the cultural mosaic, which unfortunately forces the Indo-Caribbean and other immigrants to perceive themselves as tiny individual tiles kept peripheral, if contiguous, to the prominent central tile of the mosaic. None of the novelists portrays major characters who are seriously contemplating a return to India; they create a few secondary characters who feel alienated in the Caribbean and dream of India but hesitate to make the final commitment to return, fearing that they no longer would be at home even in India.

The early attempts at assimilation by the East Indian pocket of Trinidadian society are a primary concern of such fictional studies as Seepersad Naipaul's *Gurudeva and Other Indian Tales* (1943), Samuel Selvon's *A Brighter Sun* (1952), V. S. Naipaul's *A House for Mr. Biswas* (1961), and Ismith Khan's *Jumbie Bird* (1961). The East Indians' relationship with the wider society in Trinidad and Guyana, the two countries in the Caribbean with a high East Indian population, was a theme in Caribbean literature long before the appearance of works by Khan, V. S. Naipaul, Selvon, and even Seepersad Naipaul, whose *Gurudeva and Other Indian Tales* is the first collection of short stories published by an Indo-Carribean writer. A.R.F. Webber's *Those That Be in Bondage* (1917), a historical romance, Alfred Mendes's short story "Boodhoo" (1932), and Edgar Mittelholzer's *Corentyne Thunder* (1941) all discuss East Indian women's relationship with Creoles, but they are concerned with the Creoles', not the women's, psyche and, written from the Creoles' point of view, portray not the East Indians' growing awareness of the wider society but the Creoles' awakening to the East Indians' presence in the Caribbean. Moreover, the depiction of the East Indian women in these works tends to be, if not patronizing, at least flat. For instance, of Webber's portrait of Bibi in *Those That Be in Bondage* as "that smooth-skinned, bare-toed East Indian young lady" (4), Jeremy Poynting rightly observes that it adheres to the "prurient estate stereotype" (14).

In the fiction of the Indo-Caribbean writers, many of the descendants of the indentured Indian immigrants, who came to the Caribbean as adventurers and fortune-hunters and who perceived themselves initially as temporary dwellers, are now realizing that they are in the Caribbean to stay and must learn to relate to the culture beyond their narrowly circumscribed society. Others resisted relinquishing their language, culture, and tradition and created virtually transposed Indian communities. This led to the inevitable division between the assimilationists and the traditionalists, or, to put it in the Caribbean idiom, between those for and against creolization. In *A House for Mr. Biswas*, Naipaul's portrayal of Hanuman House, the traditionalist Tulsi family home, as a "white fortress"— with thick "concrete walls," closed "narrow doors," and "windowless" facades that create a "bulky, impregnable" (73) appearance—is an appropriate metaphor for a mentality that sought to isolate and insulate the East Indians against the alien culture around them. Structural fissures, however, begin to appear in the white fortress as the culture of this traditional Hindu household is challenged by such reluctant occupants as Mr. Biswas, who finds Hanuman House too constricting.

The conflict between the assimilationists and the traditionalists often disrupts community and family life, with traumatic consequences for the individuals. Selvon's short story "Cane Is Bitter" offers a moving account of such a family that resides in a South Trinidad sugar estate appropriately named Cross Crossing. When the story opens, Romesh, the son and protagonist, has espoused, while attending secondary school in the city, values and aspirations different from those of his family. He is set apart from his tradition-bound peasant Hindu parents, who implore him to return to their world. A major confrontation with his father makes him decide to leave the family fold. Selvon's phrasing puts the breach between father and son in an ancestral context: "As the wind whispered in the cane, it carried the news of Romesh's revolt against his parents' wishes, against tradition and custom" (72). What happens to Romesh after is not examined in this story, but, of another generation and on the periphery of his own family, Romesh now moves to the margin of an enigmatic society, of which, he tells his sister, "there are many things I have yet to learn" (71). In *A Brighter Sun*, set in postwar Trinidad, Selvon examines the experiences of Tiger, a protagonist who appears to be a latter-day Romesh. The sixteen-year-old Tiger, recently married, moves away from his rural Indian home to live in the suburban Creole world. The novel is an account of Tiger's sexual, intellectual, and social development and his initiation into manhood. In learning to relate to the Creole society, Tiger is very much aware of the entrenched differences between himself and his new society, and though he and his wife learn much and make new friends, they are not comfortably at home here. At the end of the novel, Tiger considers "going back to the canefields" (215) but knows that he does not belong there either. His friend Boysie, a fellow assimilationist, is leaving the island for New York. Tiger envies him, and though he attempts to make the best of his lot in his new environment, the likelihood is that, with little to hold him to his former and present societies, he himself will soon be migrating.

Seepersad Naipaul's stories in *Gurudeva and Other Indian Tales*, which are set primarily in the early decades of twentieth-century Trinidad, have as a prominent motif the germination of the lines drawn between the assimilationists and the traditionalists. He has a weakness for the happy ending, however, and tries to evade the ugly aspects of confrontation and its consequences. In "Sonya's Luck," for instance, he tells of Sonya's reluctance to agree to an arranged marriage to a man she has never met. She loves someone else and plans to elope with him the night before her wedding. When she meets him at their trysting place, he is dressed as a bridegroom, and they realize that what they are fleeing is their own marriage to each other, which by happy coincidence was arranged by their parents. Naipaul often shows the protagonist of the long, episodic title story, Gurudeva, in situations where he is caught between his East Indian values and customs and those of the encroaching Creole society. In the concluding episode of the story, a middle-aged Gurudeva falls in love with one of his students, a Westernized young woman, and has to choose between her and his tradition-minded wife, whom he married when he was just fourteen. The council of village elders decrees that Gurudeva should return to his wife, and Gurudeva, once a "badjohn," now a reputable teacher and temple devotee, accedes to their injunction, avoiding, unlike the young Romesh of the next generation in Selvon's "Cane Is Bitter," a breach with his community.

One of the ironies of the assimilationists' lot is that they are often sent on their journeys into the Creole world by tradition-bound parents, who, secure in their own culture and values, are unaware of the emotional pulls and tugs awaiting those who venture beyond the walls of the white fortress. Mrs. Tulsi of *A House for Mr. Biswas* and Romesh's father of "Cane Is Bitter" send their children out to the larger society, anticipating economic gains for them but expecting them to remain psychically unscathed by their excursion into the alien environment and not become estranged from their parents' world. One of the most evocative instances of this occurs in Ladoo's *Yesterdays* (1974), a novel that recreates through stark, ugly, scatological imagery a rural Indo-Caribbean world of rampant sensuality and brutality. The protagonist, Poonwa, is sent when he is five years old to a Canadian Presbyterian mission school by his father, a Hindu devotee, who feels that the boy should be educated to improve his prospects in his poverty-ridden village. The boy and his fellow Hindu students are flogged repeatedly for refusing to become Christians. The punishment is administered by a Canadian white schoolmistress and a Madrassi teacher who has converted to Christianity. Eventually, to avoid further flogging and humiliation, the boy accedes to the wishes of his teachers. His father, however, cannot accept his conversion and in turn whips him. Brutalized at home and in school, the boy spends his schooldays hiding in the school's latrine. Ladoo relates these incidents through Poonwa's recollections as an adult. The obsessive, nightmarish nature of these recollections clearly indicates that Poonwa has been emotionally damaged by his childhood experiences with the alien society. As an adult, he is now possessed by the idea—which sets up the novel's main narrative—of travelling to Canada with the Hindu bible and starting a Hindu mission school equipped with whips and torture chambers. At the end of the novel, the psychotic protagonist has persuaded his father to mortgage his house to finance his mad scheme. Ladoo's premature death soon after completing this novel may have robbed readers of a sequel that could have provided a fascinating resolution of Poonwa's undertaking.

In their study of the conflict between the assimilationists and the traditionalists, the Indo-Caribbean writers tend to focus on the experiences of the assimilationists, with whose lot they invariably sympathize. However, the traditionalists are not ignored, since they constitute the world within which initially, and against which later, the assimilationists are in conflict. And they are extended empathetic treatment by the authors, who show how deeply affected they can be by the rifts with their estranged kin. Neil Bissoondath's *A Casual Brutality* (1988) provides a brief portrait of the protagonist's grandmother, who is shown dreaming of a traditional Hindu family. But her dream recedes as she is "defeated by a world evolved out of her reach and by possibility created by the success of [the] grandfather's store. He could afford to send his children away to foreign universities, to expose them to the wider, more promising world beyond Casaquemada" (124). The author points up the irony of the traditionalists themselves initiating the assimilationists' journeys of estrangement—an irony of which the grandmother is oblivious. These traditionalists cope with estrangement from kith and kin by developing even stronger attachment to their culture, which accentuates their isolation. If affluent, they garrison themselves, assuming a sense of superiority to the Creole society that has beckoned their loved ones. In *A Casual Brutality*, the young assimilationist protagonist, Raj, recalls with embarrassment his affectation as a youth of his grandfather's patronizing treatment of a Creole yardboy. Embarrassment enables him to recognize how different is his approach to the Creole society from his grandfather's, though his occasional ambivalent response to this society indicates that he is not as free of the traditionalist response as he believes himself to be. In Ismith Khan's *Jumbie Bird* (1961), the patriarchal Kale Khan derives strength from his belief that he will return to India, his birthplace, and persuades his grandson to abandon Trinidad and consider India his home. He urges the boy to reject his assimilationist father's nihilistic response that "we ain't belong in Hindustan, we ain't belong in England, we ain't belong in Trinidad" (55). The traditionalists employ folktales to caution their children against the pitfalls of creolization. In *Indian Folk Tales of the Caribbean: Salt and Roti* (1984), Kenneth Parmasad retells a traditional East Indian folktale, "Rites of the Dead," which didactically shows how easily children of East Indian immigrants can lose their cultural and religious heritage.

None of the protagonists who try to assimilate Creole and Western beliefs and values seek to escape their peripheral lives in the Caribbean by returning to India, which evidently is perceived as a metaphor for the traditional life. Ralph Singh of V. S. Naipaul's *The Mimic Men* dreams of the Aryan warriors of Central Asia, but he yearns to be not there but "in Liege in a traffic jam, on the snow slopes of the Laurentians" (175). He eventually flees Trinidad for Europe rather than Asia. Naipaul himself, though he knows that he "cannot reject" India or "be indifferent to it" (*India*, ix), admits that in India he is "a stranger" (xi) and that he does not see it as home. Significantly, none of Naipaul's Indo-Caribbean protagonists has travelled or contemplated travelling to India. Naipaul records in his autobiographical sketch, "Prologue to an Autobiography," that, as a boy, his father, who becomes an assimilationist, refused to return to India when his family was approved for repatriation there. On the day of departure, he hid on the dock "until his mother changed her mind about the trip back to India" (*Finding the Center*, 62). Even the traditionally inclined are reluctant to venture to India. In *A House for Mr. Biswas*, Naipaul captures the romantic yearnings of the older East Indian immigrants to return to India; however, despite their harsh life on the periphery of the larger society, they, like Naipaul's father, would hesitate if actually offered repatriation. "They could not speak English and were not interested in the land where they lived; it was a place they had come to stay for a short time and stayed longer than they expected." Gathered together in the evenings, they "continually talked of going back to India, but when the opportunity came, many refused, afraid of the unknown, afraid to leave the familiar temporariness" (174). Kale Khan of *The Jumbie Bird*, who obsessively instills in his grandson a love of India, is himself ambivalent about returning there, for deep within he hates "India from which he had fled, and hated Trinidad to which he had come to find a new life" (2).

Many of the fictional pieces, like "Cane Is Bitter," conclude with the assimilationists' rejecting their constricting traditional life and abandoning their family and society. Subsequent portrayals, such as V. S. Naipaul's "A Christmas Story" (1964), record the tormenting ambivalence of those who leave the fold. Randolph, the protagonist of the story, wants to believe that he has done the right thing in rejecting Hinduism for Presbyterianism, but he is assailed by doubts on Christmas Eve. Fear that his embezzlement of church funds will be discovered accentuates his insecure relationship with his half-assimilated religion. His hesitancy and passivity are antithetical to the assurance and assertiveness of his relative Hori, a traditionalist, who constantly belittles him and his adopted culture. In *A House for Mr. Biswas*, Mr. Biswas rejects the suffocating traditionalism of Hanuman House. He ventures into the unfamiliar, enigmatic Creole world of Port of Spain, from which he has to seek refuge in the Tulsi home, which he comes to realize can be as much a haven as a cage. His son, Anand, living on the periphery of his extended Hindu family and of his Creole community, flees to what he considers the ordered world of London, only to find, like the assimilationist Indo-Caribbean narrator of Naipaul's "Tell Me Who to Kill" and Ralph Singh of *The Mimic Men*, that he is relegated to the margin of that society as well. The narrator of "Tell Me Who to Kill," lost and abandoned as a resident of an asylum for the insane, is appropriately unnamed. Unlike Ralph Singh or G. Ramsay Muir or Naipaul's *The Mystic Masseur* (1957), he does not even have an anglicized rendition of his name—a simple technique that Naipaul employs to underscore their assimilationist character. The unnamed protagonist emerges from his asylum in the company of his keeper to attend his younger brother's wedding, and he narrates in a diffused but evocative style the story of his flight from an existence on the margin of his extended Hindu family in Trinidad to an even more marginal life in London, where he goes mad. The cosmopolitan, creolized Ralph Singh discovers soon after arriving in London that it is not the home he envisaged as a schoolboy in the Caribbean. He returns to his island only to learn once more that he belongs neither to his extended Hindu family nor to the Creole world, and yet again he "arrives" in London, where he is marginalized in a boarding house, spending his time observing frivolously the foibles of his fellow residents while aspiring to write a history of the British empire—a futile aspiration but one which shows him still yearning to move from the periphery to the center. In Naipaul's *The Enigma of Arrival* (1987), the Indo-Caribbean protagonist, as he observes the Salisbury countryside where he is temporarily dwelling, reviews his life as artist and man and concludes that he is in a state of detachment, of not belonging, of arriving at harbors, a setting that provides an apt metaphor for his unanchored condition. He is like the group of Indo-Caribbeans who sought repatriation to India which, for them, was a "dream of home, a dream of continuity after the illusion of Trinidad."

But when they actually got there, they waited at the harbor for a ship to take them back to Trinidad: "All of India that they had found was the area around the Calcutta docks" (*Finding the Center*, 61).

The metaphor of the perpetual traveller, of the modern nomad, is dominant in Bissoondath's *A Casual Brutality*, as it is in his collection of short stories, *Digging Up the Mountains* (1985). Raj of *A Casual Brutality* belongs to the contemporary generation of Indo-Caribbean assimilationists, whose conflict with the traditionalists has diminished in intensity but not abated with the passage of time. Raj, for instance, as a boy, protests against studying Hindi. He prefers to read about King Arthur even though his uncles urge on him the epic stories of the Hindu gods. The novel examines Raj's estrangement from both the Caribbean Creole and the Canadian society to which he flees after the brutal murder of his wife and child in Casaquemada, which appears to be the fictional counterpart of Trinidad. At the end of the novel, he passively accepts his lot of not belonging anywhere. Returning to Canada, he is asked by an acquaintance at the Casaquemada airport where he is going. He listlessly responds that he is "travelling," observing self-reflexively that "the words *going home* came to mind but I resist them" (6). Bissoondath often equates Raj's ongoing personal odyssey with that of the Indo-Caribbean people. He describes as "a melancholy epic" the East Indians' journey to Trinidad. Of his return to Canada, Raj says: "What began so long ago as a flight from a dusty and decrepit village in India brings me now to a flight on a jet [to Canada]. . . . The important thing is to keep moving on" (377). The novel concludes with Raj lamenting his and his people's state of perpetually being forced to move on, prophetically and incantatorily saying: "So it has been. So it is. So it will remain" (378).

As a student in Canada, Raj befriends an old creolized Guyanese East Indian, a former primary school teacher working illegally in Canada. He is one of the perpetual travellers who are never allowed to "arrive." When Raj asks him if he will ever return home to Guyana, the old man repeats the word "home" as if, Raj observes, it were "a word alien to him, a word without meaning," and he proceeds to describe him as someone "cut hopelessly adrift" (233). The old man's story could readily be included in *Digging Up the Mountains*, in which Bissoondath's imagination is engaged in portraying various other peoples—black Trinidadians, Japanese, Latin Americans—who have rejected hobbling traditions and customs and are now alone and adrift. Bissoondath is evidently using the assimilationist Indo-Caribbean experience as a metaphor for this aspect of the human condition. He has stated in an interview that the Canadian policy of multiculturalism is a mild form of apartheid, and in both *Digging Up the Mountains* and *A Casual Brutality* he introduces this perception of the Canadian society as a sociological motif. He shows that the Indo-Caribbeans' and other recent immigrants' sense of not belonging in Canada is aggravated by the Canadian government's advocacy of the concept of a Canadian cultural mosaic that augments the isolation of each group from the others, forces the individual into his ethnic mold, and frustrates assimilation into the mainstream.

The Indo-Caribbean assimilationists' experience as treated by Caribbean fiction writers of East Indian extraction has been set against the traditionalists' recurringly in this study. The assimilationists' experience could be further set against their fellow Afro-Caribbeans'. While the Indo-Caribbean assimilationists try to escape an entrenched culture that cocoons and imprisons them, the Afro-Caribbeans, whose ancestors virtually lost their culture under centuries of British cultural domination, seek their identity by going back to Africa and by rediscovering the folk, where their Africanness lies in vestigial form. While the Indo-Caribbean assimilationists anglicize their names (Ranjit Kripalsingh to Ralph Singh in *The Mimic Men*, Ganesh Ramsumair to G. Ramsay Muir in *The Mystic Masseur*, and Baijan into Charles Christopher in *Corentyne Thunder*), the Afro-Caribbeans take on African names ("Kamau" Brathwaite). While ambivalence characterizes the Afro-Caribbeans, like Derek Walcott, who is divided between Africa and Britain to "the vein" ("A Far Cry from Africa," 18), the Indo-Caribbean assimilationists know what they want to reject, though they may not be aware of what they want to espouse; if they are ambivalent, it is about their decision to reject community and family. And while the Afro-Caribbeans are, to use Edward Kamau Brathwaite's term, *arrivants*, however dislocated and ambivalent, the Indo-Caribbean assimilationists are perpetual *arrivers*, who find themselves at the harbor contemplating the enigma of their arrival.

WORKS CITED

Bissoondath, Neil. *A Casual Brutality*. Toronto: Macmillan, 1988.

———. *Digging Up the Mountains*. Toronto: Macmillan, 1985.

Khan, Ismith. *The Jumbie Bird*. 1961. London: Longman Caribbean, 1974.

Ladoo, Harold Sonny. *Yesterdays*. Toronto: Anansi, 1974.

Mendes, Alfred, "Boodhoo." In *From Trinidad*. Ed. Reinhard W. Sander. London: Hodder and Stoughton, 1978. 142–72.

Mittelholzer, Edgar. *Corentyne Thunder*. London: Secker and Warburg, 1941.

Naipaul, Seepersad. *Gurudeva and Other Indian Tales*. Port of Spain: Trinidad Publications, 1943. Republished as *The Adventures of Gurudeva and Other Stories*. London: Deutsch, 1976.

Naipaul, V. S. "A Christmas Story." In *A Flag on the Island*. London: Deutsch, 1967. 24–26.

———. *The Enigma of Arrival*. London: Viking-Penguin, 1987.

———. *Finding the Center: Two Narratives*. New York: Knopf, 1984.

———. *A House for Mr. Biswas*. London: Deutsch, 1961.

———. *India: A Wounded Civilization*. London: Deutsch, 1977.

———. "Jasmine." In *The Overcrowded Barracoon*. London: Deutsch, 1972. 23–29.

———. *The Mimic Men*. London: Deutsch, 1967.

———. *The Mystic Masseur*. London: Deutsch, 1957.

———. "Tell Me Who to Kill." In *In a Free State*. London: Deutsch, 1971. 63–108.

Parmasad, Kenneth. *Indian Folk Tales of the Caribbean: Salt and Roti*. Trinidad: Sank Productions, 1984.

Poynting, Jeremy. "East Indian Women in the Caribbean: Experience, Image, and Voice." *Journal of South Asian Literature* 21, no. 1 (1986): 12–22.

Selvon, Samuel. *A Brighter Sun*. London: Wingate, 1952.

———. "Cane Is Bitter." In *Ways of Sunlight*. 1957. London: Longman Caribbean, 1985.

Walcott, Derek, "A Far Cry from Africa." In *In a Green Night*. London: Jonathan Cape, 1962. 18.

Webber, A.R.F. *Those That Be in Bondage*. Wellesley, Mass.: Calaloux, 1988. Orig. pub. Georgetown, Guyana: Daily Chronicle Press, 1917.

8

History and Community Involvement in Indo-Fijian and Indo-Trinidadian Writing

Helen Tiffin

There are at least two obvious limitations implied by the topic explored here.[1] First, the nature and treatment of contemporary community involvement in Indo-Fijian and Indo-Trinidadian writing, except where it is directly related by writers to the concept of history, is not considered here; therefore, much writing concerned with community interaction generally is not considered in this chapter. Second, the comparative basis itself: there is an enormous difference in the amount of material available from the two areas. In Trinidad there are over fifty novels, prose works, poems, and short story collections—major works spanning the period from the early 1940s (the first notable work being Seepersad Naipaul's collection of stories, *Gurudeva*, published in 1943) to V. S. Naipaul's *A Turn in the South* (1987) and Ismith Khan's recently published *The Crucifixion*. Indo-Fijian writing, by contrast, is approximately twenty-five years old, and so far consists mainly of poetry and short stories. Yet I think there are enough interesting tendencies in the work of writers like Subramani, Sulochana Chand, Raymond Pillai, and Satendra Nandan for critics to hazard some fruitful comparisons and contrasts between the two literary traditions—as the Trinidadian has developed, and as the Indo-Fijian seems to be developing.

At the risk of oversimplifying the situations, I wish to begin by making a couple of points of historical comparison and contrast that have a bearing on the writing from the two areas, and on the creative use of history and community involvement in their literatures. In both areas Indians came as indentured laborers under contracts that promised repatriation to India after the period of indenture expired, and that were rarely honored. In many cases Indians were misled or swindled outright in the information they received about their destinations and the conditions there. Pramesh Chand from Fiji in "A Promise" reports from an account by an indentured laborer on the kind of recruiting trickery that often occurred:

He [the white recruiter through an interpreter] told them that he had bought some land on an island in the Bay of Bengal and needed people to work the plantation there; he promised the crowd a house, food, clothes, and plenty of money; he promised to make them rich men. (Chand, 77)

Gradually Indian populations imported to work the sugar estates became populations in permanent ancestral exile, suffering the psychic dislocation and disruption inevitably a part of the experience of transplantation. In both cases, too, Indians were taken to tropical islands and to places culturally and linguistically dominated by Britain, but where another race—in the case of Fiji an indigenous people, in the case of Trinidad a kidnapped and imported population of African descent—was numerically in the majority. One would perhaps expect that such comparable experiences might produce in the literature similar emphases, concerns, and even patterns of imagery, and this is to some extent true. Dislocation and disorientation have in both areas predisposed writers toward treatment of the fragmentation of the psyche, emphasis on a sense of abandonment, dislocation, and dereliction, the imagery of shipwreck and imprisonment. Indo-Fijian and Indo-Trinidadian writing also share with colonial and postcolonial writing generally a number of specific colonial concerns, and the experience of indenture, like that of convictism in Australia, has frequently attracted the transferred metaphor of slavery.

But historical dissimilarities and differences in the new environments are also important, as a very brief (and oversimplified) summary indicates. The first difference influencing literary orientation in the developing traditions is one of time. Indians arrived in Guyana in 1838, and in Trinidad a couple of years later, while the first Indian laborers came to Fiji in 1879. By 1879 the era of European empire slavery was over, but in the 1840s both the psychic memory of slavery and its institutional apparatuses were immediately available to the indentured laborer, and Indian labor was expected to occupy the old slave niche in the plantation economy. The Indians of Trinidad thus inherited a system designed centuries earlier for African slaves. But while Indians were brought to the Caribbean to replace slave labor, they were brought as laborers to Fiji partially in order that native Fijian lifestyles and customs might be preserved.[2] In Subramani's story "Marigolds," the narrator, Mr. Chetram, finds that Eroni the native Fijian "affirms the historical basis of my existence" (137). Historically, the black West Indian population might be said to do the same for the Indo-Trinidadian, but it is a different kind of history and a different sort of affirmation. Second, the role of colonial overlord was in Fiji deputed to Australians and New Zealanders, themselves profoundly colonial, and Empire loyalty and ethos at second hand is not likely to carry the same weight as when it is directly applied.

Thus the centrality of England and of London, so important in the early West Indian literary tradition, is in the Indo-Fijian almost entirely absent.

As well as differences in time of arrival and in conditions of indenture, differences in the history of the areas to which laborers were taken have had a profound effect on the existing literary tradition of Trinidad and on its developing emphases in the Fijian. Caribbean history has been, at least since European contact, long, bloody, and spectacular. The virtual extermination of the native Caribs and Arawaks, the rapacious race between the European powers to find the legendary El Dorado, and the subsequent rise of the slave plantation system gave the area "a history" long before the arrival of Indian indentured labor. In Fiji, however, while the native Fijians were renowned as fighters, the details of their history were regarded by Europeans, and subsequently Indian immigrants, as negligible. Fijians, in European terms, had legends and myths, but no history. Thus, for the imported Indo-Fijians there appeared to be no real competing local history, as there was in Trinidad, where the African and European encounter was already legendary and had peopled the land of the decimated Caribs with historical ghosts of its own. But in terms of literary and cultural emphases, perhaps the most important difference was that Fiji, though apparently "historyless," retained a sizeable native population, while the majority black population in Trinidad was not an indigenous one, but was, like the imported Indian, one in ancestral exile.

History, like the novel, is not a traditional Indian pursuit or mode. The obsession of Indo-Trinidadian and Indo-Fijian imaginative writers with it, like that of most other colonials, is at least in part a product of their journey across the black waters, the *kala pani*. In colonial situations, history frequently becomes the source of psychic affirmation and continuity or, as group genesis, becomes the focus of a developing communal self-consciousness. History and cultural self-consciousness are necessarily aligned, and the idea of history is often closest to the hearts of those whose traditions and legends have been disrupted.

There have been at least five ways in which colonial peoples have deployed history as a means of psychic adaptation to transplantation and exile.[3] The colonial has looked back to the ancestral homeland as a source of historical or even legendary continuity for a time, or has adopted willingly or enforcedly the history of the homeland of the ruling classes (in this case England). Alternatively, the colonial has opted for the history of the new place to which s/he has been transported and adopted the collective history of its peoples. Another approach has been to concentrate on establishing the history of the race from the moment of departure from the "old" home to arrival in the new land. Finally, the colonial has invoked the legends and traditions of the new land by attempting to close the gap between his or her own colonial exile and the nondisjuncted traditions of an indigenous people regarded as being perfectly attuned to that place after centuries of unselfconscious interaction with it.

In the case of Indo-Trinidadian writing it is largely the first three options that have been adopted. I am here referring exclusively to attitudes to history to be found *in the literature*, but as is true of any relationship between literature and society, there are direct (and indirect) correlations between literary and social realities. But works of literature (and history) deal with myths as well as with the immediate sociopolitical concerns; and the complex relationship between group self-perceptions (whether historical, political, or social) and nationally or internationally dominant discursive formations necessarily vitiates any attempt at a purely reflective correlation between literary (and historial) texts and "life." Nevertheless, some degree of correlation might be hypothesized, and some apparent contradictions noted.[4] In general, Indo-Trinidadian writers have, like V. S. Naipaul,[5] looked to the ancestral homeland of India in an often vain search for a sense of continuity and wholeness, thus opting out of wider involvement with other race groups on the spot; or they have, like Selvon[6] and again Naipaul, looked to England for the shared roots of West Indian history; or they have adopted the European and African history of the Caribbean as their own and, like Naipaul in *The Loss of El Dorado*, investigated a shared Indian and black history of dereliction, decay, and failure on Trinidadian soil.

By contrast, Indo-Fijian writers like Satendra Nandan and Subramani have already begun to concentrate on the last two options: focusing on the history of Indian indenture in Fiji, the journey across the black waters to the new land, and the *Girmit* psyche this history produced; or making deliberate attempts to identify with the timeless world of the native Fijian through association with indigenous legend and mythology. Product of a different era of British colonial administration and in contact often with the secondhand imperial colonials of Australia and New Zealand, Indo-Fijian writers have produced no works comparable with the "escape to an autumn pavement" tradition in the West Indies. The linguistic tension, impositions, and creative potential of the Empire remain, but there are no works like Selvon's *The Lonely Londoners* (1965) and *Moses Ascending* (1975), which deal with West Indian life in exile in England. Neither has any Indo-Fijian writer shown interest in creating an exclusively English world, as Naipaul did in *Mr. Stone and the Knight's Companion*. Where the mini-colonial power of Australia is mentioned, as in Satendra Nandan's "The Guru," the effect is humorous. The narrator has returned to Fiji (and the direction is significant) from his sojourn in that Timbuktu of the south, Tasmania. In Subramani's "Dear Primitive" the New Zealand girl who is the central character in the story remains in Fiji after her parents return.

Return to the ancestral homeland (i.e., India) has not so far provided a dominant psychic pull in Indo-Fijian writing, perhaps because there is no surrounding community comparably in exile. (However, since the Rambuka coup of 1987, Indo-Fijian writers have evinced increasingly greater interest in the ancestral Indian connection, and their visits to India perhaps presage a literary revolution of this kind.) The black power movement in Trinidad had significant repercussions on the Indian cultural revival there (Samaroo, 84–98), the shared experience of exile with the surrounding black community perhaps providing one reason for this difference between Fiji and Trinidad. V. S. Naipaul's *An Area of Dark-*

ness (1964), *India: A Wounded Civilization* (1977), and *India: A Million Mutinies Now* (1991) attest to a complicated love-hate relationship on the part of the ancestral exile for the motherland. The tension involved in Naipaul's encounter with India (in part an expression of his deep involvement with it) is absent from the Indo-Fijian Vijendra Kumar's "Through the Time Tunnel." With rather self-conscious confidence, Kumar writes: "Like Alex Haley, I was looking for my roots. . . . India is another country in another age, I thought. It was a pleasant and exciting Wellsian sojourn. And now I was eager to return home" (Kumar, 86, 90). The angst (and the interest) of Naipaul's encounter with India is totally absent.

The major contrast in historical orientation in the writers of the two areas occurs, however, in the relation of the very different histories they stress or emphasize. Indo-Trinidadian writers have the European and African historical background of the Caribbean firmly in mind—either European history in the Caribbean or English history itself—and the devastation of the Caribs and Arawaks or the appalling history of slavery and the plantation system. In marked contrast, Indo-Fijian writers have concentrated on the history of Indian indenture itself—on the trickeries of recruiting, the crossing of the black waters, the wreck of the *Syria* in 1884, life in the *bhut len*, the haunted lines, and the complicated legacy of the indenture period, the Girmit psyche. There is little mention of or interest in European history or Indian history except in contemporary political allusions. The reader of Indo-Fijian stories and the growing body of criticism of these works finds himself/herself involved not only in the experience of indenture, but in its language—words and phrases like *kala pani*, *narak* (hell), *bhut len*, *girmit* become an essential part of the literary vocabulary. In Trinidad, the strength of the history of the previous African slave experience seems to have outweighed the vocabulary and metaphors that might have arisen out of Indian indenture itself. In Naipaul's *A House for Mr. Biswas* (1961), the metaphors of the slave experience are readily grafted on to an indenture history and psychology which they as effectively express.[7] In the Indo-Fijian tradition, however, Satendra Nandan in "The Old Man and the Scholar" uses Fiji Hindi to create both the journey from India and the new world of the indentured laborer:

> *bhaiya, rowat-gawat*
> *heelat-dolat*
> *adat-padat*
> *hum sub ain.*
> (Brother, crying singing,
> shifting swaying,
> eating farting,
> we all came.)

(Nandan, Faces in a Village, 26)

In "Sautu" and "Gamalian's Woman" Subramani not only recreates the period of indenture itself, but in the deliberately fragmentary narrative method both expresses the nature of that history and suggests its contemporary legacy in the Indo-Fijian psyche. This view of history is a far cry from the *English* history so humorously, ironically, yet lovingly and familiarly presented in the Trinidadian Selvon's *The Housing Lark*. Selvon's West Indian characters are on an excursion to Hampton Court and are discussing history:

"I must say you boys surprise me with your historical knowledge. It's a bit mixed up, I think, but it's English history."
    "We don't know any other kind. That's all they used to teach we in school."
    "That's because OUR PEOPLE ain't have no history. But what I wonder is, when we have, you think they going to learn the children that in the English schools?"

And the retort is:

"Who say we ain't have history? What about the Carib Indians and Abercromby and Sir Walter Raleigh?" (Selvon, *Housing Lark*, 125)

The characters involved here, though created by an Indo-Trinidadian author, are not, with one exception, Indian characters. But it is characteristic of Selvon that race division is eschewed, and characteristic of Indo-Trinidadian writing that the history here alluded to is European and indigenous Caribbean history, not the history or meaning of *Indian* indenture. In *A Brighter Sun* (1952) Selvon deliberately juxtaposes European historical events and local Trinidadian happenings, brilliantly diminishing in the process the centrality of the history of the culturally dominant European world. History for Selvon is Caribbean and racially collective—being created in the present through a complex (if often antagonistic) relation between British history and Indian and black integration in the islands and in England. In Ismith Khan's *The Obeah Man* (1964) the history alluded to is a combination of Aboriginal and European:

The island was a burial ground after many, many battles . . . bones bleached chalk-white in the tropic dust grew out of the earth after a heavy rain. Zampi did not fear the dead whose ash-white bones were plentiful as stone. The Caribs, the Arawaks, the Spaniards, the British. An ancient history had walked this land. (Khan, 29)

Zampi, the Obeah man, represents a deliberate attempt on Khan's part to amalgamate all racial interests and to give the post-independence Caribbean a local and potentially racially integrated tradition by placing the events of the novel during Carnival time, a festival in which all imported communities increasingly participate. In his earlier *The Jumbie Bird* (1961) Khan had dealt with the disappearance of the old Indian way, symbolized by the death of Kali Khan which, like Mr. Biswas's liberation from the Indian world of Hanuman House, releases the next two generations of Jamini and Rahmin into the Caribbean present. *The Jumbie Bird* is one of the very few Trinidadian works to make substantial reference to the indenture period, but, characteristically, the whole direction of the novel (and the title) is away from the Indian past toward a Caribbean present. Even in Harold S. Ladoo's *No Pain Like This Body* (1972), where the novel is set exclusively in the tiny Indian settlement of Tola Trace in 1905, the island on which the village is situated is called *Carib* island, indicative again of the stress on aboriginal or "new land" history.

Other Indo-Trinidadian writers like V. S. Naipaul have stressed the general colonial aspect of history, and where Indo-Trinidadian writers have humorously or bitterly inverted its hierarchies, it is the slave or general colonial pattern that is reversed, not a specific indenture model. In Selvon's *Moses Ascending* the shared nature of colonial slave history is stressed, and Moses Aloetta of *The Lonely Londoners* again becomes the focus of West Indian life in exile in London. Brenda's black power literature in the basement may be to Moses "in my way to stand up by the window" (Selvon, *Moses*, 147)[8]—but it is black Caribbean and international black movements generally that are both lampooned and endorsed in the novel. The climax of the various revelations for Moses is his discovery that his English Midland man Friday, Bob (the metaphors of shipwreck persist, though they are inverted), cannot read or write. Kindly, Moses sets about teaching Bob his own language, reversing the general colonial metaphors of Crusoe/Friday and Caliban/Prospero. In Harold Sonny Ladoo's *Yesterdays* (1974), Poonwa is persuading his father to sponsor him on a Hindu mission to Canada where he will reverse the course of slave/colonial history. His specifics are Hindu, but his general intentions and the reverse colonial metaphor invoked have affinities with postcolonial writing generally:

In my Mission, all children will have to learn the Hindi alphabet. They will study only Indian History and Hindi Literature. They will have to dress like East Indians. Then I will build more schools and open Hindu temples for the white people to worship the Aryan gods. . . . My Mission . . . is to make white people good Hindus. I am going to make them feel that their culture is inferior; that the colour of their skin can justify their servitude. Within a few decades I will teach them to mimic Indian ways. Then I will let them go to exist without history. I will make East Indians buy up all their lands and claim all their beaches. Then I will drain all their national wealth and bring it to Tola. (Ladoo, 77–78)

Throughout his work V. S. Naipaul has been consummately interested in history, in the relations between the past and present, in finding an answer to his now infamous question, "How can the history of this West Indian futility be written?" (Naipaul, *Middle Passage*, 29). But in *The Loss of El Dorado*, where he assesses the responsibility of the past for the present West Indian condition, Naipaul turns to two incidents in the European Caribbean past: the end of the search for El Dorado, and the slave/plantation past in the trial of Louisa Calderon. Though indenture is briefly mentioned, it is only a further "violation" and "dereliction," its significance and nature amply accounted for by the European and black experience, with indenture as a postscript to intrigue, piracy, and slavery.

In *The Mimic Men*, protagonist Ranjit Kripalsingh, using the familiar metaphor of shipwreck, describes what he calls his desert island shoreline self-consciously but revealingly as a place where the appearance of the gracefully waving palms is offset by the "cages of mangrove roots" that fringe the shoreline. It is as if in the West Indies the horror of the slave past has absorbed, metaphorically, the history of indenture, but it is also as if the atrocities of that history have cut the present-day populations off from any possibility of unselfconscious union with a landscape which, because of the nature of Caribbean history, remains unremittingly alien:

I had been able at certain moments to think of Isabella as deserted and awaiting discovery. Browne showed me that its tropical appearance was contrived; there was history in the vegetation we considered most natural and characteristic. . . . In the heart of the city he showed me a clump of old fruit trees, the site of a slave provision ground. . . . Our landscape was as manufactured as that of any great French or English park. But we walked in a garden of evil among trees, some still without popular names, whose seeds had sometimes been brought to our island in the intestines of slaves. (Naipaul, *Mimic Men*, 146–47)

The literary reality of Indo-Trinidadian writing is, then, an absorption of the writers with black African, British, Caribbean, or general colonial history rather than with specific Indian indenture history. This contrasts with the Fijian situation, and the language and indeed the very metaphors of the two literatures reflect this difference. But there is a further important distinction. While the European and African ghosts of Caribbean history continue to haunt the Indo-Trinidadian imagination, it is increasingly the Fijian spirits of place that beckon the Indo-Fijian in spite of political rebuttals from the indigenous population. Trinidad lacks a people through whose agency the haunted past might be reconciled with the present, and whose age-long association with the landscape might mediate, for the exile, an accommodation to place. But in Indo-Fijian writing, for example in Subramani's "Dear Primitive," a tentative movement toward such a possibility is explored. The central character, Elaine, remains in Fiji, the country of her childhood, after her parents leave. For them "time became historic again," but their daughter, staying on, drifts away from this linear concept of time toward landscape and a union with the timeless—and therefore legendary rather than historic—spirits of place. Her initiation into this world is begun by her contact with her spiritual half-sister, the Fijian Senibulu.

Seni initiated Elaine into the mysteries of the sea. Together they collected cowrie shells or followed her sea snakes bobbing in the waves and she tried to imagine Medusa's head: Elaine learnt from Seni the art of changing every situation into a legend. Sometimes Seni transformed herself into a sea goddess and raced away from her side, squealing with laughter, because she was nudged by a local demon. (Subramani, "Dear Primitive," 30–31)

A passage like this one contrasts markedly with Kripalsingh's associations of landscape, locality, and history, quoted above. The conflict within Elaine's psyche is imaged in the story in, on the one hand, the world of the tourist Ronnie, for whom time is historic—his sojourn on the island brief, his real, rational life elsewhere, the same world, implicitly, as that of Elaine's parents'—and on the other hand, the world of Senibulu and the Fijian spirits of place. In moments of apparent unreason, seemingly snatched from logical, rational time, Elaine experiences, without understanding—since such experiences cannot be reasoned or placed in time—a glimpse of the world of Senibulu. Torn between two worlds, Elaine finally lapses into a creative madness where the reefs break open; barriers are broken down and the former half-foreigner experiences a oneness with her world.

In Subramani's "Gamalian's Woman," the background is the indenture period, and Mrs. Gamalian is mad at the end of the story. But her madness in one sense sustains her and enables her to recoup in dreams, out of historical time, her indenture losses in it. Eating the bizarre soup she concocts of what she thought to be money, Mrs. Gamalian is consuming, as she has been consumed by, the false promises of wealth on which indenture depended. In a state of living death, however, she can only adjust to the disruption and psychic fragmentation caused by history through fantasy and madness. As in "Marigolds," the writer's method of presenting Mrs. Gamalian's story reflects and expresses the individual psychic disruption that is for the Indo-Fijian writer the present legacy of that history. In "Dear Primitive," Subramani very tentatively suggests that beyond fantasy and madness there is the possibility, for the imported populations, of real adaptation and growth in a multiracial Fijian present. But it is only a very tentative beginning. The present is depicted in terms of a *future* potential, growing out of the divisive past toward a fragile contemporary truce. Mrs. Gamalian's Girmit dislocations are more characteristic of the present position.

Most of Subramani's stories depict a people clinging precariously to islands that they have been unable to "inhabit," even after one hundred years. His recent novella "Gone Bush," like "Dear Primitive," tentatively explores the possibility of an Indo-Fijian indigenization through identification not with the land, but with the Polynesian concepts of oceanic origination. The narrator is taken on a journey around the countryside of Vita Levu by his friend, but fails to find a point of genuine psychic recognition. Instead, he identifies an *origin* in the journey of indenture across the black waters: "In the beginning was the sea" (Subramani, "Gone Bush," 77). This again suggests the potential for a confluent Indo-Fijian and Polynesian "myth of origin" focused on the surrounding sea (in spite of apparently irreconcilable community tensions and persisting racism) *and* underlines the tenacity of Indo-Fijian literary interest in an indenture history that begins with the journey out of India—the *kala pani*, which effectively exiled the Indo-Fijian from that history and from an Indian philosophy by whose terms s/he must now be declared outcast. But even if the sea offers the prospect of meeting ground, it remains an ambiguous symbol in "Gone Bush," unreliable and unstable in spite of its potential.

In *Finding the Centre* (1984) and *The Enigma of Arrival* (1987) V. S. Naipaul returned to the three loci of his quest for origins and reexamined the relationships between Trinidad, England, and (significantly) Africa in the Indo-Caribbean psyche. But in these later works Naipaul moves further toward an investigation of the constructedness of history and the value ascriptions of concepts like "exile" and "indigenization" as they were and are embedded in dominant discursive formations. Subramani's "Gone Bush," with its hints of a nightmare world already *constructed* for the Fijian indentured laborer by various intersecting discourses of "otherness" ("Paradisal Pacific," "Oriental," "Preservation of Indigenous Cultures," etc.), hints at a similar shift. The origin, or center, for both Indo-Trinidadian and Indo-Fijian writers seems to be coming increasingly to lie in the interrogation and destabilization of Old World ontologies and epistemologies with their investment in racial purity and in notions like the "indigenous." Only when the discursive constraints imposed by imperial "his/story" have been challenged will hybridized community involvement in a New World present be seen as possible.

For imaginative writers in Trinidad and Fiji, adjustment to a new world has seemed to involve an escape from colonial history into the potentialities of a racially hybridized present. Whereas in Trinidad there is no native population to mediate this process through legend and landscape, and where indenture history has been largely swamped by the greater nightmare of slavery and the extermination of a native population, the accommodation to the new place has involved an exploration of shared qualities of exile and dislocation, and eventual rejection of the divisive and destructive legacies of that history in favor of a hybridized experiential present. Until recently, the native Fijian population provided the Indo-Fijian writer with potential access to a "timeless" world where history is transformed into legend, and the journey and indenture become only a remembered dream. But with the increasing interrogation of values naturalized by the dominant discourse, and in Fiji, the Rambuka coup of 1987, much of this may change. The constraints on writing since that coup, involving active censorship of creative work (and even of literary criticism and book reviews), have drastically curtailed Indo-Fijian publication. If and when this can be resumed, questions of history and community involvement will undoubtedly be central, though the perspective of the Indo-Fijian writer may well have altered. To understand to what degree, and in which directions, we will have to await the restoration of democratic rights in Fiji.

NOTES

1. An earlier version of this chapter was published in Satendra Nanden, ed., *Language and Literature in Multicultural Contexts* (Suva: University of the South Pacific, 1983), 326–35.

2. See Morton Klass, *East Indians in Trinidad: A Study in Cultural Persistence* (New

York: Columbia University Press, 1961). Klass examines the persistence of features of the plantation "niche" into which Indian labor was slotted. See also Brij V. Lal, "Fiji *Girmitiyas*: The Background to Banishment," in *Rama's Banishment*, ed. Vijay Mishra (London: Heinemann, 1979), 12, for an account of the reasons behind the British decision to introduce indentured Indian labor in Fiji.

3. Even the categories teased out here necessarily overlap.

4. Indo-Fijian life does not reflect the integration optimism of some of the literature. Commentators, including Vijay Mishra in his introduction to *Rama's Banishment* (1979) and Subramani in *The Indo-Fijian Experience* (1979), have projected this as the future *cultural* direction. Whether this is still a real possibility remains to be seen.

5. V. S. Naipaul's works provide examples of each "category" and are used here because they are generally better known than those of, say, Khan or Ladoo.

6. From the beginning of his writing career, Samuel Selvon has deliberately dealt with non-Indian as well as Indian race groups in Trinidad.

7. For an elaboration of the metaphor of slavery in *A House for Mr. Biswas*, see Gordon Rohlehr, "Character and Rebellion in *A House for Mr. Biswas*," *New World Quarterly* 4, no. 4 (1968): 66–72.

8. In *Moses Ascending* Selvon's racially integrated imaginative world of village and suburban Trinidad is extended to a London setting through the metaphor of the house Moses owns—a kind of crackpot "Hanuman House" of Commonwealth nations.

WORKS CITED

Chand, Pramesh. "A Promise." *Mana Annual* (1974): 75–83.

Khan, Ismith. *The Obeah Man*. London: Hutchinson, 1964.

———. *The Crucifixion*. Leeds: Peepal Tree Press, n.d.

Klass, Morton. *East Indians in Trinidad: A Study in Cultural Persistence*. New York: Columbia University Press, 1961.

Kumar, Vijendra. "Through the Time Tunnel." In *The Indo-Fijian Experience*, ed. Subramani. St. Lucia: University of Queensland Press, 1979. 81–90.

Ladoo, Harold Sonny. *Yesterdays*. Toronto: Anansi, 1974.

Lal, Brij V. "Fiji *Girmitiyas*: The Background to Banishment." In *Rama's Banishment*, ed. Vijay Mishra. London: Heinemann, 1979. 12–39.

Mishra, Vijay. *Rama's Banishment*. London: Heinemann, 1979.

Naipaul, V. S. *The Middle Passage*. Harmondsworth: Penguin, 1969.

———. *The Mimic Men*. Harmondsworth: Penguin, 1967.

Nandan, Satendra. *Faces in a Village*. Suva: Viti, 1977.

———, ed. *Language and Literature in Multicultural Contexts*. Suva: University of the South Pacific, 1983.

Rohlehr, Gordon. "Character and Rebellion in *A House for Mr. Biswas*." *New World Quarterly* 4, no. 4 (1968): 66–72.

Samaroo, Brinsley. "Politics and Afro-Indian Relations in Trinidad." In *Calcutta to Caroni*. Ed. John La Guerre. London: Longman, 1974. 84–98.

Selvon, Samuel. *The Housing Lark*. London: MacGibbon and Kee, 1965.

———. *Moses Ascending*. London: Davis-Poynter, 1975.

Subramani. "Dear Primitive." *Kunapipi* 1, no. 2 (1979): 26–35.

————. "Gone Bush." In *The Fantasy Eaters: Stories from Fiji*. Washington, D.C.: Three Continents Press, 1988.

————. "Marigolds." In *The Indo-Fijian Experience*. Ed. Subramani. St. Lucia: University of Queensland Press, 1979. 132–39.

9

Staying Close but Breaking Free: Indian Writers in Singapore

Kirpal Singh

Singapore is a bustling island-city of about 2.8 million people, most of whom are of Chinese origin. In this complex, highly modernized city-state, people of Indian origin constitute about 6 percent of the total population. By "Indian" is meant those Singaporeans who are perceived to be, or commonly taken to be, of subcontinental origin. Among these will obviously be those who trace their actual origins to Sri Lanka, Bangladesh, Pakistan, and, of course, mainland India. Singapore is a densely plural society, and its history has shown a remarkable capacity for transformation—not only in terms of its landscape, but more significantly in terms of what may be called its "humanscape." Over the years this multiracial, multilingual, multireligious, and multicultural island has seen the emergence of a new breed of Singaporeans, many of whom will be of mixed parentage. Very common are Chinese-Indian marriages, with the male usually being Indian.

The Indian experience in Singapore goes a very long way back into history. During the times of the Sri Vijaya and Majapahit empires, Indians were already busy in this part of the world, especially in the Indonesian islands. From about the fifteenth century it seems clear that Indians were quite well established in peninsular Malaya and, indeed, the early founder of Singapore bears an Indian name: Parmeswara, who gave Singapore its name: Singapura, the Lion City. With the British colonization of Singapore in 1819, and its subsequent modernization, the island saw the coming of thousands of Indians who eagerly sought to better their fortunes. Some were brought in as indentured laborers, mainly to build roads and government or semi-government buildings (including churches), and others were brought in by the British administration to serve as policemen or military personnel.

Generally the Indians seem to have kept very close links with mainland India, with thousands of men having their wives and children in India while they worked in Singapore. In recent years this practice has been rapidly declining as the Singaporean Indians acquire a distinct identity and realize that Singapore, and no longer India, is their home. However, ties with countries of origin are perhaps never wholly severed—and maybe for very good reasons. By and large the Singapore Indian regards Singapore as home but nevertheless feels a strong link with the subcontinent. Political loyalty often vies with cultural loyalty, and this interesting emotional mix gives occasion for some intense literary expression.

Before the widespread acquisition of English, the more literate Indians in Singapore wrote in their own mother tongues (e.g., Telegu, Tamil, Punjabi, Kannada, etc). As more of them became fluent in English, their literary expressions too began to be in English. Indeed, of the three main non-Caucasian groups in Singapore (the Chinese, the Malays, and the Indians), it is, I think, the Indians who have felt most comfortable with the English language. The exact reasons for this deserve a separate study, but perhaps the central reason is the long exposure of Indians to British rule and to the English language in India itself. Among the more significant writers of plays, fiction, and poetry in Singapore, it is the Indians who feature prominently.

Indian writers in Singapore do not, as it would appear to be the case in some other countries (e.g., Fiji), form a group as such; rather, like the writers from other ethnic groups, the Indian writers regard themselves—and are regarded as such by others—as Singaporean writers. Better known among these are writers like Edwin Thumboo, Gopal Baratham, Chandran Nair, Rosaly Puthucheary, Nalla Tan, Philip Jeyaratnam, and Kirpal Singh. They write in a variety of styles, their themes are multifaceted, and their technical achievement is not uniform. Their main strength has been in poetry, though of late, considerable recognition has been accorded their fiction as well. In drama, the Indians have made an impact more through acting and directing than through actual script-writing. Their writing perhaps reveals more of the influence of their Westernized education than it does of their Indian origins. Perhaps it is in the values and attitudes contained in their writing that their Indianness manifests itself.

Of all the Indians writing in English in Singapore it is Chandran Nair, I believe, who may be said to be the most "Indian" in terms of literary expression. His two collections of poetry, *Once the Horseman and Other Poems* (1972) and *After the Hard Hours This Rain* (1975), reveal fairly explicit references to Indian myths, legends, landscape, and spirituality. In an early poem written for his grandfather, Nair clearly registers the Indian nostalgia felt deeply in contemplation. The poem is suggestive also of the position Nair himself seems to have adopted in relation to living in an environment which does not always appreciate the commitment becoming of a sensitive soul:

the seventy six years beneath his eyes
burst like rain, flood my earth with desolation;
his seventy six years have compromised my eyes
into a hardness that grows on me,
the imprint of his frown I wear
without his laughter.

grandfather walks the bounds of seasons
ploughing, sowing and harvesting years.
in drought stricken months
he wears old age as lightly as his beard,
his smile transcends.
to be born from unlucky seeds,
a friend once wrote, is tragedy;
the curse flows unmuted, immutable.

only the hot stares of the gods persuade the proud.
gods bothered him
but temples missed his sacrifice.
he found truth, relief, away from divinity,
spacing out years in padi fields,
unfolding particular nuances, lack of attainment.

like the padi stalk once green, easily bent,
he grew with age, aged to ripened toughness
to resist anger, misfortune of stricken years
with dignity unpersuaded.

(Nair, "Grandfather," 8–9)

The slight cynicism evident in the poet's identification with the grandfather offers an insight into the telling portrait of a man misunderstood. Loneliness and barrenness feature large in Nair's work, and both find expression in this poem. The biographical-autobiographical rendition is deliberate and offers depth to an otherwise simple emotion. Ostensibly there is nothing Singaporean about the poem but the fact that it is by a Singaporean. However, to those in the know, the "friend" in the third stanza is a reference to Mohammed Haji Salleh, a Malay poet who studied at the University of Singapore when Chandran Nair himself was there. Nair's poem aptly sums up the twin paradox suggested by my title; in wanting to break free, Nair feels very strongly the weight of staying close. In other of his poems, such a realization finds complete expression in the very easy and casual manner in which Nair manages to draw upon Indian myths (as a love poet Nair relies heavily on the Rama-Sita story) and incorporate these into poems dealing with themes pertinent to contemporary Singapore.

Edwin Thumboo is commonly seen as the most achieved of the Singapore poets. His Indianness is more successfully camouflaged, though when it surfaces it does so openly and in quite interesting ways. Several of Thumboo's poems

refer directly to Indian cultural practices or myths, and the following poem—
though again written expressly for someone close—is evidence of the emotional
contact that marks a certain truth about Thumboo's poetry as a whole:

> I greet your temple door
> With pomegranate seeds:
> The mind too nimble, sore
> Seeks the lotus in the reeds.
>
> I came to see your priest,
> To lay that ghost in my eye:
> To watch your altar fire
> Burn a hole in the sky.
>
> I saw a pattern there,
> A rhythm in the evening sun:
> Your dancing feet will tear
> The fibres of the drum.
>
>   (Thumboo, "Shiva," 16)

As always with Thumboo, the ambivalence is eloquent, the subjective mood
tempered by the craft, the emotions by the preciseness of the language. Unlike
Chandran Nair, whose "Grandfather" subtly hints at a sense of loss and dislocation, Thumboo's "Shiva" plays upon the intellectual apprehension of the
mighty god's dancing prowess. Perhaps too clever for itself and too neat as a
poem, "Shiva" nevertheless does announce a certain Indian presence in the
work of Edwin Thumboo. In other poems, too, Thumboo has utilized Indian
materials, but always there seems to be the apprehensiveness that arises out of
a fundamental reluctance to own openly and completely the compelling values
enshrined in the great myths. For Thumboo the Indian element is significantly
less important than its usefulness in enhancing the metaphoric quality and imagic
dimension of the verse.

While the poetry written by Indians in Singapore is highly emotive and technically quite impressive, it is in the fiction that the Indianness has most manifested
itself. Thus in the many stories of Gopal Baratham the Indian Tamils come in
for comment and incisive scrutiny:

In his seven years abroad Krishna had cultivated a belief in the sanctity of privacy and
developed an abhorrence of demonstrativeness, an attitude which had significantly contributed towards his acceptability in Britain. He pursued under all circumstances a policy
of non-intervention in the affairs of others and, if commitment was demanded, assumed
an indifference which he felt was the only basis for a civilised society. At the wedding,
however, he was sure to be bombarded with intimate inquiries about his personal life.
Moreover, several older members of the family would impose upon him their views on
how he should improve it. He would, he supposed, get by with noncommital smiles and
would, if they got too near the bone, exercise the restraint he had learnt in Britain. What
he dreaded most was the outrageous behaviour to which Tamils felt committed at wed-

dings. Tears, intimate exposés, hysterics, drunkenness, unwarranted affection or animosity—every known form of display histrionic and several new ones which the more
creative members of the family would improvise for the occasion. (Baratham, 6)

This short extract, taken from the story "Wedding Night," tells of the distance
between Krishna, with his English education, and the other Tamils of Singapore.
The theme is a common one: how the young respond to the older, more traditional
modes of living and behaving. It is obvious in the story that Krishna feels
awkward and very embarrassed at the manner in which relatives and friends
carry on at a typical Tamil wedding. Baratham's stories, though superficially
seeming to poke fun at the Indians of Singapore—especially the Tamils—at a
deeper level embody the anguish facing many Singaporean Indians: how to
reconcile inheritance with modernity. The Indian writer in Singapore is acutely
aware of the gap between his or her own orientations and those of the elders;
sometimes, caught in between, the writings reflect an impasse: an inability to
do more than record the problems. Constructive and meaningful answers, if any,
still await literary flowering. In the meantime plenty of self-searching goes on,
intimately tied up with larger political and linguistic issues.

   In my own work I have tried to articulate the feelings of a very small minority
group among the Singapore Indians, the Sikhs. Thus, in my short story "Jaspal,"
the protagonist is highly conscious of his Sikhness even as he grows up in healthy
cosmopolitan society. The Sikhs stand out everywhere by token of their turbans
and their characteristic manner of dressing.

From the start Jaspal had been made conscious of the fact that he was a Sikh. His parents
had instilled in him the fundamental belief that he was very different from the Malays,
Tamils, Seranees, Chinese and others of all description that lived in the same kampong.
And what about Goondoo's people, he had asked. Oh yes, they are Sikhs, his mother
had replied, but not very good ones. We are good Sikhs, no one in our family has cropped.
Look at Goondoo's family. His elder brother smokes nonstop, his mother's brother is
totally cropped, his uncle married a Tamil woman. In our family, nothing of this sort
happens. And you, being our only son, you Jaspal, must make sure never to bring disgrace
to our family. We come from a proud race, even now the English sing our praises, and
our ancestors will be grieved if you, or any one of us, ever do anything to mark the
family name. Being a Sikh, when one was six, meant being able to keep one's own anus
clean and being able to walk with pride with that little knot of hair on one's head. (Singh,
23)

Being a very closely knit group, the Sikhs are highly critical of lapses in behavior
and attitude. The tenacity of the Sikhs is well known, as is their stubborn
adherence to beliefs that die very hard. The matter of keeping the hair long, for
instance, is a source of very serious social problems, and though someone like
myself has tried to address the issues in my work, it is not easy to convince
others to modify their stand on such deep-seated questions. It is easy for the

Sikhs in Singapore to remain distinct, but this could also lead to isolation and alienation.

Because Indians form such a small part of Singapore society, they are very sensitive to the fact of assimilation. Different subgroups have adopted different strategies to prevent this: integration is desired, not assimilation, and even integration has to be undertaken gently, without upsetting the customary rituals and ceremonies. The younger Indian writers (Bilahari Kim Hee, Elizabeth Alfred, Qirone Haddock, Shirley Dhillon) have given utterance to difficulties they face in reconciling their Indianness with the demands made upon them by their being nationals of Singapore, an island society in which productivity is more usually measured in terms of dollars and cents than in terms of spiritual or creative progress. Problems peculiar to minorities anywhere also find expression in the writings of these Singaporean Indians. Though not frequently bitter or even cynical, many of the new literary works indicate a growing need to break free from bonds brought over from India through years of direct, intimate contact.

I believe that because Indians have always ultimately been prepared to take risks, the Singapore Indian writers (Philip Jeyaratnam is a classic instance here) will voice their frustrations and their aspirations so that the other ethnic groups will realize Indian sensitivities. The Indian sensibility is usually more than willing to accommodate variances and even, sometimes, to encourage these. When the Indian finds himself neglected, he is inevitably going to resort to ways of making his presence felt. Because of his facility with the English language, creative expression here comes almost naturally. If good writing comes out of a sense of desperation or of celebration at being accepted on equal terms, then the Singaporean Indian writers have nothing to be anxious about. Staying close but breaking free might sound pithy, but within the context of contemporary Singapore—and with direct relevance to Indians writing in English in Singapore—the profundity of the paradox cannot lend easy escape. It is this tension within that will surely promise a good harvest in the years to come.

WORKS CITED

Baratham, Gopal. "Wedding Night." In *Figments of Experience*. Singapore: Times Books, 1981. 1–12.

Nair, Chandran. "Grandfather." In *Once the Horseman and Other Poems*. Singapore: University Education Press, 1972. 1972. 8–9.

Singh, Kirpal. "Jaspal." *Solidarity* No. 108. Manila: Solidaridad Publishing House, 1988. 22–30.

Thumboo, Edwin. "Shiva." In *Ulysses by the Merlion*. Singapore: Heinemann, 1979. 16.

10

Sam Selvon's Tiger: In Search of Self-Awareness

Harold Barratt

Although the decades before the 1950s produced important writers—Herbert George de Lisser, C.L.R. James, Alfred Mendes, and Edgar Mittelholzer, for instance—a substantial body of distinctive and distinguished West Indian literature, the kind produced by novelists and poets such as V. S. Naipaul, Derek Walcott, Wilson Harris, and George Lamming, all of them writers of the first order, was yet to come. By the end of the sixties Naipaul had already written some ten books, including the brilliant *A House for Mr. Biswas* and *The Loss of El Dorado*; Lamming's *In the Castle of My Skin*, Harris's Guiana Quartet, several collections of Walcott's poems, and six of Sam Selvon's novels had also appeared.

The Indian diaspora from the Gangetic plain contributed 143,939 indentured workers to Trinidad from 1845 to 1917, when the last boatload of largely agricultural workers arrived. By 1871 Indians had become the backbone of the sugar industry and made up some 25 percent of Trinidad's population. Of this number 4,545 were locally born (Brereton, 105). Sam Selvon is a product of this monumental diaspora, which altered, profoundly and permanently, Trinidad's economic, social, and cultural complexion. Selvon, born in Trinidad in 1923 of an Indian dry goods merchant and a half-Scottish, half-Indian mother, is one of those distinguished writers who contributed to the remarkable emergence of a vibrant West Indian literature in the fifties and sixties. In his London fiction Selvon explores with sensitivity and perception, and a humor brilliantly mixed with pathos, the vicissitudes of the largely unskilled, displaced West Indians who are merely surviving in a hostile society that does not welcome them and confines them to menial jobs.[1] None of Selvon's expatriate West Indians, including the charismatic Moses, who functions as the group's father and mentor and whose withers have long since been wrung through the London mill, feels that he belongs in Mother England, the promised land for all good colonials. The three novels and the short stories that comprise the London fiction, together with *A Brighter Sun* (1952) and *Turn Again Tiger* (1958), guarantee Selvon a permanent place in the history of West Indian literature.

A Brighter Sun can of course be read and appreciated separately from its sequel, *Turn Again Tiger*; since, however, the internalizing of Tiger's identity, which is the central focus of *A Brighter Sun*, is continued and indeed consolidated in the sequel, it is appropriate, and certainly rewarding, to study both novels together.

A Brighter Sun is a historically important work because of Selvon's use of Trinidadian dialect. It would appear that his use of the dialect was not a studied stylistic device, since he has said that he "did not even know the full meaning of the word dialect" when he wrote the novel. He was more concerned with "the translation of the emotions, feelings and situations than with reproducing a historically accurate language. If I find a language form that works," he added, "I will use it" ("Sam Selvon Talking," 100–101). *A Brighter Sun* is also a pivotal novel because its central theme is the main character's quest for what has become the most compelling issue in West Indian literature: identity, self-awareness and wholeness in a colonial and pluralistic society infected with a good deal of self-contempt, and still showing the psychic scars of slavery and the equally dehumanizing indenture system.

Selvon drew his portrait of Tiger from his acquaintance with an old Indian man of the same name who symbolized for him "the young peasant who starts off by gradually discovering about life." The old man's voyage of discovery, one may suppose, also served as the catalyst for the two novels, and indeed may have helped to shape Selvon's philosophy: "You have to discover yourself, then only can you be of some use to humanity" (Fabre, 69). *A Brighter Sun* is a careful and uncommonly sensitive examination of the growing sensibilities of an Indian youngster who is suddenly wrenched from the canefields of Chaguanas, where many of the indentured Indian workers settled, and the security of parents and playmates and finds himself a married man having to fend for two people in Barataria, a considerably more complex community a few miles outside of Port of Spain, Trinidad's bristling capital. At first Tiger is a clumsy innocent who is ignorant to the point of stupidity and blindly obedient to his parents' wishes. Even though he is married, he is of course still a child, and his urge to return to the protection of the womb when life becomes too problematic is not surprising. And his idea of manhood is adolescent: "Men smoked: he would smoke" (11). At the same time one can discern in Tiger a potential for growth and wisdom. As he and his wife Urmilla, who is equally young and callow, begin to establish the basis of a life together, they are prematurely confronted by adult responsibilities; and Tiger gradually rejects the adolescent philosophy, "all of we is Indian," and replaces it with a tentative self-assertiveness, as well as a social and political awareness and a restless urge to enlarge the horizons of his limited education. For instance, shortly after his arrival in Barataria he must negotiate for two lots of land. The transaction is at first disconcerting, and he "wished his father or one of his uncles was there with him." But this desire, Selvon writes, "made him ashamed. He was married, and he was a big man now. He might as well learn to do things without the assistance of other people" (13). Meanwhile, racially mixed Barataria gives Tiger the opportunity to broaden his relationship with blacks and other ethnic groups. Three of these neighbors, Joe, Rita, and old Sookdeo, are particularly important in Tiger's education. Old Sookdeo, an eccentric but deceptively wise Indian, says to Tiger, "Haveam some ting yuh learn only by experience" (78). Tiger learns from experience that manhood does not mean possessing a wife and fathering a child; nor does it mean smoking and drinking rum. Manhood means awareness of one's identity as a unique individual; it also means satisfying one's hunger for knowledge. In one of his many brooding soliloquies Tiger asks, "Ain't a man is a man, don't mind if he skin not white, or if he hair curl?" (48). But this new-found wisdom is abhorrent to Tiger's parents, for whom the preservation of their son's Indian identity is mandatory, and they are shocked by Tiger's friendship with Joe and Rita, whose blackness threatens to creolize their son. As Tiger's perceptions mature, as his experiences become increasingly complex, he eventually recognizes that "it was what you was inside that count" (204).

Several factors contribute to Tiger's social and political awakening. Of these, his day-to-day experiences, especially his relationship with the non-Indian members of cosmopolitan Barataria, are important factors in his growing consciousness. Two of these experiences are particularly enlightening. Tiger's humiliating encounter with a salesgirl in a fashionable Port of Spain store is instructive. When she ignores him and waits on a white woman instead, Tiger, who had believed that his Indianness gave him at least second-class status in the island's racial hierarchy, discovers that in the eyes of those for whom whiteness is the ultimate measure of excellence, Indian and black are equally unimportant. The second experience is equally, if not more, disconcerting and traumatic. When, during a rainstorm, he tries to get medical aid for Urmilla, the Indian and black doctors give his pleas for help short and rude shrift. But an English doctor from Port of Spain's elite St. Clair district comes to Urmilla's aid. The experience teaches him that good and evil are everywhere, and, furthermore, that people are neither black nor white, only gray. And there is more: Tiger is forced to consider the possibility that the "wite man must always laugh at we coloured people, because we so stupid" (189). The next day Tiger confronts the Indian and black doctors and verbally abuses them in the presence of patients and onlookers. His anger is partly displaced, and it is certainly fueled by his sense of shame and guilt for his brutal treatment of Urmilla after the dinner scene with the two Americans. Muzzy with drink, Tiger attacks the pregnant Urmilla, who, wishing to please his guests, has put on makeup and instead of obsequiously withdrawing to the kitchen, which she had tried to do at the start of the evening's entertainment, has a drink at the insistence of the Americans. This is too much for Tiger, to whom Urmilla looks "like a whore in Port of Spain" (175); and when he kicks his pregnant and defenseless wife in the face and stomach, it is undoubtedly the nadir of his young life. But Tiger's anger also brings to the surface issues that have been subconsciously troubling him: What is the connection between individual and national integrity? How can the island achieve national independence in the absence of individual integrity? In the encounters with the salesgirl and the doctors a seed has been planted, and it will eventually grow into Tiger's nagging desire for personal and, later on, national identity.

Tiger's questions and anxieties about the need for national independence point to his growing maturity, and they match his own hunger for personal independence and identity. One thinks here of his desire, notwithstanding some initial anxiety, to strike out on his own as soon as he has arrived in Barataria; and not too long after his confrontation with the doctors Tiger asks Joe: "But listen, it ain't have a way how we could govern weself? Ain't it have a thing call self-government?" (196). Tiger's questions and conversations with Joe emphasize his growing preoccupation with self-awareness. His confusion and doubts are not unlike Selvon's. In more than one interview Selvon has betrayed his strong sense of displacement. In an interview with Peter Nazareth, Selvon refers more than once to his rootlessness, to his sense of being a displaced writer, as well as the amorphousness of his identity (Nazareth, 83). Unlike his compatriot V. S. Naipaul, Selvon did not grow up in the sort of closed yet disintegrating Hindu world Naipaul has described more than once.

It is not surprising that rootlessness is a strong theme in Selvon's *An Island Is a World* (1955) and *I Hear Thunder* (1963), which have been unfortunately neglected, but nonetheless aid one's understanding of *A Brighter Sun*. Both novels are finely focused and accurate pictures of Trinidad society in the forties and fifties. It is a society of petty racism, with men and women lost in the void of colonial neglect, the kind of society with which Selvon is intimately familiar and from which he himself escaped. Many of the characters in these novels, such as Adrian and Mark of *I Hear Thunder* and the Indian men of *An Island Is a World*, are complex and fully embodied; and Selvon's best female portraits can be found in both novels. The Indian characters resemble Tiger to the extent that they are ready to philosophize at the slightest encouragement. Like Tiger, they are also introspective and melancholy. More important, they too are seeking some sort of fulfilling wholeness. Foster, "the lost soul groping in the dark" (*Island*, 92), is cabined, cribbed, and confined by his island home, and he desperately flees Trinidad in search of fulfillment in London. But the promised land only exacerbates his alienation and hopelessness. Rufus, Foster's brother, also flees Trinidad and a loveless marriage for America's greener pastures. His search ends in failure and bigamy. Although he has lived, raised a family, and prospered in Trinidad for several years, Johnny, the Indian jeweller whose daughters Foster and Rufus marry, stubbornly regards India as his spiritual home. Becoming increasingly alienated from his family, to say nothing of the frustration he suffers when he fails to achieve his eccentric goal of harnessing the force of gravity, he turns to excessive drinking and then to the government's plan to return disaffected Indians to Mother India. But even as he departs for India, Nehru, to whom the disaffected have written for support, responds with no encouragement and indeed sees no place for Johnny and the other victims of the diaspora in postcolonial India.

While he struggles to find a significant place in his racially divisive and amorphous society, to say nothing of trying to understand the place of his seemingly insignificant island in the world, Tiger loses some of his links with his tenuous Indian heritage. Tiger's increasing creolization, however, does not mean the total disintegration of his Indianness. The experiences of Pariag, the Indian outcast in Earl Lovelace's *The Dragon Can't Dance*, will point a useful comparison. Pariag abandons the narrowness of a predominantly Indian sugar estate and dependence upon an overbearing uncle for Port of Spain, "where people could see him, and he could be somebody in their eyes" (78). He, too, is in search of an awareness beyond that of Indian and black; but the dominant black community of Calvary Hill, where he and his wife have come to live, rejects them out of hand. Pariag's Indianness makes him an interloper. He is deliberately excluded from the Christmas festivities and, more important, the Carnival celebration, the community's central ritual, which is a complex amalgam of rebellion, fantasy, drama, and escapism and a symbolic embodiment of the quest for identity. Pariag experiences a symbolic crucifixion on Calvary Hill—a crucifixion adumbrated in Lovelace's skillful use of Ash Wednesday imagery and the farcical crucifixion of a religious crackpot at the start of the novel—when his neighbors, convinced that his purchase of a new bicycle is his attempt to rise above "the equalness of everybody" (103), smash the machine to pieces. Lovelace, however, turns Pariag's symbolic death into a victory and rebirth, for his stoic acceptance of his victimization makes him "alive and a person" to his hostile neighbors. The symbolic crucifixion, furthermore, is said to be "a sacred moment for it joined people together to a sense of their humanness and beauty" (141).

This sense of a primal, inviolable humanness, a theme also noticeable in Lovelace's *The Wine of Astonishment*, is implicit in Tiger's desire for an identity that transcends racial divisions. Put another way, Tiger seems to be aiming for a West Indian identity that would not assimilate, but incorporate, his Indian being. Tiger's relatives are products of the diaspora, displaced in a disconcertingly pluralistic society; and they are ferociously Hindu: "Nigger people all right, but you must let creole keep they distance," his uncle advises (48). Tiger has been spawned by this threatened Hindu world; but he is also palpably West Indian. He is indeed an early West Indian hero whose quest for integrity and personal independence is a reflection of the individual's desire to overcome the colonial neglect so deeply embedded in the West Indian psyche, the sort of syndrome that bears some resemblance to George Lamming's term "psychic shame" ("West Indian People," 69).

Lamming has emphasized Selvon's importance as an explorer of the social situation in the West Indies, and he has drawn attention to the peasant roots of Selvon's fiction (*Pleasures of Exile*, 45). But Lamming does not discuss the intimate bond between Selvon's peasants and the land they cultivate. Some commentators, unfortunately, have given Tiger's bond with the land short shrift; recognition of this bond, however, is essential for an understanding of Tiger. It is true that Tiger is indeed happy to give up small farming in order to earn a higher income working with the Americans who are building a road through Barataria; but Tiger's bond with the land is considerably more than a mere economic necessity. The land helps to mold his growing sensibilities, and Selvon emphasizes the power of this bond in strategic periods in Tiger's life. Consider, for example, an early period in his life, a time of confusion and bewilderment about the war raging in Europe, a time of doubt about his self-worth and capacity for growth and understanding. All of these anxieties are alleviated when he turns to the land for relief and understanding. Tiger feels, and in fact participates in, the power "throbbing in the earth, humming in the air, riding the night wind" (113). These moments of communion with the land demonstrate Tiger's abiding love and respect for a power he does not fully comprehend but of which he is nonetheless fully cognizant. Wordsworth and Coleridge, one feels, would have understood Tiger's oneness with the land, sky, and sun. Union with the land, furthermore, gives Tiger the solace he needs and the strength to persevere. "Whenever big things happen," he reflects, "I does go out and look all about, at the birds, at the hills, and the trees, and the sky. . . . And I does get a funny feeling, as if strength coming inside me. That must be God" (117–18). When he rebels against Barataria's narrowness and yearns to escape to the seductive world of Port of Spain, Selvon, we notice, counterpoints this restlessness with Tiger's compelling sensitivity to the land and its fetching nuances.

Two other crucial periods in Tiger's life are worth noting. Although it will provide needed jobs, the building of the road is disruptive and brings uneasiness to Tiger and his neighbors. Immediately, however, Tiger counteracts his anxieties through a simple communion with the land. The second important moment is at the end of the novel. The war in Europe, whose long and devastating arms have also embraced Trinidad, has ended, and Tiger has built a new house. The promise of a sunlit day that he detected in the sky has been realized, we may say. At once Tiger thinks of returning to the canefields of his boyhood; but the thought makes him "laugh aloud" (215). The laugh signals the end of his innocence, and not a turning away from the land. The novel's final words— " 'now is a good time to plant corn,' he muttered, gazing up at the sky" (215)— drive this point home. Tiger's words confirm his continuing attraction for the land as the source of an undefined, yet certain, power. Tiger, furthermore, experiences a regeneration in the reaffirmation of his value and the power of the land over his earlier materialistic hunger. Selvon also matches Tiger's bond with the land with his recognition that one pays a price for adulthood: "It ain't always a man does be able to do the things he want to do" (213). This acceptance of responsibility contrasts sharply with Joe's complacency. Tiger rejects Joe's attitude—"dey have plenty people who can't write and dey living happy" (42)—out of hand. "The great distance which separated him from all that was happening" (75) is at the heart of Tiger's restlessness, and the following exchange between Tiger and Joe clearly shows this:

"You mean to say, Joe, that you never had ambition to go to college or get a good office job?"
   "But why, papa? Ah man cud live happy without all dem things."
   "Well, Joe, that is you, but as for me, I can't be happy until I find out things." (111–12)

Tiger's determination to find out more about himself and his world continues in *Turn Again Tiger*. His communion with the land is no less intimate than in the earlier novel. Although he is older and presumably wiser, he still turns to the land for comfort, recognizing a superior wisdom in its shifting moods. But the sequel is even more finely focused upon Tiger's quest for self-possession; and the novel has several important links with Selvon's *Those Who Eat the Cascadura* (1972). Both novels explore the vicissitudes of a central Indian character in a tiny and isolated village. Five Rivers, the setting of *Turn Again Tiger*, is a sleepy village where Tiger and his family are temporarily living with his father, who, now that he is foreman at an experimental cane plantation managed by the Englishman Robinson, needs his son's help. Like the bucolic Sans Souci, the setting of *Those Who Eat the Cascadura*, Five Rivers is a microcosm of pre-independent, colonial Trinidad. The three-tiered racial hierarchy, complete with antagonisms and divisiveness, is firmly entrenched at Five Rivers and Sans Souci. There are, however, one or two differences: the social and political center of Five Rivers is the Chinaman Otto's rumshop, and the village is a more cohesive community than Sans Souci. Racial tension in Five Rivers, moreover, is subordinated to Tiger's quest: "But when I come a man in truth, I want to possess myself" (155).

Tiger's continuing hunger for self-possession can be seen in his interminable brooding and deliberately assertive posture in the presence of the formidable Robinson. His assertiveness is all the more noticeable because of its sharp contrast with his father's obsequiousness. Tiger's hunger is effectively dramatized in his violent sexual encounter with Doreen, Robinson's coldly provocative wife. It is the novel's central scene, and it brings to the surface all of Tiger's ambivalence and disingenuousness. Tiger's self-esteem and fragile dignity are shattered when, in a moment of panic, he flees from the sight of Doreen bathing naked in the river. His explanation for his shameful action is glib and disingenuous: "It had nothing to do with colour or the generation of servility which was behind him. He had fled because she was a woman, a naked woman, and because he was a man" (52). The truth is that Tiger has fled from the bogey of the luscious, forbidden white female, and fear has reduced him, the man "who drank rum with men and discussed big things like Life and Death'' (51), to a terrified, cringing boy. When he does make love to Doreen—it is brutally cold and as ferocious and impersonal as Sarojini's copulation with the Englishman Johnson in *Those Who Eat the Cascadura*—his motives are not as simple as he at first imagined. First, there is the obvious *frisson* of interracial sex, to say nothing of the revenge motive, a feature of the black male–white female syndrome often explored in West Indian literature. There is, too, as Tiger puts it with blunt directness, an even more basic motive: "I wonder," he asks himself, "if under all the old-talk, all I wanted to do was to screw a white woman?" (149). None of these is as important, one feels, as his need to restore his shattered self-esteem and free himself of the paralyzing fear of the untouchable but eminently desirable white fruit.

Tiger's frenzied possession of Doreen ought to be read as a symbolic killing. He himself senses this: "Over here," he tells Joe when he visits his friend in Barataria, "some of we still feel white people is God, and that is a hard thing to kill" (158). The possession of Doreen should be set alongside Otto's fight with Singh, who has cuckolded him. The Chinaman must thrash Singh in order to exorcise the jealousy destroying his soul and heal the wound inflicted upon his ego. Tiger must possess Doreen in order to exorcise his own devils. The act brings relief and victory to both men. For Tiger it is the peace he had been subsconsciously seeking. Singh's broken hand, meanwhile, can be fixed by a doctor, but Otto "had to get well inside." This happens when he conquers "the hate and jealousy in his heart" (181). Tiger must also come to his own sense of the matter; and he does so with noticeable finality:

His life had impinged on hers, but only for one purpose. There was no pleasure in the memory for him; afterwards he had shrugged like a snake, changing skins. No triumph, no satisfaction, no extension of desire to make him want to do it again. Just relief, as if he had walked through fire and come out burnt a little, but still very much alive. (180–81)

For Doreen too, the act has been final: she has also rid herself of the twin torments of hate and lust.

If Joe's and Tiger's attitudes toward the encounter with Doreen are compared, its psychological significance for Tiger is at once clear. When he relates the incident, Joe dismisses Tiger's irritating consternation with what appears to be trenchant common sense: "Men screwing women all over the world every day, Tiger, why you have to make a problem out of this one?" (155). But Tiger sees the incident as a test which he has failed: he has failed to possess himself. Furthermore, he can see in his failure a more universal problem: if Joe is correct and Tiger is merely a drop of water in a river, then he is destined to "just sit down on his arse and float with the tide" (156); and this destiny Tiger has consistently rejected. Tiger's exorcism is immediately followed by his symbolic purification in the river. A symbolic purification is also suggested after the brutal coupling of Johnson and Sarojini; and here again a comparison with Sarojini's symbolic rape of Johnson will shed some light on Tiger's experience. Sarojini sees union with the Englishman as her highest achievement. But the raping of Johnson is an obvious reversal of the white overseer's raping of Indian girls in the canefields of Trinidad. Nor does her sexual union with Johnson bring Sarojini any insight or self-awareness. Her childlike dependence upon Johnson is still intact, and at the end of the novel she is a pathetic figure desperately clinging to an obeahman's incantations and rituals and living in the hope of Johnson's unlikely return. Unlike Sarojini, who will never free herself of Johnson—she is carrying his child—Tiger's encounter with Doreen has enlarged his sensibilities, if not matured him. The experience is not unlike the land's continual changes and growth: "It just like we," he says of the land; "we finish one job, and we got to get ready to start another" (181). Tiger's life changes dramatically after the encounter with Doreen: he gives up the crutch of heavy rum-drinking; and the profound change in his life is metaphorically suggested when, walking off the trail one day shortly after the incident, he at once "righted his direction" (162).

At the end of the novel Tiger comes to terms with his obsessions and anxieties. To this extent he resembles other tormented West Indian heroes, such as Aldrick, the brooding, questing hero of Lovelace's *The Dragon Can't Dance*, whose regeneration is the victory of the self over his escapist fantasies. Unlike men such as Galahad and Battersby, two of Selvon's feckless exiles who are trapped, it would appear, in a permanent stasis, Tiger is driven by a strong sense of purpose, and he achieves an integrity when he realizes that he must turn inward to his own inner resources for strength.

NOTE

1. Sam Selvon's London fiction consists of the following: *The Lonely Londoners* (London: Allan Wingate, 1956), *Ways of Sunlight* (London: MacGibbon and Kee, 1957), *The Housing Lark* (London: MacGibbon and Kee, 1965), and *Moses Ascending* (London: Davis-Poynter, 1975).

WORKS CITED

Brereton, Bridget. *A History of Modern Trinidad 1783–1962*. London: Heinemann, 1981.
Fabre, Michel. "Samuel Selvon: Interviews and Conversations." In *Critical Perspectives on Sam Selvon*. Ed. Susheila Nasta. Washington, D.C.: Three Continents Press, 1988. 64–76.
Lamming, George. *The Pleasures of Exile*. 1960. Reprint. London: Allison and Busby, 1984.
———. "The West Indian People." *New World Quarterly* 2, no. 2 (1966): 63–74.
Lovelace, Earl. *The Dragon Can't Dance*. London: Deutsch, 1979.
———. *The Wine of Astonishment*. London: Deutsch, 1982.
Nazareth, Peter. "Interview with Sam Selvon." In *Critical Perspectives on Sam Selvon*. Ed. Susheila Nasta. Washington, D.C.: Three Continents Press, 1988. 77–94.
Selvon, Sam. *A Brighter Sun*. 1952. Reprint. London: Longman, 1971.

———. *I Hear Thunder*. London: MacGibbon and Kee, 1963.

———. *An Island Is a World*. London: Allan Wingate, 1955.

———. "Sam Selvon Talking: A Conversation with Kenneth Ramchand." In *Critical Perspectives on Sam Selvon*. Ed. Susheila Nasta. Washington, D.C.: Three Continents Press, 1988. 95–103.

———. *Those Who Eat the Cascudura*. London: Davis-Poynter, 1972.

———. *Turn Again Tiger*. 1958. London: Heinemann, 1979.

11

Indian Writing in East and South Africa: Multiple Approaches to Colonialism and Apartheid

Arlene A. Elder

> On account of our Indian Empire we are compelled to reserve to British control a large portion of East Africa. Indian trade, enterprise and emigration require a suitable outlet. East Africa is, and should be, from every point of view, the America of the Hindu.
>
> —Harry H. Johnston, 1901 (Gregory, 96)

The imperialist attitude toward land and cultures expressed above by the British governor of Uganda accounts, in large part, for the presence of Indians in modern and present-day East Africa; similarly, they were lured to South Africa to serve as cheap labor. Contemporary Indian writers in English from both these areas have responded to their historical situation in a multiplicity of genres, focusing upon four central subjects: the history of Western imperialism against India and Africa; traditions and changing cultural perceptions within the African Indian communities; the corruption of politicians both pre- and post-independence; and the continuing conflict between the races in Africa. This survey of Indian-African writing in English begins with a brief historical background intended to clarify the historical/political situation of the Asian communities, then points out the responses to that history by a number of Indian writers employing a variety of genres, and ends with a detailed look at the contribution of Peter Nazareth and Bahadur Tejani of Uganda and Ahmed Essop of South Africa.

BACKGROUND

Although Indians in Africa are, typically, classed together and referred to popularly and in the general literature simply as Asians, this population is composed of many different cultural groups and is certainly aware of its own diversity. Muslims, including the Ismaili followers of the Aga Khan, Isnasheries, Bohras, Memans, and Baluchis, various castes of Hindus, and Catholic Goans have been the most numerous and influential. Much of their literature reveals conflicts among them due to religious and/or cultural differences.

East Africa was the focus of Indian trade. Both in eastern and southern Africa, Britain ultimately predominated in the "European scramble," acquiring control, first, of Zanzibar, then of what was to become Kenya and Uganda, then, after the First World War, of German East Africa, principally Tanganyika.

Three early schools of thought emerged about India's role in Africa and the situation of the Indian immigrants there:

One can be called imperialist because of its advocation of an Indian colony to serve as an outlet for India's surplus population. . . . Most of those interested in East Africa comprise a second group which stressed the Indians' right to equality of status and treatment throughout the Empire. . . . For this group, which was mainly Liberal in political affiliation, the Indians' struggle for equality in the British overseas dependencies was closely tied to the nationalist movement at home. . . . The third group was humanitarian in that it subordinated Indian interests in East Africa to those of the African majority. (Gregory, 503)

These conflicting points of view were debated throughout the colonial period in East Africa, Britain, and India alike.

For a considerable time, India's role as a trading partner, especially with Kenya and Uganda, was extensive, greater even that that of Britain or Germany; therefore, its influence upon the situation of the immigrant Indians was also significant. However, most of its attention was commanded by the more discriminatory government in South Africa.

The first large group of Indians arrived in southern Africa in 1860, principally in the then British colony of Natal, to provide labor on the newly established European sugar plantations (Gregory, 81). Primarily Hindus, these indentured workers were bound for three, and later five, years and at the end of this tenure could renew their original contract, return to India at government expense, or accept a piece of crownland equal in value to the cost of a return passage. The majority took the land, remaining in Natal as free citizens, becoming market gardeners, fishmongers, venders of fruits and vegetables, artisans of various sorts, moneylenders, small shopkeepers, and traders (126). "Passenger" Indians followed, British subjects paying their own way, mostly Muslims who chose to emigrate to Natal for commercial purposes. In addition to agricultural work, the unskilled Indians engaged in labor in the coal mines and on the railways.

The Indian community in Natal thrived and extended to Transvaal and Cape Colony as well. Needless to say, its growth provoked resentment among the Europeans, and various discriminatory laws were passed to restrict Asian power, for instance the Indian Immigration Act of 1895 in Natal and even harsher regulations in Transvaal. Gregory reports that Indians were not attracted to the Orange Free State because of the extreme discrimination that had existed there all along against all non-Europeans: "The constitution of 1854 expressly conferred the benefits of citizenship only on 'white persons,' and Indians were subsequently regarded as 'coloureds' '' (128).

According to the 1980 census, there are 795,000 Indians in South Africa, more than on the rest of the African continent (*South Africa 1983*, 82). Traditional and colonially inspired economic, language, cultural, and class barriers exist among them, but the South African government generally deals with the Indian community as a homogeneous unit, legally restricting its living areas and employment opportunities, but recently allowing them, along with the Coloreds, representation in the Tricameral Parliament.

With the exception of South Africa, it was in Kenya that the British government's policy of favoring European interests most threatened Indian welfare and sharpened their understanding of their fortunes being linked to those of the black Africans, since both were, in reality, colonized peoples. By 1939, however, their situation throughout the region was one of relative privilege:

The Indians' place in the Government and society of Kenya had become fairly well stabilized, somewhere in the scale of privilege, power, and prestige between the position of the European community at the top and that of the Arab and African communities at the base. (Gregory, 455)

Before reaching this position of segregated but comparable economic and social comfort, however, the Kenyan Indian population found itself faced with discrimination resulting, primarily, from European greed for the best land and fear of Indian/African political affiliation against them.

It is true that in both Tanganyika and Uganda, the non-European populations cooperated to resist European hegemony. In 1906 at Kilwa in Tanganyika, a number of Indians were convicted of smuggling arms and supplies to the African Maji Maji rebels attempting to overthrow the harsh German rule (103), and in Uganda, where there was also a relatively small European population, the Indian planter class generally cooperated with the Africans, especially the Ganda (400). It was in Kenya, however, where the imperialist tactics of the British were the keenest, that the most cohesive African and Indian political cooperation developed. The alliance between Manilal A. Desai of the Nairobi Indian Association and the Gikuyu reformer Harry Thuku resulted in the formation of the East African Association (Gregory, 205).

As might be expected, European reaction to this cooperation was swift; it took two forms, direct suppression and subversion. An extremely effective tactic was

Britain's pitting of African political interests against Indian in the region. After the First World War, when both anti-European and pro-European sentiments in Kenya were speeding toward revolution, the cry for "native paramountcy" was raised repeatedly by white settlers and encouraged by Winston Churchill, who had succeeded as Secretary of State for the Colonies in 1921. This sudden concern with African rights was offered as a justification for denying Indians equal citizenship with whites and free entry into the colony. Clearly, it served the useful purpose of undermining the collective strength of the non-European populations.

The political wedge forced between the African and Indian communities was particularly effective, because their unity had always been primarily political, not economic. From the beginning of Indian immigration, because of the frequent use of influence by India to support its emigrants and the political use to which Indians increasingly could be put in the maintenance of British "indirect rule," their economic situation was a privileged one.

Africans became increasingly aware over time that the proposition that at least a portion of East Africa become a colony of India was being seriously entertained; that Indian/European political equality was slowly being approached; and, especially, that the Indian merchants with whom Africans dealt were sometimes almost as unscrupulous as the European settlers and bureaucrats in their dealings with them. In both Uganda and Kenya, instances of Indians taking advantage of Africans in business transactions occurred, and local clashes resulted. Some Indians, too, were attacked during the Tanganyika Maji Maji rebellion (104). On a larger scale, friction developed between the two communities throughout East Africa because legal restrictions on landholding and farming practices guaranteed the Indians' dominant economic position (401). Rumors of extensive areas in the lowlands being set aside exclusively for Indian colonization as well as what appeared to be plans gradually to decrease differences between the legal status of the Indian and European communities, but not the African, despite Churchill's pronouncement, exacerbated this resentment.

It is predictable, however, that the main opposition to Indian advancement came not from the Africans but from the Europeans, who saw their own place of privilege threatened (494). Ironically, this European recalcitrance and greed fueled the fires of independence movements in both East Africa and India and has led to longstanding, outspoken Indian opposition, like that of Mahatma Gandhi, to apartheid in South Africa. In East African countries after independence, Uganda being the most noticeable example with its expulsion of Asians in 1973, efforts to Africanize the economies have led to sometimes violent, always destabilizing effects upon the Asian communities.

THE LITERARY RESPONSE

Contemporary Indian-African writers in English have produced works in every Western literary genre, reflecting both their training at universities such as the influential colonial institution, Makerere University College in Uganda, and their reaction to that training.

David Cook's *Origin East Africa* (1965), subtitled *A Makerere Anthology*, contains undergraduate poetry and fiction from three such Asian writers, including Peter Nazareth, who will be treated more fully below. M. M. Haji from Zanzibar, who took an arts degree at Makerere in 1958, contributed two short stories, "When the Walls Came Tumbling Down" (11–15) and "Nothing Extraordinary" (15–21), maturation tales focusing on the growth through painful love experiences of a young Asian man. Romantic love is also the subject of Tilak Banerjee, who migrated to Uganda from Calcutta in 1947 and entered Makerere in 1960. "Poem" (112) offers a conventional atmosphere of heaviness and inertia as it reveals the longings of an expectant lover, but "An Orissan Love Story" (113–18) engages the reader in Banerjee's version of a traditional, tragic tale, which nevertheless ends with its blinded protagonist waiting for his youthful lover. Only Peter Nazareth's brief play, "Brave New Cosmos" (167–78), reflects in any detail the political situation in East Africa, focusing upon two self-deceptive and self-important undergraduates who have received no real wisdom from their education. Nazareth has commented about the "heavy colonial pall" that hung over Makerere while he was there, "which made it quite hard to be creative instead of imitative to challenge any of the norms" ("Interview" with Lindfors, 84).

Cook's and David Rubaderi's 1971 *Poems from East Africa* features four more Indian writers, Bahadur Tejani, Jagjit Singh, Parvin Syal, and Saroj Datta. Tejani's work will be discussed at length elsewhere in this chapter, but "In the Orthopaedic Ward" (173) deserves mention for its expression of unified humanity; "On Top of Africa" (176–77), in contrast, for the speaker's sense of competition with both nature and his black companion; and "Wild Horse of Serengeti" (178–79) for its vivid recreation of the power and freedom of nature. Singh's "No Roots, No Leaves, No Buds" (152) is a young man's bitter lament against a lover who has rejected him, and "Death, etc., etc." (152) leaps unconvincingly from the killing of a cockroach to musings about the genocidal destructiveness of warfare and collective guilt. His more successful "Public Butchery" (160) ironically approves the public execution of four alleged conspirators, reflecting the political turmoil of his time. "Portrait of an Asian as an East African" (156–60), in particular, compels interest because of its comparison of the African Indian to the Wandering Jew, condemned by colonial purposes to limit his expectations to commerce. Because of impending independence, this perpetual wanderer soon will be forced into new lands, where the poet sees a repetition of the hostility against him. Syal, who also writes in Hindi, powerfully reflects the constant awareness of Asian writers of their marginal status in East Africa. Both "The Pot" (167) and "When I Came Here" (170) concern this rejection, although the latter poem could as easily be about a failed romance as about the political situation. More straightforwardly, "Defeat" (168) assumes a female persona, recreating the humiliation of a young woman on display at a slave auction after her people have been defeated in war. Datta, the one Asian woman among these writers, offers in "The Dead Bird" (35), a skillful but, finally, conventional nature poem about the death of natural beauty and the speaker's emotional response.

In addition to poetry, drama has been particularly attractive to East African Indian writers. Jagjit Singh is also a playwright, whose "Sweet Scum of Freedom" was chosen to be included in *African Theatre: Eight Prize-Winning Plays for Radio* (1973). "Sweet Scum of Freedom" concerns three conflicts: the debate between Sunma, an older prostitute, and the younger Anna about Asian exploitation of Africans; the muted disagreement between Anna and her Indian lover, Keval, about his leaving Africa for London; and the attempted assassination, allegedly by a prostitute, of Dr. Mosozi Ebongo, a hypocritical government minister who uses his power unfairly against Asians and has recently cracked down on "the scum that is today disgracing the heroic freedom struggle of our people" (44).

Ebongo, reflecting Idi Amin's ideology, declares: "We still have a lot of foreigners in our country. I am referring of course to the Asian community now" (45). The intense feeling against Asians seems to stem from the conclusion that they did not fight wholeheartedly against British colonialism and that they are not totally committed to independent Africa, but are keeping "one foot in Britain, the other foot in India and only their hands in Africa playing like prostitutes with our commerce and trade" (45). Ebongo's publicly stated solution, however, is not for Asians to leave the country, but to become citizens, even to intermarry with Africans. The assassination attempt against the minister, which has occurred before the play begins, sparks a revealing conversation between Anna and Keval suggesting that, because of resistance on both sides, both citizenship and intermarriage are doomed. Keval admits:

We are frightened. The Asians are such a frightened people. They're so pure and clean—must say their prayers and wash their bodies every day. And they're so rich—most of them and they have such big cars and you don't. So they'll never marry you. Besides Black is so untame and dangerous for them. And they'll always call half-caste children chotaras. (46)

These are the same cultural and economic conflicts treated at length by Bahadur Tejani in *Day After Tomorrow* (1971). Tejani's other major charge, sexual repression and denial of feelings within the Hindu community, accounts for Keval's agonized response to Anna's questioning him about his guilt in coming to African malayas, prostitutes. Furthermore, while the Asians are emotionally self-destructive and in political flight, the African politicians are depicted as bleeding all the people they can, regardless of ethnic origin.

Kuldip Sondhi, twice winner of the Kenya Drama Festival Playwright's Award, also addresses the racial tensions aroused by both Africanization after independence and rivalries promoted by the colonialists. "Undesignated" introduces the contentious Majid, who challenges African privilege under the new government. Majid's complaint is twofold. He sees the educated black man as able to secure any position he chooses simply by virtue of his education and color. Moreover, as an educated Asian-African, he feels doubly discriminated against, a second-class citizen first under the British, and now under the independent black African regime.

His successful black business associate, Solomon, to whom most of his remarks are addressed, reminds him that under the old government, he and other Africans were third-class citizens; understandably, Solomon insists upon individual merit as the key to advancement. At this assertion, Majid scoffs bitterly, but he is clearly outnumbered by his fellow Asians, who admit that the present situation is unfair to them but are prepared to accept it.

"Of Malice and Men" by Ganesh Bagchi shifts this conflict to the personal sphere, concentrating upon an Asian-white love triangle. For the first time in these works, sympathy for the displaced colonial retainer is expressed. Michael, a Britisher, is returning to England, because he is increasingly uncomfortable with the realization that his black and Asian co-workers at his office are waiting for him to go. Either his departure will represent a new job opportunity for one of them to move into, or it will end the humiliation of being reminded of the former British dominance. Sona, his Hindu girlfriend, is a curious character who seems extraordinarily apolitical, even naive. She claims not to understand what the controversy is about, insisting that people should be able simply to live peacefully together, without constantly referring to their ethnic origins.

The actual political issues surface vividly when Sudhin, also in love with Sona, appears at Michael's apartment to take her back to her father's house. The white man, a self-proclaimed former idealist, has already expressed his disillusionment with Britain's motives for being in Africa but, in subsequent dialogue, reveals that he maintains his sense of cultural superiority. Sudhin's contention that the British have created a civil service bourgeoisie among the Africans to aid and conceal their continued exploitation is dismissed as old political jargon by Michael, who claims to love Africa and to feel displaced and betrayed by having to leave.

Ironically, Sona is essentially dismissed by both men. Despite her apparent inability to engage in political analysis and to recognize historical consequences, she, in turn, finally takes a firm, if overly emotional, feminist stance against both Michael and Sudhin. The problem with her characterization is that Bagchi presents her as a good-hearted, sincere, but simplistic thinker who unwittingly contradicts her own statements and theories. Nevertheless, at the end, it is in Sona's mouth that the playwright places his most important conclusions. She refuses to see members of her generation as either victims or heroes and attributes the current racial tension to a subversive plan of the continuing colonial system. Additionally, she urges Michael and Sudhin and, by extension, all those caught up in ethnic antagonism to work together as individuals in order to fight neo-colonialism. Despite Michael's insulting opinion, expressed at the beginning of the play, that no Hindu woman is capable of sorting out what she herself thinks, a feeling with which Bagchi largely appears to agree, the Britisher decides to remain in Africa if Sona will stay with him. She agrees.

In contrast to this study of interracial romance, the larger social issue of bribery and its effect on the common people is the subject of the brief two-act sketch, "Bones" (*Short East African Plays in English*, 47–49), written in Swahili and translated by Sadru Kassam from Mombasa.

As have their black African counterparts, Indian African writers have turned to the novel as a natural method of expressing their concerns. *The Gunny Sack* (1989) by M. G. Vassanji, who was born in Nairobi and currently lives and teaches in Toronto, through evocations of both orature and written history, traces the intwined stories of four generations of Indians in East Africa. His concern is both with the individuals, the descendants of Dhanji Govindji, and with their inevitably changing Asian heritage due to cultural conflict under colonialism. A collection of his short stories, *Uhuru Street*, is due to appear soon.

THREE WRITERS: NAZARETH, TEJANI, ESSOP

> I am an African. . . . I'm an African writer of Goan origin.
> —Peter Nazareth, "Interview" with Irby, 3, 5

> Lord! Lord!
> Let the brown blood
> rediscover the animal
> in itself,
> and have free limbs
> and laughing eyes of
> love play.
>
> Lord, make these men
> and their women
> feel
> that each to other
> is not an untouchable.
> —Bahadur Tejani, "Lines for a Hindi Poet"
> (*Poems of Black Africa*, 132–33)

> Though I have been, like many other people, profoundly affected by the immensity of the human tragedy, I have tried to keep my poise in the act of writing.
> —Ahmed Essop, Comments in *Momentum*, 21

Peter Nazareth and Bahadur Tejani of East Africa and Ahmed Essop of South Africa are the focus of the third part of this study. As their comments composing the epigraphs to this section suggest, their works reflect in very differing ways the historical realities of the Indian experience in Africa. Not only do their emphases and conclusions about the African-Asian situation differ, the contrasts in their formal expression indicate the variety of literary possibilities employed by African Indian writers in English.

Peter Nazareth, who writes novels, short fiction, radio plays, and criticism, was born in Uganda of Goan parents and was educated at Makerere; a schoolmate of Ngugi wa Thiong'o, he was one of the editors of the literary journal *Penpoint*. Like Ngugi, he did postgraduate work at Leeds University in England. Nazareth returned to Uganda to join the Ministry of Finance in Entebbe, his hometown, where he worked for five years under the government headed by Milton Obote and for two more under the rule of Idi Amin. In 1973, his Ugandan citizenship taken away from him, he accepted a fellowship to study at Yale. From there he joined the English Department and the Afroamerican Studies Program at the University of Iowa, where he continues to teach at the present time and to serve as advisor to the International Writing Program.

Bahadur Tejani, "born on the slopes of Kilimanjaro" (*Poems from East Africa*, 201), also studied literature at Makerere, sharing with Nazareth the distinction of being sports editor on *The Makererean*, then travelled to Cambridge University to read philosophy. Returning to East Africa, he taught for a period of time at the University of Nairobi and now resides and teaches in the United States. In addition to his novel, *Day After Tomorrow*, he has published a volume of verse, *The Rape of India and Other Poems*.

Ahmed Essop was born in Dabhel, Surat, India, and educated at the University of South Africa, Pretoria. He has taught at secondary schools and colleges throughout Johannesburg, where he presently resides in the Indian suburb of Lenasia. Under the pseudonym Ahmed Yousuf, he published a collection of poetry, *The Dark Goddess*, in 1959, and a novel, *The Emperor*, about the downfall of Mr. Dharma Shoka, an Indian headmaster with an "unquenchable thirst for power" (*Contemporary Authors*, 96), in 1984. *The Hajji and Other Stories* (1978), an earlier version of the collection of his short fiction, won the Schreiner Award from the English Academy of Southern Africa in 1979.

While all three writers come from the same continent, and their artistic concerns are similar in that they reflect a colonial or postcolonial world of oppression, their focuses are very different, as are their solutions, styles, and ultimate views about the individual and society. Reflecting the experience of his people, the Goans of Uganda, Peter Nazareth's novels present an African world in flux, where the individual, willingly or not, must finally exile himself for personal and economic survival. In contrast, Tejani's solution to the political upheaval of the twentieth century is closer bonding of the races, a recognition in social and personal action of the actual unity and complementarity of black and Indian cultures. Essop, in contrast, presents a picture of ancient cultural differences among the Asians of Johannesburg and suggests that individual growth, rather than social, can come only through suffering. To demonstrate their common subject matter as well as their different approaches to Asian-African life, I will discuss Peter Nazareth's *In a Brown Mantle* (1972), followed by Bahadur Tejani's *Day After Tomorrow* (1971), then Nazareth's *The General Is Up* (1984) and Ahmed Essop's *Hajji Musa and the Hindu Fire-Walker* (1988).

In both *In a Brown Mantle* and *The General Is Up*, Nazareth centers upon the Goan community of Uganda; therefore, a brief explanation of the origins of this community, which was severely disrupted by Idi Amin's expulsion of all Asians in 1973, will be helpful. Goa, the homeland from which Nazareth's particular community of East African Asians came, is located on the west coast of the Indian subcontinent and has experienced colonialism itself since the sixteenth century. In 1510, it was taken over by the Portuguese, a rule that brought an immense change to Goan Culture and lasted until 1961, when Goa was captured by India. Since 1962, Goa, along with the other islands of Daman and Diu, has formed a Union Territory of the Republic of India ("Interview" with Irby, 1).

A Catholic, like most of the Portuguese-influenced Goans, Nazareth was very active in Goan social and intellectual life in his hometown, serving several times as the president of the Entebbe Goan Institute. Even his joining the civil service is true to the experience of many members of his community, that occupation being one of the niches carved out for them by the British. Encouraged by both Ngugi and Mali novelist and poet David Rubadiri, whom he also met at Makerere, to write something out of his own background and about his own people, Nazareth, after returning to Uganda from Leeds, struggled with a novel that would divide its interest between the Goan experience and the overall political situation in Uganda. A fragment of the work was published in a special issue of *East African Journal* edited by Ngugi: "But eighteen months passed, until the morning after the assassination attempt on Obote. That's when the novel began to come, and I couldn't stop writing. I finished the draft within six weeks, in January, 1970" ("Interview" with Lindfors, 90).

Set in Uganda (called Damibia), *In a Brown Mantle* centers upon the Goan community, both accounting for its presence in East Africa and revealing its uncomfortable relationship with the African majority after independence. Nazareth offers three contrasting protagonists, each representative of actual figures in recent Ugandan history or of historical impulses within their communities: the narrator, Deo D'Sousa, a young Indian bureaucrat turned political aide; Pius Cota, an outspoken Goan political leader; and Robert Kyeyune, the African spokesman for Damibian independence who becomes the country's first president, only to see corrupting forces working to undermine both the people's prosperity and his own career. The correspondences between events in the novel and recent occurrences in Uganda are clear.

Nazareth's characterization of the Damibian Goan community is of an insular group that is superstitious, socially conformist, and politically complacent. Predictably, it is resentful and fearful of the ideas of a radical spokesman like the fiery Pius Cota. The novel begins with an explanation by D'Sousa of why Goans are in East Africa and an attempt to explain the particularly conservative nature of their society. He reveals the continuation of ancient beliefs like that in "dist,"

or the "bad eye," despite its efficient, bloody work of the Portuguese mission-
aries at the time of conquest to convert the Goans to Catholicism. Moreover,
he posits that brutal historical experience as an explanation for the present desire
of the Goans in Damibia not to "rock the boat" politically.

Pius Cota, whose last name, Nazareth subsequently discovered, means "fort
or . . . the place with a key fort, the fall of which led to the conquest of the
whole country" ("Interview" with Lindfors, 93), represents a frightening threat
to their quiet security. Even though Cota points out that the racial and economic
injustices in their society hurt Goans as well as Africans, he is rejected, even
by D'Sousa at first, as a troublemaker. Cota's message to the Goan elders at the
Institute, to throw in their lot with the growing freedom movement among the
Africans, meets with a reminder of "the grand and glorious progress brought
about by the British. . . . Schools, houses, offices, hospitals, shops" (*In a Brown
Mantle*, 10). His rejoinder that most Africans and Asians cannot even go into
these places and that the Goan lack of response, in actual fact, cooperates with
this exploitation leads to cries of " 'Shame,' 'Troublemaker,' 'Get out,' 'Who
do you think you are?,' and 'Throw him out' " (12). Explaining further, Nazareth
shows that a concept much deeper than the fear and admiration instilled by
European colonialism reinforces the Goan desire for conformity. Rejecting the
caste system of "decadent Hinduism" and recognizing the community's economic status as uniformly lower middle class, the Goans, according to D'Sousa,
are especially quick to attack any evidence of individualism or elitism.

Cota's African counterpart is Robert Kyeyune (modeled on Milton Obote),
who has effectively organized labor strikes and boycotts against British firms
and expertly plays the political game. Much of the political analysis crucial to
the book is placed in the mouth of Cota or Kyeyune, not in that of the naive
narrator.

Their observations lead D'Sousa to further analysis on his own and to political
maturation and activity. Although, as a predictably conservative Goan, he had
originally judged Cota a madman and mistrusted Kyeyune for being "a radical
in the typical African manner" (25), D'Sousa, renamed Mr. Brown, goes to
work as a speech writer for the black politician, independent Damibia's first
president. Nazareth wishes to distinguish between African and Asian cultural
traits; therefore, it is precisely D'Sousa's Goan reserve, even detachment, that
makes him valuable to Kyeyune and offers the author an opportunity for reflection
on cultural ambiguities. After watching the difference between his own and his
boss's responses to prostitutes, D'Sousa ponders the question whether

this difference between Kyeyune and myself [was] purely a personal difference? Or was
it a racial difference? Is it true, as somebody has said, that Africans are short-visioned
and only live in the present whereas Asians are long-visioned and only live in eternity?
If so, how did my ancestors explore every avenue of sensuality and sexuality five thousand
years B.C.? (56)

The reader is never offered answers to these questions of identity born from stereotypes fostered by a racist colonial system. Nazareth devotes his attention in the latter part of the book to D'Sousa's isolation within Kyeyune's government because he is Indian and to his eventual co-opting by Damibia's increasingly dishonest politics.

An important secondary character is Gombe-Kukwya, popularly known as The Cow. While Robert Kyeyune is unable to control Damibian political corruption, he remains relatively untainted by it. His minister, Gombe-Kukwya, however, offers a clear fictional picture of an active agent in the historical exploitation of the Ugandan people by their newly elected black officials. Agreeing with D'Sousa that The Cow is an exploiter, Kyeyune points out, however, that he is also powerful, popular with his tribe, and has the backing of rich African businessmen. Therefore, he must be brought into the government so that he will not play the destructive role of leader of the opposition. "So I had to accept Kyeyune's thesis that the end justified the means. This was the world of politics after all. One had to compromise" (78).

D'Sousa also receives a quick lesson in practical politics during Kyeyune's election campaign when he learns of the dirty tricks used to intimidate supporters of the other party and helps to falsify the vote in favor of his own, sometimes bribing ordinary voters with booze, but chiefs with gifts like bicycles, motorcycles, cows, or even cars (79). Moreover, he learns how Kyeyune has manipulated "a certain Western power" (79) to contribute large sums to his campaign by convincing it that the other party is a front for the Communists.

These lessons do not prepare him for the difficulties of running the country once Kyeyune has won. Every sector in the economy retains the weaknesses left over from colonialism, and independence brings its own set of difficulties; conflict between the older politicians and the young, educated African elite; the hidden hand of European economic control; Damibia's secondary position within the East African economic community; and the rapid influx of so-called experts, followed by "the biggest bunch of crooks, thugs, thieves, and rogues one could find anywhere" (107). "When we woke up four years later, the country was in the quagmire of corruption" (113).

In his explanation of Kyeyune's mistaken privileging of the military, particularly his decision to allow it to be semi-autonomous, Nazareth provides an extremely useful inside explanation of the rise of Idi Amin. In the fictional account, D'Sousa discovers a plot by The Cow and the army to overthrow Kyeyune as he himself is slowly sliding into dishonesty.

D'Sousa's illegal activity and his desperate hope of hiding it from Kyeyune coincides with the assassination of Pius Cota. Ironically, Cota has discovered an extensive bribery scheme in the government of Azingwe (Kenya) and is threatening to expose the entire mess. When D'Sousa goes to Kyeyune with this news, he discovers that not only does the Damibian president already know about the bribery network, but he intends to do nothing about it for fear of antagonizing Azingwe. Moreover, he threatens to remove D'Sousa from the party if he informs

Cota that his knowledge has been discovered. Consequently, Deo is silent, and Cota is killed. "Sickened beyond cure" (149) and afraid of the exposure of his own dishonesty, D'Sousa takes his first opportunity, being sent to represent Damibia at a conference in Jamaica of nonaligned nations, to leave the country permanently. In a last monologue, Nazareth returns his protagonist to a concern with the precarious identity of the Asian in Africa: " 'Goodbye, Mother Africa,' I said, as the plane lifted off. 'Your bastard son loved you' " (150).

Despite this late return to the subject of Deo's Goan ancestry and other isolated scenes where his or his community's racial identity is the subject, Nazareth's main interest in *In a Brown Mantle* is the larger issue of African politics during the critical transition to Ugandan self-rule. In contrast, Bahadur Tejani's novel, *Day After Tomorrow*, while also set in the same country right after independence, specifically in Kampala in 1964, focuses upon particular characteristics of the Asian community, especially the Hindu, that the author finds both self-destructive and limiting socially and politically. Unlike Deo D'Sousa, Tejani's Samsher is a rebel from his Asian society, the prototype of a new African of universal sensibilities, incorporating the best in both Indian and African cultures.

Day After Tomorrow presents a community still stinging from the cynical colonial manipulation of the Indians as buffers between white power and black labor. Tejani's concern is not only with imperialist exploitation, however, but with traditional weaknesses within the Asian community itself, especially what he portrays as its anti-intellectualism, sexual repression, materialism, conservatism, isolation, and fearfulness of anything or anyone different. The solution he posits is intermarriage between blacks and Asians, thereby creating a new race, children "of a new civilization" (6).

It would be helpful in clarifying Tejani's perception of the differences between Asian and African societies to recall a striking passage from *In a Brown Mantle* in which Deo is contrasting African and Goan public dances. Nazareth's image of a typical Asian dance is one of formality and decorum, but ultimately, except for an occasional fight at the bar, unexciting. The scene in an African nightclub, in comparison, is chaotic, erotic, and completely involving:

Go to an African nightclub and you are assailed by electronic wailing before you get in. The guitars send out signals to the neighbouring areas so that all may come to the dance. You pay a couple of shillings at the gate to a brightly painted woman, and enter into a sleazy hall.

The hall is dark and full of music. There is movement everywhere, people dancing or drinking. They are dressed as they like and do what they like. The atmosphere is charged, as though the uninhibited human being is inescapably erotic. (*In a Brown Mantle*, 19)

Tejani's desire to appropriate some of this vitality and joy for the conservative Asians is explicit in his depiction of Samsher's conflict with his merchant father. Like his father before him, Samsher's father works from dawn to dusk in his small shop, waiting on African customers whom he mistrusts and is contemptuous of, stopping this routine only to instruct his son in the methods of sharp trading. In the village where the protagonist grows up, the Asian community is strong, but its cohesiveness is born out of fear. After moving to Kampala, Samsher realizes::

The traders in the city, he saw for himself, were no different from those in the village. If anything a little more frightened and callous. . . . Here too, the traders locked their doors and windows with ingenious bolts and chains. They put ground glass on the wall of their houses, turning the buildings into ugly gnashed fortresses. (*Day After Tomorrow*, 31)

Boarding the steamer coming from the village to the city, Samsher witnesses a violent scene in which prospective African passengers are not permitted to board until the ship is almost under way and are then beaten back and shoved into the water. When the young boy asks Mohemadali why this brutality has occurred, his father explains quietly that it is because they are Africans and, also, third-class passengers. While one senses that Mohemadali is sensitive to the injustice of this treatment, he does not condemn it to his young son. We are told that the Asian traders are obsessed with the Africans around them but only as objects of trade or sources of fear, certainly not as fellow victims.

The scene on the steamer so outrages Samsher that, in contrast to his passive, possibly even approving, father, the boy resolves, "Someday when I grow up I shall help them" (29). Even more problematically for his own sense of identity, he also feels "disgust of his father and mother and people who looked on, as the black men were kicked and beaten when they tried to get on board the ship" (29). This rejection of his parents' racism and/or fear and apathy is a significant factor in his rejection of their way of life altogether and his growing appreciation of the world of the Africans, whom he had recognized back in the village as living "a life close to the earth and the elements. Who had no consciousness of shame because of the fullness of their natural dignity. Men and women at one with their surroundings" (32).

Education is of utmost importance to his parents, but only education of a useful sort. Samsher's community sends its children to school so that they can grow up to be more skilled traders, but does not want the school to supercede the home or school work to be brought into the shop. After a while, the Asian parents begin to fear the school as a fragmenting force and "always tried hard to rid them of what they learnt in the magical circle of the school. Talk about school was discouraged. The children were not allowed to do their school-work at home" (29). It is at school, after being unfairly beaten by the white headmaster for defending a hapless classmate while the Indian teachers remain silent, that Samsher remembers his earlier resolution at the steamer always to treat others fairly. He receives no maturing influences from his day-to-day experiences in his own community; on the contrary, what he observes of his family's neighbors is more cruelty, born of fear. Especially repugnant to the adolescent boy is his growing awareness of Asian sexual repression and consequent debasement and sterility. The subsequent street scene represents Tejani's strong condemnation of sexual codes of behavior he considers unnatural and socially destructive; Samsher "wanted to escape them badly" (112).

Not only has Samsher rejected the life of trading his father has carved out for him, opting instead to pursue a teaching certificate, but his youthful experience with African customers in Mohemadali's shop in the village invites him to a more natural, positive mode of existence than that of his own people. Significantly, he comes to sexual awareness while observing the delicate touching and word play of an African couple. It is no surprise, then, that he marries the outspoken, self-confident African woman Nanziri, who herself has had to weigh the warnings against racial intermingling angrily presented by her friend Jane. Jane's reminders represent the negative African attitude toward the Asians in Uganda, "full of money and arrogance" (122), at the time of independence.

Charles Sarvan observes of *Day After Tomorrow*: "It is ironic that the novel was published in the year Idi Amin seized power. The *Day After Tomorrow* brought indignity, expulsion, and exile, even to the Samshers of Uganda" (103). He notes further that two weeks after *In a Brown Mantle* was put on sale in Uganda, General Idi Amin served an expulsion order on the country's Asians. In his first novel, Nazareth presents a prophetic, angry exchange between The Cow and Deo, ending with the black politician's warning, "We can do without your kind here. We have had enough of exploiters" (74–75).

While Tejani romanticizes the Africans in *Day After Tomorrow*, characterizing them not only by their natural ease, unfair victimization, and healthy communal relations, but also by a "rich heritage of humanism" (145), Nazareth presents a much more complicated view of urbanized Africans and their interaction with the Asians in *The General Is Up* (1984). The expulsion of the Ugandan Asians forms the backdrop to this historical novel. Uganda is still called Damibia, and the General who is "up" is obviously Idi Amin.

Like Tejani in *Day After Tomorrow*, Nazareth focuses most of his attention in this book upon strengths and weaknesses within the Asian community itself, emphasizing, too, its caution, resistance to change, sexual double standards, and exaggerated respect for authority. Although one of his major subjects is the antagonism and suspicion between the Africans and Asians, more surely than *In a Brown Mantle* and in contrast to *Day After Tomorrow*, *The General Is Up* insists upon cultural and historical links between the two groups.

One of Nazareth's consistent techniques is to highlight his characters' individual struggles, always keeping in mind their relationship to the political situation of the country as a whole. The seemingly endless, but ultimately futile, efforts of David D'Costa to acquire Damibian citizenship offer a Kafkaesque image of the general experience of Asians in the country after independence. His runaround is comic and predictable but reflective of the real frustration and insecurity of Asians at a time when neither the British nor the Ugandan authorities were sensitive to their plight.

While D'Costa's personal war against the bureaucrats is being lost, Damibia is attacked by guerillas from neighboring Leshona (Tanzania), which is offering asylum to the country's first president, overthrown by the General:

The next day, the General's soldiers slaughtered hundreds of people in the areas where the guerillas had appeared to be successful on the grounds that they had helped the guerillas. Many of the killings were done in public as a lesson to the people who survived. (58)

Such incidents are presented in a detached, reportorial style and serve primarily as a backdrop against which the situation of Nazareth's protagonists can be judged.

In the light of such political upheaval, David D'Sousa is able acutely to analyze the Goan dilemma. He is particularly struck by his people's continuing sense of exile and dislocation and does not blame present-day Africans, despite the General's order, instead looking behind the present political situation to the continuing influence of British colonialism. David realizes that the British were very skillful in shifting the appearance of exploitation onto the Asians in East Africa, and that the present animosity against brown people on the part of ordinary Africans is testimony to the whites' ability to camouflage their own actions and motives.

Despite all the attempts to separate Asians and Africans, however, Nazareth insists upon their ultimate similarity, in both human and political terms. He presents Roland, who, like Deo and Samsher, remembers that he had been trained to believe in African inferiority. Experience, however, has taught him the similarity of both colonized peoples:

Ronald once again said, "Bastard," cursing the unknown African for wasting his money on a petrol-guzzling, tyre-chewing Benz, and then added, "Bastards tool", cursing the Goans in Damibia who hoarded almost every cent, as though the whole aim of life was to accumulate every coin and note. Though the one wanted to hoard it and the other to spend it, Goan and Damibian were two sides of the same coin in their excessive devotion to money. (288–29)

It is in the conflict and ambivalent friendship of David D'Sousa and the African George Kapa that the genuine cultural and political differences between their communities are brought into high relief. Shortly before he is to go into exile, D'Sousa makes a farewell visit to George, an old college friend and present fellow member of the former Goan Institute. He is stunned to be accused by George of cowardice and naive idealism for refusing to take the risk of staying for the good of the country, even without citizenship papers. George's identification with the new bourgeoisie on the make, according to David, is raised as a major factor in the General's seizure of power:

"*Wacha* Daudi!" shouted George, his blood rising. "You are only rationalizing your Goan habit of thinking small. . . . "

"No, but you have class feelings. Why did you not get involved in a mass movement! You had the easy-going liberal tolerance that is purchased by privilege. If you had started a mass-movement, I would not be sitting here trying to say Goodbye! I am leaving because of you—''

"Goddammit it!'' said George, leaping up. "You are passing the buck, blaming me for your own cowardice. Aren't you as a Goan a member of the privileged class!''

"Yes, and that is why you like the Goans—because they are still, to your not-yet-decolonized mind, the privileged class!'' (122–24)

George's weak attempts to defend himself and other Africans who have prospered immoderately since independence are only half-hearted, and he admits, at least to himself, that he failed to attend the Institute for the farewell parties for his Indian friends for fear of being perceived as "fraternizing with the expellees" (126). This conversation suggests ambivalence of both racial and class feelings present at this period in East Africa and returns to Nazareth's concern with the political complicity post-independence politicians found so difficult to resist.

Despite Nazareth's disclaimer of writing of actual people, *The General Is Up* resonates with actual historical events: the attempts to murder a student leader who spoke out publicly against the expulsion of the Asians; the foiled efforts to round up the entire editorial board of the university student newspaper, which published his speech; numerous failed assassination attempts against the General; the resignations from abroad of the General's Minister of Overseas Affairs and Minister of Public Affairs; the General's suspension of his entire cabinet; and the violence against fleeing Asians by the army and theft of their possessions. The novel ends, however, with an unsatisfactory scene of wish-fulfillment, with the General being shot by General Oma, a political rival. This moment of authorial lapse strikes the reader, however, as, if not convincing, at least understandable in view of both the actual unforgettable horrors in Uganda and Nazareth's anguish about the dilemma of the Goans. There is no such loss of control, however, in Ahmed Essop's *Hajji Musa and the Hindu Fire-walker* (1988), which keeps the political reality of South Africa at a sufficient distance to allow concentration upon usually genial characterizations representative of the Johannesburg Asians.

At the beginning of *In a Brown Mantle*, the narrator, David D'Souza observes wryly:

Hardly anybody paid any attention to Goa until India decided a few years ago to re-conquer it from the Portuguese, who had ruled it for four hundred and fifty years. . . . China . . . attacked India at the border on the pretext that the land was originally Chinese. Meanwhile, having got used to the idea of being Indian once again instead of Portuguese, Goans started wondering what it would be like to be Chinese. (3)

The bemused detachment of this observation about the absurdities of imperialism occurs only occasionally in Nazareth and never in Tejani but is the dominant tone of Essop's study of the Hindu community in South Africa.

In his Introduction to this collection of short fiction, Lionel Abrahams mentions, in particular, "the subtle combination of feelings within many of the stories," revealing the author's "fascination with the endlessly varied ways of the human heart. Thence the power to amuse, delight, move and challenge us" (ii, iii). Indeed, Essop is less explicitly political than Nazareth; like Tejani, he addresses a wide range of cultural issues. Unlike the Ugandan, however, his satire of the Asian community of Fordsburg in Johannesburg is generally of the mildest, most sympathetic sort, certainly with no suggestion of the necessity of intermarriage for its enrichment or survival. Writing in *World Literature Today*, Reed Dasenbrock compares Essop's collection to V. S. Naipaul's *Miguel Street* in its creation of "a microcosm that represents the larger Indian community" but notes that "though Essop's natural gift is for comedy, the comedy in the stories of *Hajji Musa* often turns bittersweet" (355).

Ahmed Essop has commented on the danger to writers "under the pressure of a crushing social reality" like that of South Africa to become "single-voiced" and has revealed his own attempt to speak with many voices (*Momentum*, 19). In an oppressive political situation, he notes:

The voice of the comedian, the satirist, the wit, the historian, the allegorist, the lover and sensualist, the lyricist, the psychologist, the philosopher and visionary may not be heard. The writer may reduce himself to the level of the secretary, the journalist, the zealot, the demagogue; and as passionate commitment to social and political change becomes the principal end of writing, abandon the formal aspects that control creative literary performance. (*Momentum*, 19)

In contrast to the more immediate concerns of Nazareth and Tejani, Essop aims to reveal what he considers universal patterns of behavior as often as he does meanings and values that are individual to a particular group of people or a certain geo/historical locale. He does not censure other, more ideologically committed writers, however, for he recognizes that devotion to " 'universal truths,' 'literary technique' and 'aesthetic canons' [does] not guarantee any piece of writing literary validity" (*Momentum*, 20). Put simply, Essop seems intent on avoiding what he judges as the temptation to exploit fictionally the racial situation of South Africa as well as on rejecting the seductive lure of "the wasteland of avant-garde writing where experiment and form become preoccupations" (*Momentum*, 20). Essop's tight-rope act, "keep[ing} his poise in the act of writing," results in stories that, for the most part, delight the reader in their sympathetic revelation of a variety of human foibles, Asian and otherwise, but often frustrate by seeming to deflect intense engagement with the South African reality by focusing on quirks of personality and intercommunity jealousies and power plays.

Essop's tales are related by a narrator, appropriately named Ahmed, who matures from a young schoolboy to a freelance journalist through the course of the book, and whose primary thematic role is that of chorus, reflecting the attitude of the Asian community toward the various events and individuals he witnesses and meets. Essop's subjects range from interracial marriage, religious fanaticism, and fraud to responses to political directives; from studies of quirky individuals to examinations of the outrageous or self-destructive behavior of political or religious groups; the tone, too, alternates between amused detachment and quiet sympathy.

Unlike Tejani's novel, Essop's tales of interracial romance, "The Hajji," "The Yogi," "The Target," and "Black and White," suggest no enrichment in the experience for the Asian partner; in fact, reflecting the strict segregation of blacks in South Africa, the sexual mingling in these stories occurs between Asians and whites. Such a marriage in "The Hajji" leads to the Indian male partner being rejected by his brother, even when he is dying and the rest of the community has accepted him back. Revealing his primary interest to be in character rather than situation, Essop focuses here on the rigidity of the unforgiving brother rather than on the complexities of racial intermarriage. Both "The Target" and "Black and White" offer examples of adolescent love affairs crossing racial boundaries, the first being a study of a young man who would be maladjusted under any circumstances. Mahmood is the hapless victim of physical violence from both his Asian girlfriend's brothers and from white bullies presumably trying to teach him a lesson about staying away from their girls. The second story offers a white Mahmood too naive to stay away from the hostile Asian neighborhood and his fickle Asian girlfriend. The strongest contrast to Tejani's handling of this similar subject is "The Yogi," where miscegenation laws and segregated seating in the law courts are mentioned only as an aside, and the real interest is in a comic portrayal of a hypocritical and comical religious leader. Although this protagonist reappears in the novella "The Visitation" as mentally deranged, presumably as a result of his experience in prison, in this story the emphasis is on his comic hypocrisy. "Red Beard's Daughter" sidesteps the issue of interracial marriage to concentrate on an unusually rebellious young Indian woman who refuses her greedy, domineering father's choice of a husband. The half-breed, Ben Areff, is dismissed as not "the sort of man to be envied. At home neither in an Indian world nor an African world, he was a derelict socially" (101). Only "Gerty's Brother" directs attention to the inhuman consequences of apartheid laws that criminalize love between the races; significantly, after witnessing the pain inflicted by such restrictions, the narrator returns to his room "with the hackles of revolt rising within me" (128).

Questionable religious leaders besides the Yogi mentioned earlier are the irrepressible Hajji Musa of the title story and the fanatic Aziz Khan in the tale of that name. Yet, no issues of any political or religious significance are examined in Hajji Musa's tale. Ahmed is interested in creating a comic characterization. "Aziz Khan," on the other hand, contrasts conservative Muslim and Hindu religious practices, such as the growing trend for Hindus to have Western-style weddings, against which Khan has written a blistering pamphlet, although he attends such weddings himself. Aside from characterizing his comic protagonist as a hypocrite, Essop's interest is in showing the factionalism within the Muslim community, as a result of which Khan is about to be beaten up by "ambassadors" (81) hired by the Muslim Council, angry with him for also railing against beards. "Film" is equally divided between revealing Muslim fanaticism and poking hilarious fun at the segment within that community intent on engaging in a jihad against any Western importation, such as motion pictures, and especially against films like *The Prophet*, which they consider sacrilegious.

Political factionalism within the Asian community, much more divisive than any shown by Peter Nazareth among the Ugandan Goans, is the subject of both "The Betrayal" and "Ten Years." Essop's concern with this subject, however, is the personal consequences of political decisions, not the social effects. Dr. Kamal's agony, in the first story, over his bowing to political expediency and betraying his Gandhian principle of nonviolence, and the irremedial rupture in "Ten Years" between a father and a son over the ramifications of violence versus nonviolence as a strategy, plus the disintegration of their family due to its political activity, are significant and pertinent issues. Essop's concern again, though, is almost entirely personal, not completely limiting the scope of his consideration to effects on individuals rather than the community, but largely doing so.

A completely comic treatment of antagonism between the generations is "Father and Son," in which Asif is having an affair with his aged father's young wife. Similarly, "The Notice" transforms the timely issue of the forced removal of ethnic groups from one area of the city to another into a bedroom farce. Domestic relations within the Asian community are, in actual fact, one of Essop's most frequent subjects in this collection. "Dolly" and "Two Sisters" both concern turbulent relationships between the sexes, the latter, in particular, revealing the nosiness of neighbors in cramped quarters and the cruelty toward nonconformists or strangers that Tejani complained of in *Day After Tomorrow*. Unlike Tejani, however, Essop displays no outrage toward the wife abuse he depicts in "Dolly" or the "frigid contempt and outright hostility" (42) of the people in the yard against the two promiscuous sisters in the second story; his criticism of Aziz Khan, who whips up a religious condemnation of them, is muted satire, and the evicted sisters' response to their violent landlord, Mr. Joosub, who threatens one of their children, is matter-of-factly reported.

Essop's sympathetic portrayal of individuals caught in webs of society's or of their own making is his strong suit. "Obsession," "Gladiators," "Mr. Moonreddy," and "The Commandment" differ from the other stories in the collection by examining, with a minimum of humor, the pathology created in individuals living within a sick society. The slightest and most comic of the group, "Obsession," divides its energy between a slapstick tale of bumbling burglars and a study of Milo, an African haunted by fantasies about gorgeously dressed Asian women, which he fuels with exotic images from the Indian cinema. While Essop only scratches the surface of his complex protagonist's psyche, Milo squarely belongs to the small group of outcasts in these stories, unable, for whatever reason, to achieve the sense of community the author likes to satirize genially.

The racist and classist nature of imperialism is the source of the illusions shaping Mr. Rajespery, principal of the Tagore Indian High School in "Gladiators," and thrusting him into violent conflict not only with the primary school principal, Mr. Rajah, but with his entire community. Mr. Rajespery is one of those pitiful individuals who has accepted white assertions of his own race's inferiority and shapes his life around trying to belong to the "superior" group. His isolation and contempt for other Indians lead in the end to humiliation and derangement. Although our last image of him is one that could have been presented with the same distancing humor as many others of a similar nature in this collection, Essop actually paints a horrifying picture of a self-destructive individual trapped in his allegiance to European civilization, insane in his commitment to a life of assumed superior force that actually goes nowhere:

Next morning he was seen sitting in his Citroen, speaking to himself, shaking his fists at those looking at him, and refusing to come out. Many people came to see him; children milled around his car; and everybody laughed at the sight of Mr. Rajespery in his black Citroen, going up and down. (89)

Another bachelor, fastidious in his appearance and overly conscious of his social standing, is Mr. Moonreddy in the story of that name, condemned to be a waiter because of "unpropitious circumstances" (148), the poverty of his parents. Like Mr. Rajespery, Mr. Moonreddy "could not weather deprecatory remarks; they harrowed some rawness inside him" (150). After being deeply moved by a stray dog's cry of pain, his responses and behavior quickly become pathological. When he acquires a dog of his own, pampers it, and feeds it delicacies, the animal is intended to be an extension of himself, trained to prowl a wealthy Indian neighborhood and kill whatever it comes upon: "The little dog let out a howl, and then a multitude of sharp cries as the fangs gored into the flesh. Mr. Moonreddy stood under a tree, clutching a branch, bathed in sweat, tears running down his cheeks, overwhelmed by a complex feeling of pleasure and pain" (152–53). His emotional identification with both the savage animal he has trained to "Go! Go! Kill!" (152) and its victim is clear evidence of the intense psychological and social pressures under which he has lived but which Essop chooses neither to clarify nor to condemn, focusing instead, without analysis, upon their dire emotional consequences. An equally complex psychological portrait of oppression is "The Commandment." This time, however, Essop's gaze is fixed upon psychological changes in the community rather than solely in the individual. A seventy-year-old African, Moses, who "lived in the yard" (95), takes care of Mr. Rehman's children, performs small errands for other residents, and is generally well liked by the Asians he lives around, especially because he has mastered Gujerati. His quiet life is interrupted by an official order defining the old man as "alien" and ordering him to resettle in his tribal homeland. Moses's bewilderment and growing loss of reason are not

Essop's focus; instead, he traces the ironic changes, from sympathy to hatred, that occur in the Indian community as a result of the order.

A more political writer than Essop would have probed the fears that lead to this reversal and would have driven home the point that Moses is victimized, finally, not only by the impersonal state that values him only as a documented worker controlled by the apartheid labor laws, but, more ironically and tragically, by the very neighbors and friends whose language and lives he has shared and who seemingly valued him before. Essop, however, maintains his usual matter-of-fact narrative voice, detailing both Moses's and his neighbors' decline with only the most restrained emotional response from the narrator.

Essop's critical statements suggest his own struggle to maintain just such restraint in his fictional voice:

Like so many other writers I have been profoundly disturbed by the structural violence of our society. It is buttressed by many convergent forces, among them historical causes and precedents, human frailties, psychological determinants, and, on the religious plane, the Judaeo-Christian ethic of the chosen guardians of final truth. There is also the larger context: the Western world's continual display of its arrogant ego in its relations with the peoples of Africa and the East and its historical record of plunder, oppression and cultural annihilation. (*Momentum*, 19)

His novella, "The Visitation," treats none of these external forces in any explicit way, reflecting, instead, the spiritual state and growth under pressure of an individual businessman, Mr. Sufi, whom Essop presents as representative of many within the South African Asian community. Like similar characters in the short stories, this protagonist is well-to-do, self-indulgent, self-satisfied, only sporadically interested in the doings of his family, a womanizer, and a person who escapes the routine of his life by going to the movies. His story, in brief, is one of financial decline and moral and emotional bewilderment at the hands of another favorite character of Essop's, Gool, the gangster manipulating the Asian business community of Fordsburg. At the beginning of the tale, Sufi, a negligent landlord with several lucrative properties throughout the community, is paying protection money to Gool. Significantly, his economic decline, sparking an opportunity for spiritual growth, begins when Gool forces him to store in his apartment fifty, presumably stolen, boxes of Apollo light bulbs. On the level of characterization, his taking the bulbs is ironic, since, as Gool knows, "all the stairs, foyers and corridors of his apartment buildings . . . were unlit. He was obsessed by the idea that a continuously burning lamp was not only a waste of electricity . . . but a fatal drain on his bank account" (157). On the allegorical level, however, despite Sufi's attempt to rid himself of the bulbs *and* of Gool, this event is not just the beginning of his end financially but Mr. Sufi's unthinking ability to isolate himself from the reality of the sordidness in his business dealings and the stagnation in his personal and spiritual life. The narrative traces his downward spiral into Gool's clutches and his upward journey into self-reflection and supposed moral development.

By the end of the novella, Sufi has, in effect, been manipulated into turning over all his financial resources to Gool and his associates to invest as they see fit in a newly created Asian residential area to replace Fordsburg. Elysia in the novella, Lenasia in reality, represents actual housing restrictions on the part of the South African government. Fordsburg, the colorful Indian residential area of Johannesburg,

had by the late 1970's (when *The Visitation* was written) become largely an inner-city industrial and business area in which the ownership of property was . . . restricted, under the South African Group Areas Act, to the White population group. . . . The Indian community was, in fact, compelled to move en masse to the newly created satellite town of Lenesia . . . twenty kilometres south of Johannesburg. The Fordsburg where Essop himself had lived and of which he wrote with such affection . . . was little more than a memory by the time the collection was published. (Freed, 12–13)

Essop's interest, however, is not primarily in analyzing historical events as shapers of his characters' responses; he uses the evidence of apartheid as a quickly mentioned backdrop, never commenting upon the injustice of what it represents, as Nazareth does with the Asian expulsion in *The General Is Up*, but highlighting Gool's use of the event to rob Mr. Sufi.

Eugenie R. Freed correctly identifies "the unifying principle" of this novella as "the Sufi quest" (Freed, 3) for insight and spiritual growth and its form as basically allegorical, a mode that suits Essop's spare narrative style and reliance upon fictional events to carry his meaning. Another mythic mode controlling the narration is the descent into the Underworld to achieve transcendence. By the end of his story, the once popular, mundanely avaricious Mr. Sufi is involved in criminal activity, bankrupt, shunned, hiding out in his bedroom from family and former friends alike; "socially, his status and respectability were irrevocably lost" (263). Essop uses Sufi's descent, however, to trigger his salvation: "he came to realize that only in relation to [his family] did his life take on meaning" (264).

Our last image of Mr. Sufi is as he lies helplessly on the bedroom floor, clinging to his wife, "breathing convulsively, sweating profusely, seeking solace, compassion and love" (276), reaching out emotionally to his frightened children. The implication at the end is that Sufi will eventually rise, enlightened, to a better life, unencumbered by material possessions and concerns. This conclusion, however, is completely unconvincing. Mr. Sufi's passivity at the end is hardly more commendable than his previous avariciousness; his feelings for his family seem completely self-serving; further, his deliberate and knowing financial abandonment of his buildings, his tenants, his wife and children strikes the reader as both personally and socially irresponsible. Dasenbrock notes that Essop's novella "is less concentrated and less powerful than the stories that precede it" (355). The entire collection charms the reader with the author's skill at humorous depiction but leaves her eager for more of the political/historical, not just individual, context by which to explain Essop's characters.

The African world presented in the pages of Nazareth, Tejani, and Essop is one in which race and culture, rather than place of birth, are crucial. Native-born Indians, both in East and South Africa, are shown to have been treated as full citizens neither during nor after colonialism. Moreover, separatism as a social as well as political policy seems sanctioned by all the groups involved, African, European, and Asian. To a greater or lesser extent, the consequences of this historical and psychological situation are the intriguing subject of all three writers.

WORKS CITED

Bagchi, Ganesh. "Of Malice and Men." In *Short East African Plays in English*. Ed. David Cook and Miles Lee. London: Heinemann, 1968.

Banerjee, Tilak. "An Orissan Love Story" and "Poem." In *Origin East Africa: A Makerere Anthology*. Ed. David Cook. London: Heinemann, 1965.

Dasenbrock, Reed Way. Review of Ahmed Essop. *Hajji Musa and the Hindu Fire Walker*, by *World Literature Today* 63 (Spring 1989): 355.

Datta, Saroj. "The Dead Bird." In *Poems from East Africa*. Ed. David Cook and David Rubaderi. London: Heinemann, 1971.

Essop, Ahmed. "Comments." In *Momentum on Recent South African Writing*. Ed. M. J. Daymond, J. U. Jacobs, and Margaret Lenta. Pietermaritzburg: University of Natal Press, 1984. 19–20.

———. *Hajji Musa and the Hindu Fire-Walker*. London: Readers International, London, 1988.

Freed, Eugenie R. "Mr. Sufi Climbs the Stairs: The Quest and the Ideal in Ahmed Essop's 'The Visitation'." *Theoria* 71 (May 1988): 1–13.

Gregory, Robert G. *India and East Africa: A History of Race Relations Within the British Empire 1890–1939*. Oxford: Clarendon Press, 1971.

Haji, M. M. "Nothing Extraordinary" and "When the Walls Came Tumbling Down." In *Origin East Africa: A Makerere Anthology*. Ed. David Cook. London: Heinemann, 1965.

Kassam, Sadru. "Bones." In *Short East African Plays in English*. Ed. David Cook and Miles Lee. London: Heinemann, 1968.

Nazareth, Peter. "Confession of an African Bureaucrat." *Afriscope* 9, no. 4 (1979): 31–33.

———. *The General Is Up*. Calcutta: Writers Workshop, 1984.

———. *In a Brown Mantle*. Nairobi: East African Literature Bureau, 1972.

———. "Interview" with Bernth Lindfors. In *Mazungumzo: Interviews with East African Writers, Publishers, Editors and Scholars*. Athens: Ohio University Center for International Studies, Africa Program, 1990.

———. "Interview" with Charles Irby. *Explorations in Ethnic Studies* 8, no. 1 (January 1985): 1–12.

Sarvan, Charles Ponnuthurai. "Ethnicity and Alienation: The African Asian and His Response to Africa." *Journal of Commonwealth Literature* 20, no. 4 (1985): 101–10.

Singh, Jagjit. "Death, etc. etc.," "No Roots, No Leaves, No Buds," "Portrait of an

Asian as an East African," and "Public Butchery." In *Poems from East Africa*. Ed. David Cook and David Rubaderi. London: Heinemann, 1971.

———. "Sweet Scum of Freedom." In *African Theatre: Eight Prize-Winning Plays for Radio*. Ed. Gwyneth Henderson. London: Heinemann, 1973.

Sondhi, Kuldip. "Undesignated." In *Short East African Plays in English*. Ed. David Cook and Miles Lee. London: Heinemann, 1968.

South Africa 1983. Official Yearbook of the Republic of South Africa. Johannesburg: Chris van Rensburg, 1983.

Syal, Parvin. "Defeat," "The Pot" and "When I Came Here." In *Poems from East Africa*. Ed. David Cook and David Rubaderi, London: Heinemann, 1971.

Tejani, Bahadur. *Day After Tomorrow*. Nairobi: East African Literature Bureau, 1971.

———. "In the Orthopaedic Ward," "On Top of Africa," and "Wild Horse of Serengeti." In *Poems from East Africa*. Ed. David Cook and David Rubadiri. London: Heinemann, 1971.

———. "Lines for a Hindi Poet." In *Poems of Black Africa*. Ed. Wole Soyinka. London: Heinemann, 1975.

12

Kamala Markandaya and the Indian Immigrant Experience in Britain

Hena Ahmad

a time

to recollect
every shadow, everything the earth was losing,

a time to think of everything the earth
and I had lost, of all

that I would lose,
of all that I was losing.

—Agha Shahid Ali, "Snow on the Desert"

Kamala Markandaya is a Third World, postcolonial writer, an Indian who since the 1950s has lived in Britain and written novels about India or about Indians in England. This chapter attempts to examine her diasporic sensibility and its artistic and political manifestations in her seventh novel, *The Nowhere Man* (1972), in which she astutely critiques an Indian immigrant's experience in Britain. I begin with an epigraph from an Indian poet that echoes feelings of loss in order to draw attention to the loss that subsumes expatriation in *The Nowhere Man*.

Kamala Markandaya belongs to the body of writers who, by choice or otherwise, have left their countries of origin and made their homes elsewhere. She thus takes her place alongside such writers as Salman Rushdie, V. S. Naipaul, Nirad C. Chaudhri, and Ved Mehta, to name a few, all of whom trace their origins to India. In a wider context, she comes under the umbrella of postcolonial

Third World literatures written in English, encompassing writing from the Indian subcontinent, Africa, and the Caribbean. As such, she belongs with writers like Chinua Achebe, Ngugi wa Thiong'o, Jamaica Kincaid, and Anita Desai, among others, all of whom share a common heritage, colonialism, which is closely linked to immigrants and questions of their identity, questions especially significant in their relevance to Third World literatures in English written in a Western context.

Though Markandaya is technically a postcolonial writer, there is a marked difference in her diasporic sensibility from that found in some of the more recent writers. The reasons for this difference are related to the relatively recent emergence of the politics of a postcolonial identity. That she is a generation removed from many postcolonial writers now making history, like Salman Rushdie or Hanif Kureishi, is therefore significant. Markandaya's fictional concerns are different from those of these writers, in terms of their postcolonial *consciousness*. The theme of Indian and British differences, for example, which runs through most of her fiction, is not central to these writers. Their concerns with questions of a postcolonial identity, on the other hand, do not find much emphasis in her novels. This is not to say, however, that the evolution of a postcolonial consciousness is not evident in her fiction. In fact, Markandaya's novels too have evolved, in that the almost total absence of a postcolonial consciousness in *Nectar in a Sieve* (1954) gives way somewhat to a questioning of the underlying assumptions of British colonialism in *The Nowhere Man*.

What these writers of the diaspora have in common is that they are products of a dual cultural background, native and Western, and thus are able to bring a wide and rich range of experiences to their literary output. A common impulse of theirs is to examine issues arising from their immigrant condition, as does Salman Rushdie, for example, who straddles two cultures and explores the emergence of a complex identity in *Midnight's Children*, or Hanif Kureishi, who in his film script *My Beautiful Laundrette* illustrates the cold reality of immigrant experience in England. Kamala Markandaya, of course, wrote her novel about the Indian immigrant in Britain long before *My Beautiful Laundrette* (1986), which depicts similar concerns.

The Nowhere Man presents an Indian immigrant's predicament in Britain over a period of fifty years and reveals the effects of expatriation on him. The novel brings together elements of alienation and loss and combines them with aspects reminiscent of Markandaya's life, her colonial past, her immigrant present. It creates a sense of nostalgic yearning for the past and, at the same time, a sense of finality in exile which allows no return to the old country or a past identity. However, the question of identity is the crux of the immigrant's dilemma, as Markandaya so cogently describes it in the novel. She shows how the immigrant starts by retaining his Indian identity, which he then submerges in an effort to belong to the new culture; he then loses his self-identity, the implication being that the immigrant, ultimately, does not belong anywhere. He is the nowhere man.

The Nowhere Man, a scathing attack on British colonialism and racial discrimination against immigrants, is the story of Srinivas, a member of a learned, landowning family who flees India to escape the perpetrations of the British colonial regime, hoping to make a career for himself, ironically, in Britain. Markandaya shows how both colonialism and discrimination are responsible for his turmoil as an immigrant in Britain. The novel opens in 1968, when Srinivas, nearing seventy, is diagnosed as having leprosy, but the present is put on hold and the novel takes the reader back into Srinivas's history of fifty years in England, interposed into which is a flashback of his youth in India.

Srinivas arrives in Britain toward the end of the First World War, and as the novel takes the reader through all the stages of his life—as husband, father, widower—Markandaya emphasizes his growing sense of alienation. Like Hugo Baumgartner in Anita Desai's *Baumgartner's Bombay*, who does not belong to India even after living there for fifty years, Srinivas too, after fifty years in Britain, does not finally belong. As he comes more and more to see himself as outsider, intruder, stranger, as his feelings of alienation intensify after he experiences racial attacks and he succumbs to the pressure of oppressive rejection by the social system, memories of home amid "waves of loss" return. Having lost his wife to tuberculosis, one son to the Second World War, and the other to the alien culture, he seeks refuge within the four walls of his attic, which contains his teak bed, his only link with the past. Srinivas, who passively accepts his meager life in Britain, a country he has come to regard as his home, is shattered when he realizes that he is not wanted in the country he considers his own, because, as he realizes, leaving implies that there is a place to go. He, however, has nowhere to go. As he says to himself, he is "a nowhere man," a man searching for a "nowhere city" (174).

Markandaya starts by establishing Srinivas's Indianness, a factor fundamental to his immigrant experience, that which sets him apart from the natives, serves to alienate him from his neighbors, and precludes his acceptance by them. In depicting Srinivas as a small man with a brown face, serene eyes, and a thin voice, one who speaks with a precise enunciation, wears layers of ill-fitting, old-fashioned clothes, and manages to disconcert the doctor with his poise, Markandaya unequivocally establishes his difference from the Anglo-Saxon natives. His *tropical* disease, leprosy, ominous in the light of later events and symbolic as a culmination to fifty years in Britain, emphasizes—rather, exaggerates—his alienation.

Srinivas's life is presented in a series of relationships with other characters who not only serve as foils to his character but also reveal an aspect of, or are a comment on, British or Indian social culture, thus underscoring cultural polarities. As such, Markandaya juxtaposes Srinivas with various characters: Vasantha, his wife, who refuses to compromise her Indian identity, wearing nine yards of sari and sandals "irredeemably Indian" to the day of her death; Laxman, his son, who wants his Indian parents to merge invisibly into British culture so that they will not stick out like sore thumbs; Abdul, his ambitious and successful friend, who fails to persuade Srinivas that the only way to survive as an immigrant in Britain is with power and money; his friend, Mrs. Pickering, the brisk, practical islander who sees Srinivas as a dreamy man from whom she would get no help, "who like the rest of his people gave up the ghost" when practical things needed to be done (225).

Other characters in the novel, in betraying their prejudices against Srinivas, serve primarily to show the cultural wall that he is up against and the racist sentiment that confronts him: Dr. Radcliffe, who is humane but whose wife's extreme racial prejudice prevents him from helping Srinivas; Marjorie, the status-conscious wife of the doctor, who needs to disinfect her hall with a spray after her husband sees Srinivas in his surgery; Fred Fletcher, his bigoted neighbor, who, as an unemployed, unskilled worker, has determined that the blacks are responsible for all his and Britain's ills; the God-fearing Mrs. Fletcher, who believes that Srinivas has rights as a neighbor, but is prevented by her prejudice from stepping inside Srinivas's door; Mrs. Glass, Srinivas's neighbor of thirty years, who feels a fascinated repulsion for people from other countries.

Though there are times when Srinivas feels he is being accepted by his neighbors, the novel implies otherwise. For example, the Christmas tree in his home brings him a few smiles and compliments from his neighbors: "Almost one of us, the neighbors said privately, and stopped Mr. Srinivas in the street to tell him how pretty the tree looked" (68), which prompts him to think that he is being accepted by them, forgetting that in all those years not one neighbor had entered his house. The narrator tells the reader that Mr. Srinivas was "almost one of the English," as the English themselves were inclined to say in their more generous moods, "bestowing the best accolade they could think of" (76), and he was increasingly inclined to take them at their word. The implicit cynicism in the narrative voice is unmistakable. In another passage, Markandaya again underscores this situation, thus reinforcing the provincial prejudice of the neighbors. That his family was becoming accepted because the neighbors, finally, could refer to them as the "Srinivases" is negated by the implication that a mere acknowledgment of presence neither implies acceptance nor precludes prejudice.

Though Srinivas's sense of alienation intensifies after he becomes the subject of a racial attack, Markandaya shows that Srinivas is, throughout, highly aware of the inequality between himself and the Anglo-Saxon natives. For example, when Srinivas, like his neighbors, is saddened to see building construction over a patch of land which, with its "ferns and vines, buttercup and bindweed," was a source of pleasure to him, as to his neighbors, he is unable to complain or express his regret like them, "for although he was so nearly one of them he could not quite command the liberties and licences of the English" (89). Or when he listens to them indicting Asia and Africa, he does not comment, because he is restricted by his "dual affiliation." It makes him aware of incongruity "as the islanders were not, and the merging in him of them and us" demanded "an honorable consistency," which led to his keeping silent (90).

Markandaya thus invests Srinivas with conflicting loyalties which create doubts in his mind about where he belongs and make him unsure of his identity. For though he loves Britain, the country of his adoption, he cannot condone or forget its imperialist ways, much as he tries. For instance, Britain's role in the Suez crisis makes Srinivas think of it as a country which had "reverted to peremptory imperial ways," the ways that not only had formed his life, but also laid the foundation for his own anguish in the past (98). But immediately he questions his own honor in thinking disloyally of a country that had sheltered him and become finally his own (177). However, much as his conscience persuades him to be loyal to Britain, his "blood" aligns him on the side of the ones being attacked, "in automatic reaction" against those countries that had "carved up continents, calling the slices their colonies" (99).

Markandaya reinforces the immigrant's sense of alienation not only by underscoring political differences but also by setting up contrasts between first- and second-generation immigrants. Srinivas's sons reflect the second-generation immigrant ethos, as they, born and bred there, consider the alien country their own. Markandaya portrays the distance that develops between the anglicized sons and their parents. Laxman, who is referred to as "a pale brown Englishman with a pale pink wife" (34) who sees his father as a man of principles that are "sound but monumentally useless" (37–38), and who could not but look somewhat scornfully at his prim, provincial parents—"his mother with her bun, and her clothes like the robes Jesus Christ wore, only worse . . . and her English which was not the country's or his own" (35)—is the second-generation immigrant who, in his desperate effort to belong to the white social class, completely denies his Indian connection and conforms to the social values he sees around him.

Markandaya reinforces Srinivas's loss as he is forced to acknowledge his son's total alienation from him. Laxman, unlike his father, is hardened and tough, someone who has learned to fight for survival. Laxman wants his parents to assimilate British culture because he thinks that the only way to belong and be accepted is by conforming to the social ways of their adopted country. (The irony, of course, is that even thought his voice, syllables, accent, syntax, clothes, manners, style, are British, his color prevents him from being accepted.) The alien culture widens the chasm between Srinivas and his son, whose filial insensitivity reminds Srinivas of the cultural contrast as he remembers his own respectful attitude toward his father in India and accepts that, in England, speech of various kinds was used when sons spoke to their fathers.

Underlying all the events in the novel is a pervasive sense of loss. The oppressive rejection by the system, to which Srinivas finally succumbs, despite Mrs. Pickering's kindness and support, dehumanizes him. A profound sense of Srinivas's rootless existence and homelessness permeates *The Nowhere Man* as he, having lived in Britain for fifty years and come to accept it as his home and seen his sons fight as British soldiers in the Second World War, is finally told that he should go back to where he came from. What kills him in the end is not so much the shock of the fire set to his home by his white neighbor but, rather, the knowledge that he does not belong to the country that he has considered his own for fifty years.

Srinivas, told to go back to India, faces a dilemma common to many immigrants, a dilemma portrayed by other writers of the Indian diaspora as well. For example, Anita Desai's characters confront similar predicaments in *Bye-Bye, Blackbird*. And the tension between Srinivas and his neighbors is reminiscent of the tensions shown between the Pakistani immigrants and the white gangs in Hanif Kureishi's *My Beautiful Laundrette* and *The Rainbow Sign*. The kind of extreme racist violence Srinivas is subjected to is described in *The Rainbow Sign*, a succinct account of British racism of the sixties, in which Hanif Kureishi analyzes the atmosphere of fear and hatred, the kind Srinivas encounters: he is tarred and feathered by Fred Fletcher and his gang, a lynching he miraculously survives, as he does the fire, technically speaking, which Fletcher sets to his house, though he dies of shock after he is rescued from the fire. What he is not strong enough to withstand and what kills him, metaphorically speaking, is the cold, contemptuous hostility he encounters in almost everyone. For when his white neighbor, a reputed "blacks basher," brutally attacks him, Srinivas looks for reasons but finds none that would explain to him why Englishmen would like him to leave their country, though all along somewhere in "his mind had lain subliminal perception," which he had not permitted to challenge his consciousness (175). It seems as if all the questions and doubts that had lain in his subconscious for all those years—questions of alienation, home, identity, loss—emerge to haunt him and his dreams and acquire oppressive proportions with which he is not hardened enough to cope.

Srinivas's oppressive discrimination in Britain brings memories of his past oppression in India at he hands of the British colonialists. His past in colonial India, presented as a flashback and strategically centered in the novel, becomes an effective point of reference for Markandaya to make connections between Srinivas's colonial past in India and his immigrant present in Britain. As the novel moves back and forth between the present and the past, Markandaya not only makes political connections but also provides a contrast between Indian and British ways of life, thus reinforcing cultural difference as a key factor in the immigrant's sense of alienation.

Srinivas spends the first twenty years of his life in India, in a traditional extended family, under the patriarchal rule of his grandfather, marked by harmony and security, warmth and peace. This peace is shattered by the colonial authorities, who hound and persecute and jail members of his family, including him, for subversive political activity. These events persuade his family to make arrangements to send him to Britain. Just before embarking on the sea voyage, he is married to Vasantha, his childhood playmate, who follows him later.

Markandaya, also, seems to go down memory lane in this novel, rediscovering, as it were, her Indian roots through Srinivas, who remembers "sunny childhood days, in a boat, on a lake," over which, in the long years of exile, "mists had risen" (304). Pervading the whole novel, thus, is a sense of nostalgia for the past and for India as she remembers it. The description of the colonial past in India serves to recreate Srinivas's Indian home, establishing his identity in the solidity of his past, which is reinforced by images of the teakwood house, the stability of the family, and the inherent security that it provided, and highlights the poverty of his life in Britain which, by comparison, is denuded of family warmth and bereft of social interaction in any substantial sense.

Srinivas's efforts to block out the past, in order to absorb the new culture, do not succeed. For example, the uncarpeted staircase to Srinivas's attic with its "planed timber under his bare soles" gives Srinivas a pleasure which, we are told, "seldom failed to surface," even though he had once tried very hard to subdue this pleasure. It was a pleasure which "went back to an old wooden dwelling, in a country left behind" (16). Srinivas, in his efforts to assimilate British culture, cannot relinquish the past. This is brought out most acutely in the comparisons made between Srinivas's house in India and the one in Britain. Srinivas's nostalgia for his home in the past, with its teak structures, is evinced in numerous references to oak and teak and in the fact that getting used to the oak timbers of the new house is not easy for him.

Markandaya, in bringing out Srinivas's past associations, recreates their pleasure for him in myriad nostalgic memories. Even though memory cannot retrieve the actual past but only its supplement, Markandaya shows that it can create, in a sense, its own reality for Srinivas. Markandaya's constant references to Srinivas's link with the past, symbolized by his teak bed, which accompanied him on his voyage from India, reveal his need to hold on to the past as a means of reaffirming, as it were, his sense of self.

That Srinivas, despite his efforts to assimilate or to hold on to the past, belongs nowhere is underscored when he wants to celebrate a festival and can think of neither an English occasion nor an Indian one. As he tells Mrs. Pickering, one does not realize "when one leaves one's country, how much is chopped off and left behind too" (70). Trying to remember Indian festivals to celebrate, Srinivas finds blankness: "Festival lights had dimmed, and even the seasons in which they had been lit—let alone dates—had receded from memory" (70).

As Srinivas, rejected by Britain, realizes that he will always remain an outsider, he is drawn toward India, "feeling the tug of another country, which the years had rendered tenuous, to which he was nevertheless being slowly ferried" (241). But all that is left of India is his teak bed and the tin trunk in which are packed "useless things which even the dustmen would not take, sealed jars of coconut oil" (241). From this "dented but indestructible box, which smelled of metal and ancient vegetable fat that greased its hinges," he extracts the "thin white mull dhoti with the quarter-inch gold border" (241) and wears it. Srinivas's act of wearing the dhoti symbolizes his identity with India. But what does his Indian identity mean at this point? It has been whittled down to the diaphanous dhoti and the useless things that even the dustmen would not take, a silent testimony to his immigrant experience.

The Nowhere Man, in terms of Markandaya's response to her immigrant situation, reveals that the sense of loss experienced by an expatriate, a consequence of a combination of factors including uprootedness and alienation, is fundamentally a sense of lost identity. Though Srinivas is caught in a dilemma with his conflicting loyalties to the two countries, he ultimately has not much of an identity left; in contrast, characters in recent expatriate fiction emerge with complex identities, rather than as nowhere men.

WORKS CITED

Ali, Agha Shahid. *A Nostalgist's Map of America*. New York: Norton, 1991.

Desai, Anita. *Baumgartner's Bombay*. New York: Knopf, 1988.

———. *Bye-Bye, Blackbird*. Delhi: Hind Pocket Books, 1971.

Kureishi, Hanif. *My Beautiful Laundrette and The Rainbow Sign*. London: Faber and Faber, 1986.

Markandaya, Kamala. *Nectar in a Sieve*. New York: New American Library, 1954.

———. *The Nowhere Man*. New York: John Day, 1972.

Rushdie, Salman. *Midnight's Children*. New York: Avon Books, 1980.

13

Rushdie's Fiction: The World Beyond the Looking Glass

Vijay Lakshmi

It is the world of changelings, of djinns, of women turning into beasts and men changing into horned and hoofed creatures. It is a world that, as Camus would say, cannot be explained even by bad reason. Ironically, it is also the world that its creator, Salman Rushdie, has found himself thrown into—"the world beyond the looking glass, where nonsense is the only sense" (Rushdie, "Pen Against the Sword," 57). To step into this world, where the boundaries of accepted morality, reality, or reason have become blurred, where the best human efforts seem but imperfect constructs, and where there is no leap of faith, is to step into the universe of the absurd. This chapter attempts to understand the nature of Rushdie's world and to inquire if his worldview could be an offshoot of the immigrant's psyche.

Incongruous and illogical, grotesque and devoid of any "totalized explanation," this universe undoubtedly is. All the same, it constitutes the starting point for Rushdie's fiction. "The elevation of the quest for the Grail over the Grail itself," as Rushdie points out in his Herbert Reade Memorial Lecture, "the acceptance that all that is solid has melted into air, that reality and morality are not givens but imperfect human constructs, is the point from which fiction begins" ("Is Nothing Sacred?," 9).

Not a special event or an exclusive condition of human life, the absurd exists in the banal and the mundane. It can strike any man in the face, as Camus says, at any street corner.

A man is talking on the telephone behind a glass partition; you cannot hear him, but you see his incomprehensible dumb show; you wonder why he is alive. This discomfort in the face of man's inhumanity, this incalculable tumble before the image of what we are, this "nausea," as a writer of today calls it, is also the absurd. (*The Myth of Sisyphus*, 15)

To confront our own strangeness in the mirror is to realize the denseness and strangeness of the world where our gestures become meaningless, silly pantomimes. With Rushdie's characters, we descend into the irrational depths of human personality, whose dreams and nightmares projected into the daylight make no logical sense. The Cultmaster of Chupland (the land of silence and darkness) in *Haroun and the Sea of Stories* is a good example of this dark self. Obsessed with the idea of controlling the world, he is poisoning the Ocean of Stories and is having a plug assembled to stem the very source from which stories spring. Inside every story, as he explains to Haroun, and "inside every Stream in the Ocean, there lies a world that I cannot rule. And that is the reason why" (161). Ahmed Sinai, in *Midnight's Children*, dreams of dictating to secretaries in the nude, while trying curses and sorcery to kill dogs. Sufiya, in *Shame*, has things locked up in her head. "There is an ocean. She feels the tide. And, somewhere in its depths, a Beast, stirring" (237). And Farishta, in *The Satanic Verses*, wrestles with the voices he hears and the visions he sees. But beyond personality, we are confronted by another plane of absurdity, which Martin Esslin describes as "the absurdity of the human condition itself in a world where the decline of religious belief has deprived man of certainties. When it is no longer possible to accept closed systems of values and revelations of divine purpose, life must be faced in its ultimate, stark reality" (352). Rushdie's fiction interweaves the subjective absurdity with the objective; the personal, which is unique to an individual, with the universal, which is part of the human condition.

Familiar though it is in the way it is structured, the Rushdian world becomes incomprehensible in the way it operates. It keeps shifting between the objective and subjective realities. On the surface, the author seems to be satirizing the social and political systems and parodying human behavior. In doing so, he spares neither any institution nor any set of beliefs. At a deeper fictional level, however, he uses the parody to confront the reader with the absurdity of human existence itself—of an existence devoid of faith in God and in religion. Gibreel Farishta is the modern man who has lost faith in God and religion. During his illness, he hopes for a miracle cure; so he prays, then he gets angry, and finally a feeling of emptiness overtakes him as he senses the absence of God. It dawns upon him that he was talking to thin air and that there was nobody there at all, "and then he felt more foolish than ever in his life, and he began to plead into the emptiness, ya Allah, just be there, damn it, just be. But he felt nothing, nothing nothing, and then one day he found that he no longer needed there to be anything to feel" (*The Satanic Verses*, 30). No longer held together by any system of values or beliefs, Farishta descends into a schizophrenic world where, released from the bondage of time and space, he drifts into the city of Jahilia and dreams of himself as the archangel Gibreel. Totally disoriented, he talks to the dead and sleeps with ghosts and is caught between two realities, "this world and another that was also right there, visible but unseen. He felt slow, heavy, distanced from his own consciousness, and realized that he had not the faintest idea which path he would choose, which world he would enter" (351).

Such is Rushdie's world of the absurd, "the devil's version of the world," as he calls it. *The Satanic Verses*, he has pointed out, attempts "to portray a soul in crisis, to show how the loss of God can destroy man's life" ("Pen Against the Sword," 54). Once cut off from his religious, metaphysical, and transcendental roots, man, as Ionesco points out, is lost, and "all his struggles become senseless, futile and oppressive" (216).

Rushdie's other two novels, similarly, traverse both the personal and the universal worlds of absurdity. *Midnight's Children* spans the history of modern India through the lives of the children born at midnight on August 15, 1947, when the country got its freedom from Britain. The narrator, Saleem Sinai, is a parody of the nation he symbolizes and, like the nation he perceives, he is beginning "to crack all over like an old jug" (37). Into this framework are woven characters and events of all dimensions, colors, and significance. *Midnight's Children* is the story of one Dr. Aziz, who resolves never to pray after, in the act of praying, he hits his nose on a frost-hardened tussock of earth. It is the story of Saleem's parents, who are not his parents. It is the story of the people living in the Methwold Estate—another miniature India—of the widows' hostel in Benares, of Parvati-the-witch, of the socialist Picture Singh, and of the bulldozed ghettos. Events in this world happen without human control or reason. When the poet Hummingbird is assassinated, "six thousand four hundred and twenty curs" appear from nowhere and attack the killers. Ahmed Sinai descends into the world of djinns, of private nightmares, and keeps urging a caged budgerigar, "Sing, little bulbul! sing!" while his wife carries on a furtive affair with her ex-husband. It is the story of the modern man, of the midnight's children who have the privilege and the curse "to be both masters and victims of their times, to forsake privacy and to be sucked into the annihilating whirlpool of the multitudes, and to be unable to live or die in peace" (*Midnight's Children*, 552).

In *Shame*, the world becomes even more bizarre. "The country in this story is not Pakistan, or not quite," the narrator tells us.

There are two countries, real and fictional, occupying the same space, or almost the same space. My story, my fictional country exist, like myself, at a slight angle to reality. I have found this off-centring to be necessary; but its value is, of course, open to debate. My view is that I am not writing only about Pakistan. (23–24)

Whatever the country, the characters and events are even more grotesque and incongruous than those in *Midnight's Children*. Omar Khayyam, the protagonist, is a bastard child, mothered by the three Shakil sisters, who have shut themselves off from the world, both literally and metaphorically. For twelve years Omar

Khayyam's only contact with the outside world is maintained through a telescope trained at it. Even when he escapes from "Nishapur," the outside world never seems to touch him. He remains on the periphery of Raza Hyder's, Harappa's, and even his three mothers' lives. The novel deals with the lives of men and women in power, and each episode, each event, becomes more nonsensical than the last. Bariamma, the matriarch, for instance, sleeps guard over the forty young women of her family in one room. But every night their husbands steal into the room and after "the darkness acquires a rhythm, which accelerates, peaks, subsides," they leave. Begum Naveed has so many children that she has lost count of them, while her insatiable husband expands his dream of children who would fill up the place in his life previously occupied by polo, "and owing to his clairvoyant talents, he always knew which nights were best for conception" (228). Sufiya, the deranged wife of Omar Khayyam, turns into a beast that rips people into shreds and stalks the streets at night in search of prey. The three Shakil sisters make the naked General Raza Hyder carry his wife's putrefying corpse into the dumbwaiter, where eighteen-inch stiletto blades cut him to pieces.

Grim as the world is and its future without hope, the narrator does not take on a tragic voice. Like Harold Pinter, who thinks "the greatest earnestness is funny; even tragedy is funny," Rushdie seems to be inspired by the basic absurdity of the situations and finds life funny up to a point. The more grotesque, horrifying, and irrational man's actions become, the more absurd and comic he himself becomes. Rising above the level of drawing room comedies, Rushdie pushes everything to the limit where the boundaries between the comic and the tragic disappear, creating, in the bargain, a violently comic fiction where compassion and human dignity fade out as virtuous notions. Nor can death, in such a universe, be a solemn affair. This is how the watchman in *The Satanic Verses* describes Rekha's suicide after she has pushed her three children from the roof of the high-rise home. He had been walking by when the body of the eldest daughter fell.

Her skull was completely crushed. I looked up and saw the boy falling, and after him the younger girl. What to say, they almost hit me where I stood. I put my hand on my mouth and came to them. Then I looked up a further time and the begum was coming. Her sari was floating out like a big balloon and all her hair was loose. I took my eyes away from her because she was falling and it was not respectful to look up inside her clothes. (15)

Characters in such a world can only be seen as a parody of heroic figures. Not theirs the stature of a Lear or an Oedipus. The more banal and the more commonplace they get, the better they fit into the world they inherit. If need be, Rushdie is glad to distort his characters to make them look grotesque. Saleem Sinai, in *Midnight's Children*, has "a wondrously enlarged nose, a completely non-existent chin and giant stains on each temple." He is greeted with alarm wherever he goes. He is known as Snotnose, Baldie, Snuffie. Not his parents'

child, his hair pulled off by a teacher, a finger broken by a boy, an ear damaged
by twisting, memory lost after a nightmarish journey through the Sunderbans,
and the vasectomy "draining below," he is a hero whom we know very well
but never can fully identify ourselves with. Similarly, Omar Khayyam in *Shame*
is described as "dizzy, peripheral, inverted, infatuated, insomniac, stargazing,
fat," and the narrator wonders, "What manner of hero is this?" (19). Omar
Khayyam calls himself a peripheral man. "You see before you," he confides
to Iskander Harrappa, "a fellow who is not even the hero of his own life; a man
born and raised in the condition of being out of things" (18). In a discordant
and disintegrating world, all pretensions of heroism are futile. Chamcha, in *The
Satanic Verses*, has a glimpse of this reality when Gibreel stands before him
with a gun.

The true djinns of old had the power to open the gates of the Infinite, to make all things
possible, to render all wonders capable of being attained; how banal, in comparison, was
this modern spook, this degraded descendent of mighty ancestors, this feeble slave of a
twentieth-century lamp. (546)

To live in the world of the absurd is to remain unsurprised by any occurrence.
For after a point, the boundaries between the real and the unreal, the true and
the false, disintegrate. Fabulation, then, becomes a medium for the writer to
cross the conventional frontiers. Rushdie uses the fable to make the implausible
plausible. The fairy tale beginnings, for instance, at once create a willing suspension of disbelief for the reader. "I was born in the city of Bombay . . . once
upon a time. . . . On the stroke of midnight," says the narrator in *Midnight's
Children*. And then, "Once upon a time, in the far northern princedom of Kif,
there lived a prince who had two beautiful daughters, a son of equally remarkable
good looks, a brand-new Rolls-Royce motor car and excellent political contacts"
(382). And *Shame* begins like this: "In the remote border town of Q., which
when seen from the air resembles nothing so much as an ill-proportioned dumb-
bell, there once lived three lovely, and loving, sisters." The use of the fable
gives him a tool for "off-centering" reality, so that the reader will not go hunting
for the missing pieces that could make a puzzle whole. Time and again the
narrator in *Shame* reminds us of the make-believe character of this book.

If this were a realistic novel about Pakistan, I would not be writing about Bilquis and
the wind; I would be talking about my younger sister. Who is twenty-two and studying
engineering in Karachi. . . . I think what I am confessing is that, however I choose to
write about over-there, I am forced to reflect that world in fragments of broken mirrors.
(70–71)

Rushdie's "overt use of fabulation," as he admits, is a device, not "to falsify
history but to allow fiction to take off from history" ("Pen Against the Sword,"
56). The use of the fable is a way of creating a distance from actuality. But at

the same time it is not escaping from reality. "It's a way of defining and dreaming the world," as he said in an interview on London Weekend Television, "... a way of stripping away the veil of custom through which we normally look at the world which makes us think that it's somehow normal. But actually the world is a very abnormal place" (Suri, 26). To Rushdie, "a bastard child of history," as he calls himself, the nonsensical framework gives him a freedom from the "straightjacket of logic," so that he can stretch the world that has lost its unifying principle, its meaning, and its purpose to its ultimate in nonsense. Like the immigrant narrator in *Shame*, he too is a fantasist, who builds imaginary countries and tries to impose them on the ones that exist. "I, too," the narrator says, "face the problem of history; what to retain and what to dump, how to hold on to what memory insists on relinquishing, how to deal with change" (92).

If the absurd offers us a way of looking at and understanding a world gone awry, then an immigrant writer—one who is displaced, dislocated, and torn between forgetting and remembering—offers a more apt inquiry into the predicament of the modern man. Characters in Rushdie's fiction, largely people like himself, reinvent themselves in a new city. But there still remain, as Rushdie points out, "old selves, old traditions erased in part but not fully. So what you get are these fragmented, multifaceted, multicultural selves" (Marzorati, 44). The migrant, after a while, does not remain a person who has moved from India or Pakistan to England; he is man in general, who has no permanence, no stability, no sense of belonging anywhere. *The Satanic Verses*, for instance, is set in London, where the two middle-aged actors arrive after they survive a plane crash and meet more migrants like themselves. The migrant, in fact, becomes a metaphor for the modern man who eternally drifts between two worlds. "When you have stepped through the looking glass," Chamcha reflects, "you step back at your peril. The mirror may cut you to shreds" (58). Chamcha is ill at ease in Bombay; in London, he is an outsider. His transformation into a goaty, horned, and hoofy demon in the sanitarium is not to be taken as a physical transformation but as a psychological trauma. Gibreel is but another wandering soul, lost in the abracadabra of the absurd world. "He floated over the parkland and cried out, frightening the birds.—No more of these England-induced ambiguities, these Biblical-Satanic confusions!—Clarity, Clarity, at all costs, clarity!" (353). But clarity is not even a byproduct of the absurdist world. For modern man, as for the immigrants, psychological mutilation seems to be an inevitability, the world being what it is—a planet sans faith, sans charity, sans grace.

WORKS CITED

Camus, Albert. *The Myth of Sisyphus and Other Essays*. Trans. Justin O'Brien. New York: Alfred A. Knopf, 1964.

Esslin, Martin. *The Theatre of the Absurd*. New York: Anchor Books, 1969.

Ionesco, Eugene. *Notes and Counter Notes: Writings on the Theatre*. Trans. Donald Watson. New York: Grove Press, 1964.

Marzorati, Gerald. "Salman Rushdie: Fiction's Embattled Infidel." *New York Times Magazine*, January 29, 1989, 24–100.

Pinter, Harold. Interview with Hallam Tennyson. B.B.C. General Overseas Service, August 7, 1960.

Rushdie, Salman. *Haroun and the Sea of Stories*. New York: Viking, 1990.

———. "Is Nothing Sacred?" The Herbert Reade Memorial Lecture. *Granta*, February 6, 1990, 2–16.

———. *Midnight's Children*. New York: Avon Books, 1980.

———. "A Pen Against the Sword: In Good Faith." *Newsweek*, February 12, 1990, 52–57.

———. *The Satanic Verses*. New York: Viking, 1988.

———. *Shame*. New York: Vintage International, 1983.

Suri, Sanjay. "Rushdie Appears on British TV." *India Abroad*, October 5, 1990, 26.

14

Author(iz)ing *Midnight's Children* and *Shame*: Salman Rushdie's Constructions of Authority

Anuradha Dingwaney

My principal methodological devices for studying authority here are what can be called *strategic location*, which is a way of describing the author's position in a text with regard to the . . . material he writes about. . . . this location includes the kind of narrative voice he adopts, the type of structure he builds, the kinds of images, themes, motifs that circulate in his text— all of which add up to deliberate ways of addressing the reader, containing [the material], and, finally, representing it or speaking in its behalf.
                                           —Edward W. Said, *Orientalism*, 20

It is a matter of significance that Salman Rushdie's two novels about the subcontinent, *Midnight's Children* (1980) and *Shame* (1984) were greeted with excitement and considerable critical acclaim both in the West and in the subcontinent. In his review of *Midnight's Children*, Clark Blaise declared, somewhat hyperbolically, "*Midnight's Children* sounds like a continent finding its voice" (19); Anita Desai called it "a great *tour de force*, a dazzling exhibition of the gifts of a new writer of courage, impressive strength . . . and sheer stylistic brilliance" (13); Tariq Ali noted that while "Rushdie's novel will not reach the South Asian masses . . . it will be read by an English speaking intelligensia [in the subcontinent] . . . and, in that sense, it is extremely important. . . . No other novel about India has had such an impact" (91).[1] Similarly, Michael Hollington found *Shame* "a noteworthy further step in the development of a prodigious talent" (403); and Inderpal Grewal, while observing that "even in Pakistan where [Rushdie's] work could be considered subversive," notes that "the pop-

ularity of [*Shame*] . . . further indicates that Rushdie's voice is not easily ignored''
(29).

However, it is equally a matter of significance that both novels, which are
large, sweeping histories of two nations from their birth, and, moreover, bitter
exposés of what these nations have become,[2] are written by a man located outside
the subcontinent, in London. This matter, of course, has been evaluated differently by readers in the subcontinent and in the West: whereas Rushdie's location,
and, thus, his critiques have proved problematic for some readers in the subcontinent, they have not troubled his Western readers much. Nevertheless, it
remains true that although for readers from the subcontinent ''Rushdie writing
from the outside . . . has been able to recreate his subject only partially . . . [so
that] many rich aspects of the sub-continent's culture and politics are absent''
(Ali, 94),[3] his accounts of these nations' birth and development are still recognized as forceful and persuasive enough to make them difficult to ignore or
dismiss.

We might well ask, then, what are the reasons for Rushdie's success in
persuading his readers (from the West and from the subcontinent) of the ''force''
or ''truth'' or even ''legitimacy'' of his accounts? An attempt to answer this
question is intimately tied to what is at stake for Rushdie and for his diverse
readers, namely, who has the power to represent what and whom to whom?
And, I would imagine, much is at stake in this regard for writers of the Indian
diaspora, who often make what they have left behind, what they are no longer
ostensible participants in, the subject matter of their works. By focusing on
certain strategic details and passages in *Midnight's Children*, *Shame*, and interviews and commentaries by Rushdie that surround the publication of these two
novels, I will examine the ways in which Rushdie constructs his authority. I
will also simultaneously reflect upon the implications of Rushdie's constructions
of authority.

Among the ''methodological devices'' Edward Said isolates ''for studying
authority'' (see the epigraph to this chapter), he mentions what he calls ''*strategic
location*,'' which includes the narrative voice, structure, images, themes, and
motifs a writer deploys ''in representing or speaking in [his material's] behalf''
(20). To this inventory I would add as well an examination of a writer's geographical location, which then interacts with his location/perspective in regard
to his material.

In *Midnight's Children*, the hero-narrator, Saleem Sinai, is placed inside or
within the history of the nation whose history he narrates; is, in fact, seen as
both cause and product of that history. Born at the moment India achieved formal
independence from the British, he is, he says, a child ''*of the time*: fathered,
you understand, by history'' (139); the logic of Rushdie's narrative depends on
a neat fit between Saleem's life and the life of the nation: ''Your life,'' predicts
Jawaharlal Nehru's letter to ''Baby Saleem,'' ''will be, in a sense, a mirror of
our own'' (143). Saleem's narrative not only records ''familiar'' events in the
pre- and post-independence history of the subcontinent, but also is centrally

connected to, in fact, crucially dependent on, an acute insider's familiarity with
that most ubiquitous icon of the subcontinent's popular culture—Bombay cinema—all of which bespeak his insider's knowledge of the subcontinent. Since
readers are likely to see Saleem's knowledge as that possessed by his creator,
Salman Rushdie, Saleem's *inwardness* with regard to his nation's history and
culture accrues to Rushdie as well. In fact, in the marketing of *Midnight's
Children* and in reviews, readers have assumed that *Midnight's Children* is
autobiographical, that Saleem's life corresponds not just with that of his nation,
but also with that of his creator. Rushdie's own comments indicate that he is
not averse to his readers' assuming this correspondence: "The assumption of
autobiography," says Rushdie,

was partly a game that I played. Saleem and Salman are after all, if you look back
etymologically, kind of versions of the same name . . . so there are clear affinities made
in his name with my name, he's the same age as me more or less, . . . he grows up in
my house, he goes to my school, some of the things that happened to me happen in a
more interesting form to him, so it's not surprising that people should assume that an
autobiography is intended. (Rushdie, "*Midnight's Children* and *Shame*," 12–13)

Of course, "the assumption of autobiography" is not just " a game" Rushdie
plays. Clearly, one can see how the conflation of Saleem's identity with his own
helps him to establish his authority for writing *Midnight's Children*: if readers
find Saleem's narrative credible, then that credibility is extended to Rushdie as
well. The significance of this move cannot be emphasized enough for an expatriate writer, physically located in England, writing about the post-independence life of India, in which he has participated only partially. Yet, a great deal
of his authority to represent India to Indians (and, perhaps, to some readers in
the West) depends precisely on his presenting himself as more fully a participant,
that is, part of, indeed, inside the fray. This the conflation with Saleem allows
Rushdie to achieve.
    Though this conflation is useful, Rushdie also distances himself from it to
overcome one of the charges critics could level at him: Rushdie is an *outsider*,
an expatriate writer, even though he wants his readers to see him as an insider.
    Interestingly, in his comments after *Midnight's Children* was published, Rush-
die was quite explicit about his being, in a sense, an "outsider," though he
presents this differently to readers in the West than he does to his subcontinental
readers. To Victoria Glendenning, writing for the *Sunday Times* (published in
Britain), it is clear that "he will not go back to live in India now. 'You can't
go back' [Rushdie says]. There are displacement difficulties: he is not writing
in his mother-tongue—Urdu—for his own people"; and he arrogates an "international" literary ancestry by observing, "If you are an extra-territorial writer
you select a pedigree for yourself, a literary family"; his is composed of Cer-
vantes, Sterne, Gogol, Grass, Melville, and García Márquez (38). To Rani
Dharkar, who interviewed him for *New Quest* (published in India), he makes
his own location in England, and, thus, his dislocation from the subcontinent,
part and parcel of his many dislocations within the subcontinent itself:

I mean there're all kinds of dislocations. . . . First of all as you say, I live in England and I've written about India. That's one dislocation. Secondly, my family went to Pakistan so that's three countries anyway. . . . Then Bombay is not like the rest of India. People who come from Bombay anyway feel different from the rest of India and quite rightly. On top of that, my family comes from Kashmir and Kashmir is not like the rest of India. So that's four or five separate dislocations. (Dharkar interview, 353)

The net effect of Rushdie's comments is to render the notion of "representativeness" and/or "authenticity" problematic, if not altogether meaningless. Being located in Britain while writing about India is not a handicap when location within India itself—people from Bombay and Kashmir may not be the exception but the rule—does not guarantee the ability or right to speak for all of India at any juncture.

Furthermore, vying with Saleem's (and through him Rushdie's) drive for a *representative* status via his totalizing representation of his own "destinies" as "indissolubly chained to those of [India]" (*Midnight's Children*, 3), is Saleem's (and Rushdie's) equal insistence on the partiality (i.e., as in parts or made up of parts and as imbued with subjective biases) of his vision and representations of India. For instance, it is no exaggeration to say that *Midnight's Children* is haunted by fragments and their corollary, fragmentary vision. Consider, for example, the episode of "the perforated sheet," which allows Aadam Aziz to put together a "picture" of his wife-to-be Naseem (" a badly-fitting collage of her severally-inspected parts. This phantasm of a partitioned woman began to haunt him . . . glued together by his imagination" [23]). Amina Sinai, Aadam and Naseem's daughter, repeats the logic of the "perforated sheet" when she "train[s] herself to love" her husband by dividing him "mentally, into every single one of his component parts" (75). Consider, too, Saleem's literal disintegration into "(approximately 630 million [the population of India when *Midnight's Children* was written?] particles" (37).

There are other significant ways in which Saleem presents the partiality of his perspectives as well:: "There are as many versions of India as Indians" (323); or when he implicates his "version" of India with his own needs—to find meaning, for self-aggrandizement:

Re-reading my work, I have discovered an error in chronology. The assassination of Mahatma Gandhi occurs in these pages, on the wrong date . . . in my India, Gandhi will continue to die at the wrong time.

Does one error invalidate the entire fabric? Am I so foregone, in my desperate need for meaning, that I'm prepared to distort everything—to re-write the whole history of my times purely to place myself in a central role? (198)

Note how well Saleem's admission of his fallibility—a mark of his humanness—works: it shores up the credibility of his account(s) by making it (them) contingent. This move is likely to "please" readers from the West and the subcontinent, though for different reasons: the former can view this move (and other such moves) as an instance of a self-conscious individual subject (of Western modernism) reflecting not only on the "content" of his narrative, with all its gaps and uncertainties, but also on his techniques and on the business of being a novel (about India), which are, here and elsewhere, foregrounded and opened up for inspection; the latter can see it as *one* version of India, which can then take its place alongside other versions, can even be contested by these other versions.[4] Similarly, the use of fragments/fragmentariness can be keyed into the "quasi modernist aesthetic of the fragment in the West" (Sangari, 178), whereas it allows the subcontinental readers to emphasize the *partial* "truth" of Saleem's (and Rushdie's) representations of India.

As is clear from my analysis above, Rushdie's narrative is fractured by two ostensibly contradictory moves: on the one hand, it is totalizing and overdetermined in its insistent analogizing of events in Saleem's life with those in the life of the nation, whose history Saleem narrates; on the other hand, there is a simultaneous celebration of the fragmentary and contingent status of his narrative. Each move exists in a dialectical relationship with the other, and each on its own helps affirm Saleem's (and Rushdie's) authority.

Shame foregrounds and makes explicit what remains buried and is, at times, only implicit in *Midnight's Children*: Rushdie's *outsider* status. His narrator (a barely disguised stand-in for Rushdie) points out, fairly early in the novel: "I too know something of this immigrant business. I am an emigrant from one country (India) and a newcomer to two (England, where I live, and Pakistan, to which my family moved against my will)" (*Shame*, 90); or as he remarks elsewhere: "So here I am instead, inventing what never happened to me" (23).

Furthermore, unlike *Midnight's Children*, which, through at least one of its salient rhetorical maneuvers, makes Saleem's life coextensive with the life of his nation's and presents him as someone who participates in the life of *all* it classes, *Shame* focuses almost entirely on Pakistan's ruling class—its political chicaneries and shamelessness. And, with its nearly exclusive emphasis on fragments ("however I choose to write about over-there [Pakistan], I am forced to reflect that world in fragments of broken mirrors . . . I must reconcile myself to the inevitability of the missing bits" (71),[5] perspective—perspective, primarily, of the expatriate narrator—becomes all.

However, like *Midnight's Children*, where Saleem presents himself as *the* appropriate narrator of his nation's history because his life *is* the life of his nation, the narrator of *Shame* presents himself as *the* appropriate narrator of Pakistan's "post"-colonial history by remarking on the analogy between his migrant status and the status of Pakistan: "When individuals come unstuck from their native land, they are called migrants. When nations do the same (Bangladesh), that act is called secession"; "I may be such a person. Pakistan may be such a country" (91). Further, the term "Pakistan" is an acronym first "thought up" by Muslim intellectuals in England (91). Pakistan, in other words, was "dreamt" into being by "Muslim intellectuals" located in England; Rushdie's narrator, too, is located in England. His authority to write the "history" of Pakistan, finally, accrues not only from these initial analogies, but also, what is more important, from the fact that "the job of re-writing [Pakistan's] history" was "commandeered," first, by "the immigrants, the *mohajirs*. In what languages—Urdu and English, both imported tongues" (91). Thus, it makes perfect sense for another immigrant, *Shame*'s narrator in this case, to rewrite, once again, Pakistan's history.

At the same time, though, the expatriate narrator suggests that Pakistan, in the act of seceding, formed "a palimpsest on the past," thereby "obscur[ing] what lies beneath": "To build Pakistan it was necessary to cover up Indian history, to deny that Indian centuries lay just beneath the surface of Pakistani Standard Time. The past was re-written" (91). From this version of rewritten history, Rushdie (and, by implication, his narrator) also distances himself. Rushdie has always insisted on his tripartite, even multiple identities—Indian, Pakistani, British—a result of his multiple dislocations. (In "The Indian Writer in England," Rushdie unequivocally asserts that he "is not willing to be excluded from any part of his heritage" [79]). Thus, though he is like the *mohajirs*, who demanded that Pakistan's history be rewritten, be imposed, as it were, on a previous "Indian" history ("I build imaginary countries and try to impose them on the ones that exist" [92]), unlike the *mohajirs*, he undertakes to excavate what lies beneath—the suppressed histories of Pakistan, which were, and still are, covered up ("But I am dealing with a past that refuses to be suppressed" [92]). "Suppressed histories" include "excluded" histories as well—such as those of women in a traditional, patriarchal history. Thus, the narrator (and Rushdie) claims to be writing an alternate, oppositional history. In this, the project of *Shame* resembles Saleem's account of those segments of India's history suppressed in "official accounts," but aired by Saleem in *Midnight's Children* and proffered as alternate accounts. About these segments on the Bangladesh War and the Emergency, Rushdie has this to say:

The point about the Bangladesh War and the emergency particularly, it seems to me, is that what I started doing was writing a novel of memory and that it came into contact with certain kinds of events of which the official description was quite unlike the remembered, then the novel of memory became politicized. I mean simply by the act of saying that it was like this and not like that you're making a political statement because the organs of power were saying it was like that and not like this. (Dharkar interview, 356)

Rushdie asserts time and time again that "writers make alternate realities" (Dharkar interview, 360); that "books draw new and better maps of reality, and make new languages with which we can understand the world" ("Outside the Whale," 137). In fact, I would argue, this claim on behalf of writers and their works is the single most important constitutive element in Rushdie's constructions of authority in his fictional *and* journalistic prose. For instance, Saleem is not just the recorder of his nation's history; he sees himself as an active agent who

influences, *creates*, and *controls* the events that unfold in that history. Similarly,
in *Shame*, the narrator acknowledges: "I, too, like all migrants, am a fantasist.
I *build imaginary countries* and try to *impose* them on the ones that exist" (92;
emphasis added).

In a series of interviews and essays given or written around and between the
publication of *Midnight's Children* and *Shame* in the West and in the subcontinent, Rushdie invokes a complex of interrelated ideas through which he constitutes his authority *as a writer*—more specifically, as an immigrant writer.
What he has to say in these essays and interviews is especially significant for
his constructions of authority in *Shame*, which issues from the mind of an
explicitly located expatriate writer. (I have in mind, especially, the interviews
conducted by David Brooks, Rani Dharkar, and *Third World Book Review*, and
Rushdie's essays "The Indian Writer in England," "The Location of *Brazil*,"
and "Outside the Whale.") In his essay on Terry Gilliam's film, *Brazil*,[6] Rushdie
talks about the "triumph of the imagination," the "power of dream worlds" to
oppose "dark reality," and the power of politicians and government functionaries
whose business it is to suppress uncomfortable truths. The task of imagination,
therefore, is to break through "conventional habit-dulled certainties" which
make people think "resistance is useless," to transform and instill "confidence
in our ability to improve the world." Imagination is "the only weapon with
which reality can be smashed, so it may be subsequently reconstructed" ("The
Location of *Brazil*," 52–53).

The crucial move Rushdie makes in this essay is to link the abilities of
imagination described above with what he calls "the migrant sensibility" (54).
Indeed, he sees the former *as a product* of the latter. His reasons for doing so
are many:

To be a migrant is, perhaps, to be the only species of human being free of the shackles
of nationalism (to say nothing of its ugly sister, patriotism). It is a burdensome freedom.

One of the effects of mass migrations has been the creation of radically new types of
human beings: of people who root themselves in ideas rather than places, in memories
as much as in material things.

Migrants must, of necessity, make a new relationship with the world because of the loss
of familiar habitats.

. . . the location of *Brazil* is cinema itself, because in cinema the dream is the norm . . .
this cinematic land of make believe of which all of us who have, for whatever reason,
lost a country and ended up elsewhere are true citizens. Like Terry Gilliam, I am a
Brazilian. (53)

The comments above unequivocally privilege the "migrant sensibility" as the
source of, even the *site* for, an adversarial vision of history; further, they point
to a particular kind of "migrant sensibility": one that issues from self-conscious

reflection on its locations and tasks in the world; finally, and most important, they privilege the "migrant sensibility" of the imaginative creator/writer: Terry Gilliam/Salman Rushdie. The point worth underscoring here is that what Rushdie establishes in the essay on *Brazil* for the writer is no different from what he has already claimed implicitly in both novels (via Saleem and the narrator) and explicitly in his comments on his effort to write "alternate" histories. But this essay fleshes out and foregrounds in a particularly direct fashion the authority and peculiar powers of the immigrant writer *qua* immigrant writer. In this regard, this essay more fully illuminates and addresses *Shame* in a way that it does not *Midnight's Children*, where Rushdie's migrant status is suppressed, as it must be, or is not made into an issue. (*Midnight's Children*, we should remember, is Rushdie's first book about the subcontinent. Without the assurance of "authority"—a product of the critical and popular acclaim *Midnight's Children* garnered—Rushdie could hardly take the risk he takes in *Shame* when he announces himself as an expatriate, who claims to "have learned Pakistan in slices" [70]). Besides, one can also argue that for Rushdie the histories of India and Pakistan call for different rhetorical maneuvers because they issue from different attachments.)[7]

In claiming a sort of transcendent authority for the immigrant writer's imaginative (oppositional) constructs, Rushdie's essay on *Brazil* hints at what can perhaps best be described as the workings of an imperializing consciousness, and what is far more directly stated in *Shame* (a book whose project is surely retrospectively informed by this essay) when its narrator, also an immigrant writer, acknowledges that he "imposes" his "imaginary countries . . . on ones that exist" (92).[8] Saleem's can also be seen as an imperializing consciousness. Thus, the "central trope of *Midnight's Children* in which Saleem contains India's multitudes within him" (Brennan, 89) should be taken both literally *and* as a self-aggrandizing gesture whereby Saleem appropriates "multitudes" to produce a "truth" in the image of his own mind.

In fact, I would argue that the logic of writing "alternate histories," as Rushdie envisions this task, is intimately tied to the imagining or dreaming mind imposing its vision on the world and arguing for its greater validity. However, much as Rushdie's writings call upon the persuasiveness and empowering force of the imperializing mind, Rushdie is too astute and self-conscious a writer not to be open to the dangers implicit in this strategy.[9] Hence the counterclaims and methods that deconstruct this strategy of empowerment; hence his emphasis on fragments, on the contingency of his vision, and, more important, his ambivalence toward precisely that which he draws strength from as a writer. In this regard, it is difficult not to see Rushdie standing behind Saleem's recognition, as he (i.e., Saleem) enters the "illusion of the artist" whose imagination creates the world, that "with the hindsight of the lost, spent years, I can say that the spirit of self-aggrandizement which seized me then was a reflex, born of an instinct for self-preservation" (207).

For Rushdie, moreover, the freedom of the imagination is "burdensome" and requires responsibility ("The Location of *Brazil*," 53) because the imagination,

while opposed to reality, must nevertheless be anchored in reality; books must
be "about [things in] the world [otherwise] they are not interesting to people,
not even interesting to write, to me" (Brooks interview, 56); "fantasy is not
interesting when you separate it from actuality and it's only interesting as a mode
of dealing with actuality" (Dharkar interview, 355).

In my examination of Salman Rushdie's constructions of authority, I have all
along been acutely conscious of the fact that, in the two novels and the commentaries I have discussed, Rushdie never once uses the word authority. Yet,
for me, Rushdie's authority (or lack thereof) is precisely the issue, if for no
other reason than to foreground the fact that he is an expatriate writer and that
his location should enter any discussion of novels whose ambition is nothing
less than to write, or better, rewrite the histories of the subcontinent. (In this
regard it is worth pointing out that Rushdie usually presents himself as an insider-
outsider;[10] certainly my analysis of his novels concurs with Rushdie's presen-
tation.) Constructing his authority is implicated with empowering himself to
speak, with varying degrees of legitimacy, on behalf of his material.

Rushdie's constructions of authority are sensitive to the problems of authority
in a postmodern age; they are also alert to the misuse of authority by politicians
who offer their versions of history and reality in order to impose officially
sanctioned "truths" and exclude uncomfortable "truths." This sensitivity to the
problems of authority can itself be problematic for a writer to whom "moral
considerations" matter, for whom the desire to "distinguish between good and
evil, between right and wrong" cannot be avoided ("A Dangerous Art Form,"
4). Thus, his novels about the subcontinent (and his commentaries) are acute
about the need to construct ultimate fictions, which can be set off against "dark
reality." At the same time, however, they also undercut this need in the belief
that his fictions, no more than those he opposes, cannot, indeed must not, become
fascistic. It is for this reason that Rushdie both uses authority as a generative
principle and deconstructs it by insisting simultaneously on the partiality and
fragmentariness of his ultimate fictions.

The burden, I believe, for readers of *Midnight's Children* and *Shame* is to be
fully aware of and alert to the means by which Rushdie empowers himself as a
writer and constructs his authority to write about the subcontinent. Without such
alertness, readers are likely to grant him more than he can or should validly
claim (as, for instance, Clark Blaise does in his hyperbolic assessment of *Midnight's Children* as a "continent finding its voice") on behalf of his fictions.
Such alertness, then, requires that readers attend equally to both kinds of moves
Rushdie makes: the one through which he totalizes and grants a writer (especially
a writer like himself) transcendent authority; the other through which he disperses
and displaces his authority, making it contingent, partial, fragmentary.

NOTES

1. Add to this Rushdie's own comments on his reception in India and Pakistan after
Midnight's Children was published: "It was wonderful in both India and Pakistan; there

wasn't really a difference between the two countries. I was very nervous about going back, because of the expatriate problem and the suspicions that people legitimately have. . . . So I was expecting hostility or fear, and instead what happened was an extraordinary emotional event. It wasn't just that the audiences for my lectures were very large, but that there were these great waves of affection. Mostly from the young people. The book was written as a way of reclaiming India, and this was like India and Pakistan doing the same thing back" ("Author from Three Countries," 23).

2. *Shame* more so than *Midnight's Children* because of its relentless and nearly exclusive focus on a handful of members of a corrupt, immoral ruling elite, and because Pakistan represents, in Rushdie's account, "a failure of the dreaming mind," a nation "insufficiently imagined" (92).

3. Here one might include as well K. B. Rao's complaint: "Rushdie attempts to swallow all of India in his epic novel. Therein lies his ambition and his downfall. He is authentic when he writes about Bombay, the place of his birth, the city where he grew up. Probably there is no other Indian novel that captures the sights and smells of Bombay as *Midnight's Children* does, but when Rushdie writes about the rest of India, he is neither so forceful, nor so authentic" (181). Rao's complaint issues from an unexamined, and, I believe, simplistic equation between "authenticity" and "place" that Rushdie renders problematic through his book and through a variety of comments that followed the publication of *Midnight's Children*.

4. The two audiences' modes of recuperation are not necessarily mutually exclusive. I do think, however, that their motives for doing so are distinct and do not overlap.

5. It is worthwhile here to recall Rushdie's claim that although "the Indian writer who writes from outside India . . . is obliged to deal in broken mirrors, some of whose fragments may have been irretrievably lost," he "was genuinely amazed by how much came back to [him]" ("The Indian Writer in England," 76–77).

6. I focus on this essay because it includes and adds to what Rushdie has said or written in the others. Relevant page numbers for the others are as follows: interviews: with Rani Dharkar (356, 360); with David Brooks (59, 67); essays: "The Indian Writer in England" (76–79); "Outside the Whale" (137–38).

7. For example, Timothy Hyman notes: "*Shame* stands to *Midnight's Children* very much as Pakistan to India; a smaller book for a meaner world. To embody a nation in a book, yes; but the kind of book called forth by India, the ultimate "loose and baggy monster', can hardly be repeated for India's angry appendage. . . . Entering a world less known, and less loved, Rushdie discovers a wasteland" (93). Some of Hyman's "reading" is borne out by Rushdie's somewhat emotional account of the birth of *Midnight's Children*: "I, who had been away so long that I almost qualified for the title of *farangi*, was gripped by the conviction that I, too, had a city and a history to reclaim" ("The Indian Writer in England," 76); so far as I know, nothing comparable on Rushdie's attachment to Pakistan exists.

8. Timothy Brennan also addresses what he calls Rushdie's "imperial legacy" (86); see also Brennan's analysis of Saleem's "sweeping claims to be the imaginative source of history" (98–99).

9. In this, Rushdie's project is very similar to those undertaken by Romantic poets like Wordsworth, Coleridge, and Shelley, with their insistent exploration of the imagination's transcendent power, its ability to transform and counter customary responses. And they worry about imagination's imperializing propensities, even as they invoke it to empower themselves and their visions of the world.

10. A comparison of Rushdie with V. S. Naipual, who always presents himself as an outsider, an observer, an exile, is particularly instructive here. Unlike Rushdie, Naipual never displays any interest in invoking an insider's status (see Rob Nixon's excellent essay, "London Calling: V. S. Naipaul and the License of Exile"). The tone and the effects (and consequences) of their fictions are, then, quite different. Leon Wieseltier quite accurately remarks: "Rushdie is . . . not like the heartless Naipaul. Indeed, compared to Naipual the unsentimental, Rushdie is a sentimental fool. There is a good reason. He is not a man without a place. He is a man with a place that is hard to bear. The difference matters" (34).

WORKS CITED

Ali, Tariq. "*Midnight's Children.*" *New Left Review* 136 (November-December 1982): 87–95.

Blaise, Clark. "A Novel of India's Coming of Age." *New York Times Book Review*, April 19, 1981, 1, 18–19.

Brennan, Timothy. *Salman Rushdie and the Third World: Myths of the Nation*. New York: St. Martin's Press, 1989.

Desai, Anita. "Where Cultures Clash by Night." *Book World—Washington Post*, March 15, 1981, 1, 13.

Glendenning, Victoria. "A Novelist in the Country of the Mind." *Sunday Times*, October 25, 1981, 38.

Grewal, Inderpal. "Salman Rushdie: Marginality, Women, and *Shame.*" *Genders* 3 (Fall 1988): 24–42.

Hollington, Michael. "Salman Rushdie's *Shame.*" *Meanjin Quarterly* 43 (September 1984): 403–7.

Hyman, Timothy. "Fairy-Tale Agitprop." *London Magazine* (October 1983): 40.

Kaufman, Michael. "Author from Three Countries." *New York Times Book Review* (November 13, 1983): 3, 22–23.

Nixon, Rob. "London Calling: V. S. Naipaul and the License of Exile." *South Atlantic Quarterly* 87 (Winter 1988): 1–38.

Rao, K. B. "Asia and the Pacific: *Midnight's Children.*" *World Literature Today* 56 (Winter 1982): 181.

Rushdie, Salman. "A Dangerous Art Form." *Third World Book Review* 1 (1984): 3–5.

———. "The Indian Writer in England." In *The Eye of the Beholder: Indian Writing in English*. Ed. Maggie Butcher. London: Commonwealth Institute, 1983. 75–83.

———. "Salman Rushdie." Interviewed by David Brooks. *Helix* 19 and 20 (1985): 55–69.

———. "An Interview with Salman Rushdie." Interviewed by Rani Dharkar. *New Quest* 42 (November-December, 1983): 351–60.

———. "The Location of *Brazil.*" *American Film* 10 (September 1985): 50–53.

———. *Midnight's Children*. New York: Avon, 1980.

———. "*Midnight's Children* and *Shame.*" *Kunapipi* 7 (1985): 1–19.

———. "Outside the Whale." *Granta* 11 (1983): 123–41.

———. *Shame*. New York: Vintage/Aventura, 1984.

Said, Edward W. *Orientalism*. New York: Vintage Books, 1979.

Sangari, Kum Kum. "The Politics of the Possible." *Cultural Critique* 7 (Fall 1987): 157–86.
Wieseltier, Leon. "Midnight's Other Children." *New Republic* (December 1983): 32–34.

Selected Bibliography

The bibliography begins with a selection of nonliterary texts that offer broad perspectives on various aspects of the Indian diasporic experience. These works provide rich historic, cultural, and political contexts in which we may understand the literary representations of that experience. The lists of creative and critical texts that follow are, by necessity, *highly* selective.

General Works

Ali, Ahmed. *Pacific Indians: Profiles in Twenty Pacific Countries*. Suva: University of the South Pacific, 1981.

Bhana, Surendra, and Bridglal Pachai, eds. *A Documentary History of Indian South Africans*. Cape Town: D. Philip, 1984.

Bissoondoyal, U., ed. *Indians Overseas: The Mauritian Experience*. Mauritius: Mahatma Gandhi Institute, 1984.

Chandrasekhar, S., ed. *From India to Canada*. La Jolla, Calif.: Population Review Books, 1986.

Dabydeen, David, and Brinsley Samarro, eds. *India in the Caribbean*. London: Hansib, 1986.

Daniels, Roger. *History of Indian Immigration to the United States: An Interpretive Essay*. New York: Asia Society, 1986.

deLepervanche, Marie. *Indians in a White Australia*. Sydney: Allen and Unwin, 1984.

Gifford, Zerbanoo. *The Golden Thread*. London: Grafton Books, 1990.

Muthana, I. M. *People of India in North America*. Bangalore: Grangarams Book Distributors, 1982.

Nazareth, Peter. *Brown Man, Black Country*. New Delhi: Tidings, 1981.
Ramachandani, R. R. *Uganda Asians: The End of an Enterprise*. Bombay: United Asia Publications, 1976.
Ramasamy, R., and Rabindra Daniel. *Indians in Peninsular Malaysia*. Kuala Lumpur: University of Malaya Press, 1984.
Singh, Bahadur, ed. *Indians in South Asia*. New Delhi: Sterling, 1972.
Subramani, ed. *The Indo-Fijian Experience*. Brisbane: University of Queensland Press, 1979.
Tiwari, Kapil, ed. *Indians in New Zealand: Studies in a Subculture*. Wellington, N.Z.: Price Milburn, 1980.
Vaid, K. N. *The Overseas Indian Community in Hong Kong*. Hong Kong: University of Hong Kong Center for Asian Studies, 1972.

FICTION

Alexander, Meena. *Nampally Road*. San Francisco: Mercury House, 1991.
Bissoondath, Neil. *A Casual Brutality*. Toronto: Macmillan, 1988.
———. *Digging Up the Mountains*. Toronto: Macmillan, 1985.
Dabydeen, Cyril. *The Wizard Swami*. Calcutta: Writers Workshop, 1985.
Desani, G. V. *All About Mr. Hatterr: A Gesture*. London: Alder, 1948.
Dhingra, Leena. *Amritvela*. London: Women's Press, 1988.
Dhondy, Farruck. *Bombay Duck*. London: Cape, 1990.
———. *Come to Mecca and Other Stories*. London: Collins, 1978.
———. *East End at Your Feet*. London: Macmillan, 1980.
———. *Poona Company*. London: Gollancz, 1980.
———. *Siege of Babylon*. London: Macmillan, 1978.
———. *Trip Trap*. London: Gollancz, 1982.
Essop, Ahmed. *Hajji Musa and the Hindu Fire-Walker*. Columbia, La.: Readers International, 1988.
Ganesan, Indira. *The Journey*. New York: Knopf, 1990.
Itwaru, Arnold. *Shanti*. Leeds: Peepal Tree Press, 1988.
Khan, Ismith. *The Jumbie Bird*. London: MacGibbon and Kee, 1961.
———. *The Obeah Man*. London: Hutchinson, 1964.
Kureishi, Hanif. *The Buddha of Suburbia*. New York: Viking Penguin, 1990.
Ladoo, Harold Sonny. *No Pain Like This Body*. London: Heinemann, 1987.
Maniam, K. S. *Plot, the Aborting, Parablames and Other Stories*. Kuala Lumpur: AMK Interaksi, 1989.
Markandaya, Kamala. *The Coffer Dam*. New York: John Day, 1969.
———. *The Golden Honeycomb*. New York: Crowell, 1977.
———. *A Handful of Rice*. London: H. Hamilton, 1966.
———. *Nectar in a Sieve*. London: Putnam, 1954.
———. *Possession*. New York: John Day, 1963.
———. *A Silence of Desire*. New York: John Day, 1960.
———. *Some Inner Fury*. London: Putnam, 1955.
———. *Two Virgins*. New York: John Day, 1973.
Mehta, Ved. *Delinquent Chacha*. New York: Farrar, Straus and Giroux, 1970.
Mistry, Rohinton. *Such a Long Journey*. New York: Knopf, 1991.

———. *Swimming Lessons and Other Stories from Firozsha Baaq*. Boston: Houghton Mifflin, 1989.

Monar, Rooplall. *Backdam People*. Leeds: Peepal Tree Press, 1987.

———. *Janjhat*. Leeds: Peepal Tree Press, 1989.

Mukherjee, Bharati. *Darkness*. New York: Penguin, 1985.

———. *Jasmine*. New York: Grove Weidenfeld, 1989.

———. *The Middleman and Other Stories*. New York: Grove Weidenfeld, 1988.

———. *The Tiger's Daughter*. Boston: Houghton Mifflin, 1972.

———. *Wife*. Boston: Houghton Mifflin, 1975.

Mulloo, Anand. *Watch Them Go Down*. St. Port Louis: Mauritius Writers' Association, 1967.

Murari, Timeri. *The Field of Honor*. London: Methuen, 1981.

———. *The Imperial Agent*. New York: St. Martin's Press, 1987.

———. *The Last Victory*. New York: St. Martin's Press, 1990.

———. *The Marriage*. London: Macmillan, 1973.

Naipaul, Shiva. *Beyond the Dragon's Mouth: Stories and Pieces*. New York: Viking, 1985.

———. *Fireflies*. New York: Knopf, 1971.

Naipaul, V. S. *A Bend in the River*. New York: Knopf, 1979.

———. *The Enigma of Arrival*. New York: Knopf, 1987.

———. *Guerrillas*. New York: Knopf, 1975.

———. *A House for Mr. Biswas*. New York: McGraw-Hill, 1961.

———. *In a Free State*. London: Deutsch, 1971.

———. *Three Novels (The Mystic Masseur, The Suffrage of Elvira, Miguel Street)*. New York: Knopf, 1982.

Namjoshi, Suniti. *The Mothers of Maya Diip*. London: Women's Press, 1989.

Nazareth, Peter. *In a Brown Mantle*. Nairobi: East African Literature Bureau, 1972.

Rajan, Balachandra. *The Dark Dancer*. New York: Simon and Schuster, 1958.

———. *Too Long in the West*. London: Heinemann, 1961.

Randhawa, Ravider. *A Wicked Old Woman*. London: Women's Press, 1987.

Rao, Raja. *The Chessmaster and His Moves*. New Delhi: Vision Books, 1988.

———. *On the Ganga Ghat*. New Delhi: Vision Books, 1989.

———. *The Policeman and the Rose: Stories*. Delhi: Oxford University Press, 1970.

———. *The Serpent and the Rope*. New York: Pantheon Books, 1960.

Rushdie, Salman. *Haroun and the Sea of Stories*. New York: Granta Books/Viking, 1991.

———. *Midnight's Children*. New York: Knopf, 1980.

———. *The Satanic Verses*. New York: Viking, 1988.

———. *Shame*. New York: Knopf, 1983.

Selvon, Samuel. *A Brighter Sun*. London: Wingate, 1952.

———. *An Island Is a World*. London: Wingate, 1955.

———. *The Lonely Londoners*. London: Wingate, 1956.

———. *Moses Ascending*. London: Davis-Poynter, 1975.

———. *Moses Migrating*. London: Longman, 1983.

———. *Turn Again Tiger*. London: MacGibbon and Kee, 1958.

———. *Ways of Sunlight*. London: MacGibbon and Kee, 1957.

Seth, Vikram. *The Golden Gate*. London: Faber and Faber, 1986.

Tejani, Bahadur. *Day After Tomorrow*. Nairobi: East African Literature Bureau, 1971.

Vassanji, M. G. *The Gunny Sack*. London: Heinemann, 1989.

———. *No New Land*. Toronto: McClelland and Stewart, 1991.

POETRY

Alexander, Meena. *The House of a Thousand Doors*. Washington, D.C.: Three Continents Press, 1988.
———. *The Storm*. New York: Red Dust Press, 1989.
Ali, Agha Shahid. *The Half-Inch Himalayas*. Middletown, Conn.: Wesleyan University Press, 1987.
———. *A Nostalgist's Map of America*. New York: Norton, 1991.
———. *A Walk Through the Yellow Pages*. Tucson: SUN-gemini Press, 1987.
Dabydeen, Cyril. *Dark Swirl*. Leeds: Peepal Tree Press, 1988.
———. *Islands Lovelier than a Vision*. Leeds: Peepal Tree Press, 1989.
Dabydeen, David. *Coolie Odyssey*. London: Hansib, 1988.
Das, Mahadai. *Bones*. Leeds: Peepal Tree Press, 1989.
Mishra, Sudesh. *Rahu*. Suva: Vision International, 1987.
Monar, Rooplall. *Koker*. Leeds: Peepal Tree Press, 1988.
Moreas, Dom. *Collected Poems 1957–1987*. New Delhi: Penguin, 1987.
Nair, Chandran. *Once the Horseman and Other Poems*. Singapore: University Education Press, 1972.
Namjoshi, Suniti. *Because of India: Selected Poems and Fables*. London: Onlywoman Press, 1989.
Nandan, Satendra. *Voices in the River*. Suva: Vision International, 1985.
Parameswaran, Uma. *Trishanku*. Toronto: Toronto South Asian Review, 1988.
Parthasarathy, R. *Rough Passage*. New Delhi: Oxford University Press, 1977.
Singh, Kirpal. *Palm Readings*. Singapore: Graham Brash, 1986.
———. *Twenty Poems*. Calcutta: Writers Workshop, 1978.
Thumboo, Edwin. *Gods Can Die*. Singapore: Heinemann, 1976.
———. *Rib of Earth*. Singapore: Lloyd Fernando, 1956.
———. *Ulysses by the Merlion*. Singapore: Heinemann, 1979.

DRAMA

Desani, G. V. *Hali*. London: Saturn, 1950.
Dhondy, Farruck. *Romance, Romance; and The Bride*. London: Faber, 1985.
Ganesh, Bagchi. "Of Malice and Men." In *Short East African Plays in English*. Ed. David Cook and Miles Lee. Nairobi: Heinemann, 1968.
Kassan, Sadru. "Bones." In *Short East African Plays in English*. Ed. David Cook and Miles Lee. Nairobi: Heinemann, 1968.
Kureishi, Hanif. *Birds of Passage*. Oxford: Amber Lane Press, 1983.
———. *Borderline*. London: Methuen, 1981.
———. *The Rainbow Sign and My Beautiful Laundrette*. London: Faber and Faber, 1986.
———. *Sammy and Rosie Get Laid*. New York: Penguin Books, 1988.
Parameswaran, Uma. *Rootless but Green Are the Boulevard Trees*. Toronto: Toronto South Asian Review, 1979.
Singh, Jagjit. "Sweet Scum of Freedom." In *Eight Prize-Winning Plays for Radio*. Ed. Gwyneth Henderson. London: Heinemann, 1973.

Sondhi, Kuldip. "Undesignated." In *Short East African Plays in English*. Ed. David Cook and Miles Lee. Nairobi: Heinemann, 1968.

AUTOBIOGRAPHY/TRAVEL WRITING/CULTURAL COMMENTARY

Alexander, Meena. *Fault Lines*. New York: Feminist Press, 1992.

Chaudhuri, Nirad. *The Autobiography of an Unknown Indian*. Berkeley: University of California Press, 1968.

Kureishi, Hanif. *The Rainbow Sun and My Beautiful Laundrette*. London: Faber and Faber, 1986.

Mehta, Ved. *Dadaji*. New York: Farrar, Straus and Giroux, 1970.

———. *Face to Face: An Autobiography*. Boston: Atlantic–Little, Brown, 1957.

———. *Mamaji*. New York: Oxford University Press, 1979.

———. *Sound-Shadows of the New World*. New York: Norton, 1986.

———. *The Stolen Light*. New York: Norton, 1989.

———. *Vedi*. New York: Oxford University Press, 1982.

———. *Walking the Indian Streets*. Boston: Atlantic–Little, Brown, 1960.

Mohanti, Prafulla. *Through Brown Eyes*. Oxford: Oxford University Press, 1985.

Moreas, Dom. *My Father's Son*. London: Macmillan, 1968.

Mukherjee, Bharati, with Clark Blaise. *Days and Nights in Calcutta*. Garden City, N.Y.: Doubleday, 1977; Markham, Ont.: Viking-Penguin, 1986.

———. *The Sorrow and the Terror: The Haunting Legacy of the Air India Tragedy*. Markham, Ont.: Viking-Penguin, 1987.

Naipaul, Shiva. *An Unfinished Journey*. London: H. Hamilton, 1986.

Naipaul, V. S. *An Area of Darkness*. London: Deutsch, 1964.

———. *India: A Million Mutinies Now*. New York: Viking, 1991.

———. *India: A Wounded Civilization*. New York: Knopf, 1977.

Rushdie, Salman. *Imaginary Homelands: Essays and Criticism, 1981–1991*. New York: Viking/Granta, 1991.

Shan, Sharan-Jeet. *In My Own Name: An Autobiography*. London: Women's Press, 1986.

CRITICISM

Aithal, Krithriamoorthy, and Rashmi Aithal. "Indo-English Fictional Experiments with Interracial and Intercultural Relationship." In *Alien Voice: Perspectives on Commonwealth Literature*. Ed. Avadhesh Srivastava and B. N. Chaturvedi. Atlantic Heights, N.J.: Humanities Press, 1982. 54–67.

Alverez-Pereyre, Neela. "Language Practices Among Indian South Africans." *Commonwealth Essays and Studies* 8 (Autumn 1985): 73–76.

Appignanesi, Lisa, and Sara Maitland. *The Rushdie File*. Syracuse: Syracuse University Press, 1990.

Barratt, Harold. "In Defence of Naipaul's Guerrillas." *World Literature Written in English* 28 (Spring 1988): 97–103.

Bennett, Bruce. *A Sense of Exile: Essays in the Literature of the Asia-Pacific Region*. Nedlands: University of Western Australia Centre for Studies in Australian Literature, 1988.

Berman, Jaye. "V. S. Naipaul's *Guerillas* as a Postmodern Naturalistic Novel." *Perspectives on Contemporary Literature* 12 (1986): 29–34.

Boxill, Anthony. *V. S. Naipaul's Fiction: In Quest of the Enemy*. Fredericton, N.B.: York Press, 1983.

Brennan, Timothy. *Salman Rushdie and the Third World: Myths of the Nation*. New York: St. Martin's Press, 1989.

Brown, John. "V. S. Naipaul: A Wager on the Triumph of Darkness." *World Literature Today* 57 (Spring 1983): 223–27.

Bryan, Violet. "The Sense of Place in Naipaul's *A House for Mr. Biswas* and *Guerrillas*." *College Language Association Journal* 33 (September 1989): 26–35.

Butcher, Maggie, ed. *The Eye of the Beholder: Indian Writing in English*. London: Commonwealth Institute, 1983.

Campbell, Elaine. "Beyond Controversy: Vidia Naipaul and Salman Rushdie." *Literary Half-Yearly* 27 (July 1986): 42–49.

Chaudhary, Helga. "V. S. Naipaul's Changing Vision of India: A Study of *An Area of Darkness* and *India: A Wounded Civilization*." *Literary Half-Yearly* 23 (January 1982): 98–114.

Cobham, Rhonda. *"The Jumbie Bird* by Ismith Khan: A New Assessment." *Journal of Commonwealth Literature* 21 (1986): 240–49.

Cudjoe, Selwyn. *V. S. Naipaul: A Materialist Reading*. Amherst: University of Massachusetts Press, 1988.

———. "V. S. Naipaul and the Question of Identity." In *Voices from Under: Black Narrative in Latin America and the Caribbean*. Ed. William Luis. Westport, Conn.: Greenwood Press, 1984.

Davies, Barrie. "The Personal Space of a Society—Minority Voice: Aspects of the 'East Indian' Novel in the West Indies." *Studies in the Novel* 4 (Summer 1972): 284–95.

Day, Frank. "Naipaul's Vision of Wounded Civilizations." *South Carolina Review* 18, no. 1 (Fall 1985): 10–14.

Day, James. "Sexual Politics in the Novels of Kamala Markandaya." *World Literature Written in English* 21 (Summer 1982): 347–56.

Dhareshwar, Vivek. "Self-Fashioning, Colonial Habitus, and Double Exclusion: V. S. Naipaul's *The Mimic Men*." *Criticism: A Quarterly for Literature and the Arts* 31 (Winter 1989): 75–102.

Epstein, Joseph. "A Cottage for Mr. Naipaul." *New Criterion* 6 (October 1987): 6–15.

Fabre, Michel. "From Trinidad to London: Tone and Language in Samuel Selvon's Novels." *Literary Half-Yearly* 20 (January 1979): 71–80.

Freed, Eugenie. "Mr. Sufi Climbs the Stairs: The Quest and the Ideal in Ahmed Essop's 'The Visitation.' " *Theoria: A Journal of Studies in the Arts, Humanities and Social Sciences* 71 (May 1988): 1–13.

Goers, Peter. "Kink's English: Whole Language and Desani's *All About H. Hatterr*." *New Literature Review* 4 (1977): 30–40.

Goodheart,, Eugene. "V. S. Naipaul's Mandarin Sensibility." *Partisan Review* 50, no. 2 (1983): 244–56.

Gurr, Andrew. *Writers in Exile: The Identity of Home in Modern Literature*. Atlantic Heights, N.J.: Humanities Press International, 1981.

Hassan, Dolly. "The Messianic Leader in V. S. Naipaul's West Indian Works." *College Language Association Journal* 32 (December 1988): 209–24.

Healy, J. J. "Fiction, Voice, and the Rough Ground of Feeling: V. S. Naipaul After Twenty-Five Years." *University of Toronto Quarterly: A Canadian Journal of the Humanities* 55 (Fall 1985): 45–63.

Hemenway, Robert. "Sex and Politics in V. S. Naipaul." *Studies in the Novel* 14, no. 2 (Summer 1982): 189–202.

Hewson, Kelly. "Opening Up the Universe a Little More: Salman Rushdie and the Migrant as Story-Teller." *SPAN: Journal of the South Pacific Association for Commonwealth Literature and Language Studies* 29 (October 1989): 82–93.

Irving, T. B. "The Rushdie Confrontation: A Clash in Values." *Iowa Review* 20, no. 1 (Winter 1990): 175–84.

Juneja, Renu. "Representing History in *The Jumbie Bird*." *World Literature Written in English* 30 (Spring 1990): 17–28.

Katrak, Ketu H., and R. Radhakrishnan, eds. *Desh-Videsh: South Asian Expatriate Writers and Artists. Massachusetts Review* 29, no. 4 (1988). Special issue.

Kaul, R. K. "A Society Gone Sour: Naipaul's Portrayal of India." *Indian Literary Review* 4, no. 3 (October 1986): 37–41.

Kirpaul, Viney. *The Third World Novel of Expatriation: A Study of Emigre Fiction by Indian, West African and Caribbean Writers.* New Delhi: Sterling, 1989.

Kumar, Prem. "From Confrontation to Reconciliation: Kamala Markandaya's Evolution as a Novelist." *International Fiction Review* 14, no. 2 (Summer 1987): 84–88.

Lane, Travis. "I and My Creatures: Three Versions of the Human." *Fiddlehead* 31 (Summer 1989): 80–88.

Mann, Harveen. "Variations of the Theme of Mimicry: Naipaul's *The Mystic Masseur* and *The Suffrage of Elvira*." *Modern Fiction Studies* 30, no. 3 (Autumn 1984): 467–85.

Martin, Murray S. "Order, Disorder, and Rage in the Islands: The Novels of V. S. Naipaul and Albert Wendt." *Perspectives on Contemporary Literature* 10 (1984): 33–39.

Menon, Madhavi. "The Vision in Kamala Markandaya's *Nowhere Man*." *Commonwealth Quarterly* 13 (1981): 24–37.

Mishra, Vijay. "Indo-Fijian Fiction: Towards an Interpretation." *World Literature Written in English* 16 (1977): 395–408.

———. "Mythic Fabulation: Naipaul's India." *New Literature Review* 4 (1978): 59–65.

———. "Rama's Banishment: A Theoretical Footnote to Indo-Fijian Writing." *World Literature Written in English* 19 (1980): 242–56.

Mukherjee, Arun. *Towards an Aesthetics of Opposition: Essays on Literature, Criticism and Cultural Imperialism.* Stratford, Ont.: Williams-Wallace, 1988.

Mukherjee, Bharati. "Prophet and Loss: Salman Rushdie's Migration of Souls." *Village Voice Literary Supplement* 72 (March 1989): 9–12.

Myers, Lettie. " 'Bring Memory to Silence': The Celebratory Nature of V. S. Naipaul's *A House for Mr. Biswas*." *Journal of Indian Writing in English* 12, no. 2 (July 1984): 71–81.

Nachman, Larry David. "The Worlds of V. S. Naipaul." *Salmagundi* 54 (Fall 1981): 59–76.

Nagarajan, S. "R. Parthasarathy." In *Contemporary Poets*. Ed. James Vinson and D. L. Kirkpatrick. New York: St. Martin's, Press, 1988.

Naik, M. K. "Colonial Experience in *All About Mr. Hatterr.*" *Commonwealth Novel in English* 1 (1982): 57–75.

———. "A Life of Fragments: The Fate of Identity in *Midnight's Children.*" *Indian Literary Review* 3, no. 3 (October 1985): 63–68.

Nasta, Susheila. *Critical Perspectives on Samuel Selvon.* Washington, D.C.: Three Continents Press, 1988.

Nelson, Emmanuel. "Kamala Markandaya, Bharati Mukherjee, and the Indian Immigrant Experience." *Toronto South Asian Review* 9 (Winter 1991): 1–9.

Nightingale, Margaret. "V. S. Naipaul as Historian: Combating Chaos." *Southern Review* 13, no. 3 (November 1980): 239–50.

Nightingale, Peggy. *Journey Through Darkness: The Writings of V. S. Naipaul.* St. Lucia: University of Queensland Press, 1987.

Nixon, Rob. "London Calling: V. S. Naipaul and the License of Exile." *South Atlantic Quarterly* 87 (Winter 1988): 1–38.

Parameswaran, Uma. "Handcuffed to History: Salman Rushdie's Art." *Ariel: A Review of International English Literature* 14, no. 4 (October 1983): 34–45.

Perry, John Oliver. " 'Exiled by a Woman's Body': Substantial Phenomena in the Poetry of Meena Alexander." *Journal of South Asian Literature* 1 (Winter/Spring 1986): 8–18.

Poynting, Jeremy. "East Indian Women in the Caribbean: Experience, Image, and Voice." *Journal of South Asian Literature* 21, no. 1 (1986): 12–22.

———. " 'You Want to Be a Coolie Woman?': Gender and Ethnic Identity in Indo-Caribbean Women's Writing." In *Caribbean Women Writers.* Ed. Selwyn R. Cudjoe. Wellesley, Mass.: Calaloux, 1990. 98–105.

Prasad, Madhusudan. *Perspectives on Kamala Markandaya.* New Delhi: Vimal Prakashan, 1984.

Rai, Sudha. *V. S. Naipaul: A Study in Expatriate Sensibility.* New Delhi: Arnold-Heinemann, 1982.

Ramraj, Victor. "V. S. Naipaul: The Irrelevance of Nationalism." *World Literature Written in English* 23, no. 1 (Winter 1984): 187–96.

Rao, Madhusudana. "Quest for Identity: A Study of the Narrative in Rushdie's *Midnight's Children.*" *Literary Criterion* 25, no. 4 (1990): 31–42.

Rao, Susheela N. "England in the Novels of Kamala Markandaya." *Journal of Indian Writing in English* 15, no. 1 (January 1987): 1–10.

Rothfork, John. "V. S. Naipual and the Third World." *Research Studies* 49, no. 3 (September 1981): 183–92.

Sarvan, Charles Ponnuthurai. "Ethnicity and Alienation: The African Asian and His Response to Africa." *Journal of Commonwealth Literature* 20, no. 4 (1985): 101–10.

Searle, Chris. "Naipaulicity: A Form of Cultural Imperialism." *Race and Class* 2 (1984): 45–62.

Singh, Vishnudat. "Naipaul's New Indians." *Trinidad and Tobago Review Literary Supplement* 6, no. 7 (1983): 3–8, 17–23.

Slatin, John. "Blindness and Self-Perception: The Autobiographies of Ved Mehta." *Mosaic* 19, no. 6 (Fall 1986): 173–93.

Smith, Roland. "Living on the Fringe: The World of Ahmed Essop." *Commonwealth Essays and Studies* 8, no. 1 (Autumn 1985): 64–72.

Smyer, Richard. "Naipaul's *A Bend in the River*: Fiction and the Post-Colonial Tropics." *Literary Half-Yearly* 23, no. 2 (July 1982): 59–68.

Sollish, Erika, et al. *Critical Issues in West Indian Literature*. Parkersburg, Iowa: Caribbean Books, 1984.

Spivak, Gayatri C. "In Praise of *Sammy and Rosie Get Laid*." *Critical Quarterly* 31 (Summer 1989): 80–88.

Srivastava, Aruna. " 'The Empire Writes Back': Language and History in *Shame* and *Midnight's Children*." *Ariel: A Review of International English Literature* 20, no. 4 (October 1989): 62–78.

Sugunasiri, Suwanda. "Reality and Symbolism in the South Asian Canadian Short Story." *World Literature Written in English* 26, no. 1 (1986): 98–107.

Suleri, Sara. "Contraband Histories: Salman Rushdie and the Embodiment of Blasphemy." *Yale Review* 78, no. 4 (Summer 1989): 604–24.

———. "Naipaul's Arrival." *Yale Journal of Criticism* 2, no. 1 (Fall 1988): 25–50.

Swann, Joseph. " 'East Is East and West Is West'? Salman Rushdie's *Midnight's Children* as an Indian Novel." *World Literature Written in English* 26, no. 2 (Autumn 1986): 353–62.

Thieme, John. "A Hindu Castaway: Ralph Singh's Journey in *The Mimic Men*." *Modern Fiction Studies* 30, no. 3 (Autumn 1984): 505–18.

———. "V. S. Naipaul and the Hindu Killer." *Journal of Indian Writing in English* 9, no. 2 (July 1981): 70–86.

———. "V. S. Naipaul's Third World: A Not So Free State." *Journal of Commonwealth Literature* 1 (1975): 10–22.

Tiffin, Helen. "V. S. Naipaul's 'Outposts of Progress.' " *World Literature Written in English* 22, no. 2 (Autumn 1983): 309–19.

Tucker, Martin. "Peter Nazareth." In *Literary Exile in the Twentieth Century*. Ed. Martin Tucker. Westport, Conn.: Greenwood Press, 1991. 508–10.

Wirth-Nesher, Hana. "The Curse of Marginality: Colonialism in Naipaul's *Guerrillas*." *Modern Fiction Studies* 30, no. 3 (Autumn 1984): 531–45.

Youngs, Tim. "Morality and Ideology: The Arranged Marriage in Contemporary British-Asian Drama." *Wasafiri* 9 (Winter 1988/89): 3–6.

Index

About the Editor and Contributors

HENA AHMAD, who received her undergraduate education in New Delhi, is currently a doctoral student at the University of Massachusetts at Amherst. Her field of specialization is postcolonial women's writing in English.

HAROLD BARRATT was born in Trinidad, was educated in Trinidad and Canada, and is currently a Professor of English at the University College of Cape Breton in Nova Scotia. He has published several articles on Caribbean literature.

P. S. CHAUHAN, educated at Delhi, Oxford, Duke, and Yale, is a Professor of English and Director of Graduate Studies at Beaver College, Pennsylvania. He is the author of numerous articles on Indian, British, and American writers.

K. CHELLAPPAN is Professor and Head of the Department of English at Barathidasan University, India. A prolific scholar, he has written eight books, edited four others, and published over ninety scholarly articles.

C. L. CHUA is a Professor of English at California State University at Fresno. He is an expert on immigrant, particularly Asian-American, literature.

ANURADHA DINGWANEY received her doctorate in English from the University of Pennsylvania. She currently teaches courses in Anglophone postcolonial writing at Oberlin College, Ohio.

ARLENE A. ELDER holds a doctorate from the University of Chicago. Author of *"The Hindered Hand": Cultural Implications of Early Afro-American Fiction* (Greenwood), she has published several articles on African-American, postcolonial, and Aboriginal writing.

VIJAY LAKSHMI is a creative writer and the author of *Virginia Woolf as Literary Critic*. She lives in Philadelphia and teaches at Jefferson University.

VIJAY MISHRA is a Senior Lecturer at Murdoch University, Western Australia. He holds a Ph.D. in medieval Indian literature from the Australian National University and a D.Phil. in English from Oxford University.

LAWRENCE NEEDHAM is a Visiting Assistant Professor of English at Oberlin College, Ohio. He is currently at work on a book that explores the relationship between British Romanticism and empire building.

EMMANUEL S[AMPATH] NELSON received his undergraduate education in India and his Ph.D. from the University of Tennessee. During 1985–86 he was a Postdoctoral Research Fellow at the University of Queensland, Australia. Editor of *Connections: Essays on Black Literatures*, he has published over twenty articles on American and international literatures in English.

VICTOR RAMRAJ, author of *Mordecai Richler* and over three dozen articles, teaches at the University of Calgary. Currently he is coediting two collections of short fiction from the Caribbean to be published by Heinemann.

KIRPAL SINGH teaches at the National University of Singapore. A creative writer as well, he has published poetry and fiction in addition to literary criticism.

CRAIG TAPPING holds a Ph.D. in English from Trinity College, Dublin. Author of a dozen articles on Canadian, Irish, Caribbean, and African literatures, he teaches at Malaspina College in British Columbia, Canada.

HELEN TIFFIN is a Reader in English at the University of Queensland, Australia. She is the coauthor of two recent books on postcolonial critical theory: *The Empire Writes Back* and *After Europe*.